SANTAYANA'S AESTHETICS

santayana's aesthetics

A CRITICAL INTRODUCTION

IRVING SINGER

HARVARD UNIVERSITY PRESS

Cambridge, Massachusetts

1957

Publication has been aided by a grant from the Ford Foundation.

Distributed in Great Britain by Oxford University Press, London

Library of Congress Catalogue Card Number 57-9079
Printed in the United States of America

To my mother
NETTIE STROMER SINGER

PREFACE

This study has two principal objectives. First, it tries to present and clarify Santayana's philosophy, particularly his aesthetics and philosophy of art. Second, it tries to suggest a more adequate approach to several of the problems in these fields.

The book examines Santayana's aesthetics and philosophy of art, most of which was written before 1925, from the point of view of his later writings in ontology and epistemology. Part I is devoted to his distinction between essence and existence. In the other Parts, I try to show the relevance of this distinction to both his aesthetics and philosophy of art, using it as the key to his entire approach. Santayana's distinction between essence and existence is related to his distinction between an immediate aspect of experience, in which an indubitable given or datum is presented, and a mediate aspect of experience, in which the given is subjected to interpretation. In his aesthetics Santayana employs this epistemological distinction for the purpose of analyzing aesthetic and nonaesthetic elements in experience. In his philosophy of art Santayana uses the distinctions in aesthetics and epistemology as a means of distinguishing between fine art and servile art, aesthetic and nonaesthetic elements in the work of art, great art and inferior art, etc.

Santayana has himself written that his mature philosophy, especially the developments in ontology and epistemology, were latent in him from the beginning; but even if there were no historical connection of this sort, it would still be imperative, I think, to examine Santayana's aesthetics and philosophy of art in the light of the epistemology they employ. The views expressed in each of these fields are intimately related, and they characterize an intuitionistic tradition to which Santayana and many other philosophers belong.

In trying to suggest a more suitable approach to aesthetics and philosophy of art, I criticize this philosophical tradition as it manifests itself in each of Santayana's distinctions. I find that in some of the most crucial issues pragmatists like Dewey and C. I. Lewis subscribe to it no less than Santayana. But whereas Santayana is entirely committed to this approach and is *relatively* unambiguous with respect to the fundamental distinctions in epistemology, aesthetics, and philosophy of art, the pragmatists tend to vacillate. Although, in many ways, they support the tradition and contribute to it, they also deviate. Their deviations constitute a new tradition, but one that is thwarted thus far by the old. In criticizing Santayana and the tradition from which both he and the pragmatists take root, I wish to carry out the program of the new tradition, thereby elaborating an approach that is untainted by the belief in an epistemological given, a distinctive aesthetic attitude, or any uniqueness of fine art.

By way of preparing the general reader for Santayana's aesthetics, let me quote the summary statement which appears in the essay "A Brief History of my Opinions." The following passage contains most of the materials with which we shall be working:

There is in art nothing but manual knack and professional tradition on the practical side, and on the contemplative side pure intuition of essence, with the inevitable intellectual or luxurious pleasure which pure intuition involves. I can draw no distinction — save for academic programmes — between moral and aesthetic values: beauty, being a good, is a moral good; and the practice and enjoyment of art, like all practice and all enjoyment, fall within the sphere of morals — at least if by morals we understand moral economy and not moral superstition. On the other hand, the good, when actually realised and not merely pursued from afar, is a joy in the immediate; it is possessed with wonder and is in that sense aesthetic. Such pure joy when blind is called pleasure, when centered in some sensible image is called beauty, and when diffused over the thought of ulterior propitious things is called happiness, love, or religious rapture. But where all is manifest, as it is in intuition, classifications are pedantic. Harmony, which might be called an aesthetic principle, is also the principle of health, of justice, and of happiness. Every impulse, not the aesthetic mood alone, is innocent and irresponsible in its origin and precious in its own eyes; but every impulse or indulgence, including the aesthetic, is evil in its effect, when it renders harmony impossible in the general tenor of life, or produces in the soul division and ruin. There is no lack of folly in the arts; they are full of inertia and affectation and of what must seem ugliness to a cultivated taste; yet there is no need of bringing the catapult of criticism against it: indifference is enough. A society will breed the art which it is capable of, and which it deserves; but even in its own eyes this art will hardly be important or beautiful unless it engages deeply the resources of the soul. The arts may die of triviality, as they were born of enthusiasm. On the other hand, there will always be beauty, or a transport akin to the sense of beauty, in any high contemplative moment. And it is only in contemplative moments that life is truly vital, when routine gives place to intuition, and experience is synthesised and brought before the spirit in its sweep and truth.[1]

April, 1955

ACKNOWLEDGMENT

The author gratefully acknowledges permission from the following publishers and copyright holders to quote material from their publications: Constable & Co., Ltd., *Scepticism and Animal Faith, Platonism and the Spiritual Life, Soliloquies in England and Later Soliloquies*, all by George Santayana; J. M. Dent & Sons, Ltd., *The Winds of Doctrine* by George Santayana; Harvard University Press, *Three Philosophical Poets* by George Santayana; The Library of Living Philosophers and the Tudor Publishing Company, *The Philosophy of George Santayana* edited by P. A. Schilpp; *The Philosophical Review*, "The Mutability of Esthetic Categories" by George Santayana; Charles Scribner's Sons and Constable & Co., Ltd., *Dominations and Powers, Reason in Art, The Realms of Being, Interpretations of Poetry and Religion*, all by George Santayana.

CONTENTS

PART I

PART II

PART III

CONTENTS

PART I

Two persons, more than any others, have informed my thinking on the problems dealt with in this book. I cannot hope to have satisfied their high standards of philosophical analysis, but I should like to acknowledge my permanent indebtedness to Henry D. Aiken and E. Moreland Perkins.

1

MEDIATE AND IMMEDIATE EXPERIENCE

In his "Apologia Pro Mente Sua" Santayana records an opinion about his still undeveloped philosophy that Josiah Royce once expressed. The gist of Santayana's thought, Royce had said, was "the separation of essence from existence." [1] In the years following Royce's remark, Santayana's philosophy grew to a stately and unpredictable abundance. But although its mature proliferation occasionally obscured or overshadowed an earlier development, the separation of essence from existence remained at the core of all his thinking. Without a thorough examination of what existence and essence "are," and how they are to be "separated," we should find ourselves inadequately prepared for Santayana's aesthetics and philosophy of art. For he uses the distinction between essence and existence not only as a means of effecting his fundamental distinctions in aesthetics and the philosophy of art, but also as the model for further distinctions to be drawn in these fields.

I

In distinguishing essence from existence, Santayana aligns himself with the Platonic doctrine presented in the *Timaeus*. There the distinction is made between that which is self-identical, immutable, and definable and that which is in flux, unstable, and indefinable. But whereas Plato considered the Forms to be dynamic and causative, Santayana delegates all power and activity not to essence, but to the flux of existence. For him, essences are only "logical characters." As such, they constitute a different ontological realm from the underlying surd which they happen to characterize.

As an underlying surd, all existence is irrational, groundless, brute and, except for self-centered eddies in its swirling stream, devoid of purpose. Existence is constant but not directed. To this extent Santayana is clearly a "naturalist" or "existentialist." These designations must be qualified, however, by the additional fact that Santayana denies the possibility of literal or direct knowledge of existence. Substance or existence is taken to "underlie" our experience; we may, and indeed must, believe in its sustaining presence; but we can never encounter it in direct experience. Existence involves the external relations of things in flux, but our acquaintance is limited to "self-identical characters" which cannot be related to anything except internally, that is, by means of the implications of their own constitution and definition. These characters are "essences," and "existence" is defined as "essence lying in external or non-essential relations." [2]

Essences, in turn, are discovered as the last residuum of analysis. It is the function of analysis, according to Santayana, to discern these self-identical characters that are distinct from the flux of existence: "Whatsoever existing fact we may think we encounter, there will be obvious features distinguishing that alleged fact from any dissimilar fact and from nothing. All such features, discernible in sense, thought, or fancy, are essences; and the realm of essence which they compose is simply the catalogue, infinitely extensible, of all characters logically distinct and ideally possible." [3] Essences include all definite characters, not merely norms or ideals, and they are perfectly and completely instantiated whenever an existent has them as its characterization. Identity is the "principle of essence," for every essence is wholly individual: in the words of C. A. Strong, an essence is what it is — "whatever we can think of or know, considered solely with regard to *what* it is, and not as existing." [4] Since essences are neither mental nor physical, they are neutral entities; and since they can recur, they are universals rather than particulars. Finally, although they do not themselves exist, essences have a being "prior" (in a logical, not a temporal sense) to all existence. Every existent must have some character and therefore some essence; but a character that never came into existence, one that was never taken up by an existent, would still retain its being as an essence. A character is just the character that it is, whether or not it is instantiated.

Essences, then, do not exist. Facts or events that occur in nature exist, but these are not essences. Instead they are either "intuitions," including all instances of consciousness, or "physical things and occurrences." Intuitions include "pains and pleasures and all remembered experiences and mental discourse" [5] and are moments in the life of spirit; physical things are everything else in nature and constitute the realm of matter. Essences may appear as the "given" in some intuition and may be taken as evidence for the existence of an event in nature, but such existence can never be known directly or with certainty and in itself the essence is neither symbolic nor existent.

Santayana delineates four "approaches to essence": the approach through scepticism, the approach through dialectic, the approach through spirit, and the approach through contemplation. Scepticism expresses the fallibility of all belief, which is really nothing more than "animal faith." Scepticism culminates in the intuition of an essence, and concludes with the mottoes: "Nothing given exists" and "Nothing indubitable save the character of some given essence." [6] Dialectic takes one into the world of logical patterns and relations, of pure symbolism and analytic truth. It leads to the conclusion that "every term intuited or defined is an essence." [7] Spiritual discipline serves to effect a moral purgation by detaching the agent from his action and enabling him to see and understand what he is doing. Then the action is crowned by a simultaneous intuition of it. Such moral triumphs "lie in the joy of having done this: they are a passage into essence." [8] Contemplation, finally, removes us from a practical concern for facts or any consideration of how things may be used in action. Contemplation provides "aesthesis" as the sensory awareness of the feel and quality of things. The "formal arrangement" of experience then becomes clear, leading to the realization that "every intelligible pattern or harmony is an essence." [9]

Santayana's doctrine invites more criticism than need concern us at present. Here I should like only to forestall one mistaken interpretation that seems to be prevalent. The distinction between essence and existence is often taken to mean a demarcation between two kinds of things, one of which "actually exists" and the other of which "subsists" or "latently or ideally exists." Although Santayana denies any kind of existence to essences, his description of them as constituting an ontological realm all their own leads some persons who are properly hardheaded to the improper conclusion that he is offering a substitute for the actual world, a fanciful, superstitious, and baldly Platonic paradise. As a matter of fact, however, Santayana insists that the distinction between essence and existence is only a distinction of reason or analysis and that every fact includes both an existential pole and an essential one. This means that essence is "just that character which any existence wears in so far as it remains identical with itself." [10] The realm of essence is not another world; it is merely the qualitative dimension of the one we already live in.

The hardheaded critic, such as many a pragmatist, is likely to accept Santayana's distinction once it is presented in this fashion. But he will then deny that essences can have prior ontological being, that they can be anything but qualities that have actually emerged in the flow of existence. He will agree that character can be distinguished from existence, but he will deny that either term can have ontological antecedence: to conceive of essences as prior to existence is only to hypostatize a mere abstraction. [11]

Initially, I am inclined to agree with this kind of criticism. And yet, when one balances the scales between the belief in essences as abstractions and Santayana's belief in them as ontologically prior, nothing registers on either side. The pointer reads zero and we cannot find support for deciding one way or the other. Santayana claims that intuition lights

upon an essence whose being must be considered as prior unless we are to fall into anthropocentrism. Analysis *discovers*
essences, he would insist. The human mind, he says, does not
ordinarily distinguish essence from existence, but it does suppose the prior being of any character it confronts. If the analyst did not do likewise, he would never know what to look
for or how to make his distinction. The pragmatist, on the
other hand, denies that the essence could have had any kind
of being prior to its existence or instantiation. In this respect,
it is he, and not Santayana, who is the true "existentialist." At
the same time as he accepts the distinction between essence
and existence, the pragmatist will deny that the character disclosed by analysis could have had *any* being otherwise. He
will maintain that a character singled out by an analytic process cannot be presumed to be identical with any antecedent
unanalyzed character. In reply Santayana will point out that
the unanalyzed character is also an essence, whose being cannot be affected by the process of analysis. Consequently, he
will say, the essences encountered either before or after analysis must have been discovered and not created. The pragmatist will agree that "immediate experience" includes unanalyzed quality; but this pre-analytic quality, he will add, is
a mere emergent from the developmental life of an organism
and therefore cannot be ontologically prior any more than
post-analytic quality. Apart from existence, the pragmatist
will conclude, no character, quality, or essence has being. Santayana will rejoin with the insistence that essences generated
by the organism, that is, essences instantiated by an organism's
intuition, have antecedent being in their own realm independent of all existence. And he will probably end up with a vague
but withering attack on all subjectivisms, half-hearted natural-
isms, post-Hegelisms, etc. etc.

This volley or exchange, as in tennis, may have a salutary
effect upon the contestants' philosophical form, but I do not
think that it can move dispassionate judges to one decision or
another. As observers, however, we may take note of the fact
that both Santayana and the pragmatists are hitting the same

ball, although in different directions. Both accept the distinction between essence and existence, both distinguish pre-analytic from post-analytic experience, and both maintain that the essence, character, or quality that appears to an organism in either immediate experience or through analysis has been generated by the activity of the organism. Their differences amount to this: the pragmatists deny that what is generated has any being prior to generation, whereas Santayana asserts that, since essences are what they are whether or not they ever exist, generation is merely the instantiation of what has independent being anyhow.

In refusing to take sides in this issue, I reserve my forces for another, more crucial, one. Instead of arguing that essences can or cannot have prior ontological being, I shall try to show why the distinction between essence and existence is itself untenable. Once I have expounded and clarified Santayana's approach to essence through scepticism, I shall question the very foundations of his doctrine. Through an analysis of experience we shall prepare ourselves for the subsequent problems in aesthetics and the philosophy of art.

II

There are two steps or stages in the scepticism of Santayana. By taking the first step he joins forces with the traditional empirical and critical approach towards knowledge. The second step carries him to the parting of the ways between neo-realists and critical or pragmatic realists. In carrying out the program of critical realism, Santayana believes himself to have pushed the analysis to the rock bottom of "ultimate scepticism."

In the first stage of his scepticism Santayana distinguishes what he calls "facts" from "interpretation of facts." By facts he means anything in general that exists or could exist, as distinct from our opinion about it. Such opinion, a "more optional and argumentative factor," constitutes "suggestion or interpretation." [12] Empirical criticism of knowledge aspires to the correction of conventional belief; it seeks to eliminate faulty interpretations about existing things.

Santayana then moves on to the second stage of his scepticism. He now doubts the immediacy and irreducibility of facts: he doubts the reliability of interpretation itself. In order to attain certainty, he must eliminate everything in experience that is fallible: consequently, he must whittle away interpretation as a whole. Once he has pared experience of all but the given, he hopes to deny that the existence of anything whatsoever is self-evident or immediately apprehended. If he succeeds, knowledge cannot be considered direct, immediate, or certain and the intuited datum, which is direct, immediate, and "certain," cannot provide knowledge in itself. Our problem now is to discover the characteristics of this terminus of analysis, the given which is disclosed only in the furthest reach of scepticism.

The ideal sceptic, Santayana tells us, will have reduced conscious experience to a "solipsism of the present moment." The solipsist will have eliminated all memory and all expectation of the future. Gone too will be any conception of himself as a separate entity, or of the intuited object as an independent being. There will be only the intuition itself, a total experience that makes no reference beyond itself, just as it makes no distinctions between subject and object within it. Finally, and most important, the annihilation of all belief will have been effected. Belief occurs when the datum in consciousness is used as the sign of something else. Having eliminated all interpretation, the "solipsist" or perfect sceptic will not put the datum to any use at all: he will merely take what is given, with no questions asked. For, as Santayana says, "All his heroic efforts are concentrated on *not* asserting and *not* implying anything, but simply noticing what he finds." [13]

We may now see why Santayana was dissatisfied with the empirical criticism of knowledge. Empirical criticism is only an imperfect criticism; it stops with the disclosure to some animal mind of presumed facts — things that are believed in, thought to exist. But if the immediate datum excludes all belief, the notion of existence can never appear within it. Nothing, not even the object intuited, will be thought of as either existent or nonexistent. Whatever is presented will be accepted without doubt, without assent, and without assurance. The immediate datum is certain in the sense of being indubitably *there*; but we can never know with certainty that anything, even the datum, either exists or does not exist.

With this conclusion, that for the sceptic nothing exists, Santayana believes that he has taken the last step in criticism and achieved the ultimate scepticism of a vacant stare. But, as we soon discover, his analysis was only a preparation for his crucial distinction between the datum and the intuition. And this distinction carries him beyond scepticism.

Although the solipsist cannot believe in existence, the philosopher feels himself impelled to believe in the existence of the solipsist. And although the datum is given apart from all external relations, the fact remains that there was a datum. It is on the basis of this factuality that Santayana reintroduces existence. Each datum by itself would be nothing more than a pure appearance, but considered in its relations to other data, it is seen to have occurred in an intuition. As such, it is viewed "from the outside" and compared to a term or object in some other datum. Its place within a system of intuitions is defined, and the intuition that includes it is said to have existed.

Thus, at the same time as the sceptic relegates the datum to the realm of nonexistence and of mere essence, he achieves his first bit of knowledge. He knows that his intuition exists. But this knowledge, like the knowledge about physical objects which he attains as he moves further and further from the nadir of scepticism, is itself only animal faith.

As faith in a posited object, knowledge is belief in substance. Belief is always precarious since it takes the solipsist beyond his indubitable datum and confronts him with an absent object of which he can never be certain. But to avoid belief is even more precarious, not in a logical sense but in a vital one. For the solipsist cannot save his skin while he intuits essences. Vehicles are bearing down on him and missiles fill the air.

Unless he forfeits his certainty for some useful belief, the sceptic cannot survive. The needs of action underlie our faith and cause us to posit the existence of things not present. Such things, together with intuitions, form the world of substance.

As a by-product of its operation, animal faith sometimes leads us to the discrimination of essences. But because animal faith is motivated by the needs of action and survival in a material world, it does not usually allow the intuition of essences. Instead, it causes us to treat them as signals and symbols for existent substance.

Essences, then, are the only givens; but because they do not exist they cannot be taken as substantial. Substance itself is believed in but never known with certainty. Its essence is forever hidden. Still, it can be known symbolically, and such representative knowledge, distorted by the human perspective, is what the sciences actually provide. As we shall see, Santayana claims that animal faith structures the scientific attitude, whereas the aesthetic attitude depends upon the intuition of essences.

III

Santayana's analysis of experience has often been misconstrued. He has been criticized for an atomism to which he does not subscribe; he has even been accused of recommending something akin to idiocy as the only means of contacting reality. In the next few pages I shall clarify Santayana's position in an attempt to forestall mistaken criticism.

According to Santayana, the datum in immediate experience is *not* restricted to a local sensation. In eliminating interpretation, the solipsist does not fix his attention upon an *element* of his original perception. It is not a case of his seeing an instance of blueness, and nothing else, where the ordinary man sees a blue book lying on a brown table next to a chair, etc. Instead, the solipsist sees a clear and determinate picture of the entire scene. He sees it devoid of any relations beyond the solipsistic moment, but he sees it whole. When attention focusses upon a specific character like the blueness of a patch, this is all there is to the scene. But other scenes may include an indefinite number of components in all kinds of internal relations. The datum includes everything present and cannot be limited to a particular quality in the experience. Dewey is referring to the same thing when he points out that "the immediately given is an extensive qualitative situation." [14] A sceptic like Santayana analyzes experience by removing layers of interpretation, not by chopping perceived wholes into little bits.

Similar considerations apply to the datum as a temporal unit. Santayana speaks of the "solipsistic moment," but it is clear that he does not wish to limit intuition to any specific instant. Within the intuition of the solipsist there may be "long vistas," and the whole of existence, were it uninterpreted, would fit within a solipsistic moment. Nor is change, inherent in any temporal spread, excluded from the immediately given. All that the solipsist lacks is interpretation in terms of passing moments or changing events. Merely noticing what he finds, the solipsist accepts change as he accepts everything else, but he is not aware of it *as* change. For that would relate his datum with previous and succeeding ones. The given is immediately presented, but it is neither instantaneous nor unchanging. Santayana speaks of immediate experience as a picture of change and a waking dream of motion.

Finally, it is important to realize that Santayana's analysis does not deviate from common sense as much as one might initially think. Santayana's scepticism is descriptive — that is, makes reference to actual or possible states of consciousness — in two respects. First, and most obviously, it refers to the experience of a solipsist. And although a perfect solipsist may be hard to find, one might still have reason to specify the conditions for his kind of experience.* Second, and less obviously

---

* "A perfect solipsist, therefore, hardly is found amongst men" (*Scepticism and Animal Faith,* p. 18). But elsewhere Santayana tells us that "in a disillusioned analytic mind attention intently fixed on the given, far from inducing belief, induces definition of the given, and suspension of all belief; for now what in animal life was a mere incident in action has become absorption in intuition, and belief in existence has turned into contemplation of essence. I happen to be able to do this trick and to enjoy doing it . . ." ("Apologia Pro Mente Sua," p. 542).

but more significantly, Santayana's scepticism singles out an aspect in the conscious experience of ordinary human beings. Since this aspect is experience in its immediacy, the two respects in which Santayana's scepticism is descriptive are intimately related. According to Santayana, we are all solipsists *insofar* as experience immediately impinges upon us. Insofar as we interpret our experience, we are not solipsists; for interpretation belongs to another aspect of experience. The perfect solipsist is a man like the rest of us except that he restrains the interpretative aspect of ordinary experience.

Such heroic restraint is envisaged for a purpose — and that purpose is epistemological. Sceptics like Santayana analyze out solipsistic experience in an attempt to find "hard data" (as Russell calls them) which can provide a definite foundation for knowledge. By means of his analysis, Santayana wishes to show that the only indubitable aspect of ordinary experience is the aspect that corresponds to the experience of the solipsist. Only there does one discover the given content beyond which scepticism cannot go. Insofar as ordinary experience is immediate, we are confronted by a determinate datum whose presence cannot be doubted. Insofar as our experience is mediate we interpret the datum in terms of other data and construct beliefs which are inevitably fallible. Because Santayana's kind of analysis is motivated by the search for an indubitable element in ordinary experience, I shall sometimes refer to it as "epistemological scepticism." The position is summarized in passages such as the following:

Not being directed by memory upon the past, nor by animal faith upon the future or upon external things, pure intuition exercises no sagacity, no transitive intelligence, and does not think. It is merely the light of awareness lending actuality to some essence. . . . If I confine myself to the given essence without admitting discourse about it, I exclude all analysis of that essence, or even examination of it. I must simply stare at it, in a blank and timeless aesthetic trance. . . . Intuition can never yield the relation of its total datum to anything not given. It cannot refer to the latent at all, since its object, by definition, is just what is given immediately. To take the leap from one intuition to another, and assert that they view the same essence, or have the same intent, I must take my life in my hands and trust to animal faith.[15]

Once we fix the distinction between mediate and immediate experience clearly in mind, we realize that philosophers who do not consider themselves to be sceptics have held the same view. John Dewey, for instance, expresses a related position when he says:

Data are not only what is given *to* thought, but they are also the food, the raw material, *of* thought. They must be described as, on the one hand, wholly outside of thought. This clearly puts them into the region of sense perception. They are matters of *sensation* given free from all inferring, judging, relating influence. Sensation is just what is *not* called up in memory or in anticipated projection — it is the immediate, the irreducible.*

C. I. Lewis takes a similar stand:

Perceptual knowledge has two aspects or phases; the givenness of something given, and the interpretation which, in the light of past experience, we put upon it. In the case of perceiving the white paper, what is given is a certain complex of sensa or

---

* John Dewey, *Essays in Experimental Logic* (Chicago: The University of Chicago Press, 1916), p. 145, his italics. And elsewhere:
"One might think that philosophers in their search for some datum that possesses properties that put it beyond doubt, might have directed their attention to this direct phase of experience, in which objects are not a matter of sensations, ideas, beliefs or knowledge, but are something had and enjoyed. . . . But in every event there is something obdurate, self-sufficient, wholly immediate, neither a relation nor an element in a relational whole, but terminal and exclusive. Here, as in so many other matters, materialists and idealists agree in an underlying metaphysics which ignores in behalf of relations and relational systems, those irreducible, infinitely plural, undefinable and indescribable qualities which a thing must *have* in order to be, and in order to be capable of becoming the subject of relations and a theme of discourse. . . . Things in their immediacy are unknown and unknowable, not because they are remote or behind some impenetrable veil of sensation or ideas, but because knowledge has no concern with them. For knowledge is a memorandum of conditions of their appearances, concerned, that is, with sequences, coexistences, relations." *Experience and Nature* (Chicago: Open Court Publishing Co., 1926, pp. 85–86, his italics).

qualia — what Santayana calls an "essence." * This is describable in expressive language by the use of adjectives of color, shape, size, and so on. If our apprehension ended with this, however, there would be no knowledge here; the presentation would *mean* nothing to us. . . . Such apprehensions of the given are characterized by certainty, even though what it is that we are thus certain of, is something difficult of clear and precise expression when separated from the interpretation put upon it. . . . It is the interpretation put upon this presentation which constitutes belief in or assertion of some objective fact. This interpretation is imposed in the light of past experience. Because I have dealt with writing paper before, this presently given white oblong something leads me to believe there is a sheet of white paper before me.[16]

What these authorities hold in common is a belief in some immediate aspect of experience which lays a foundation for all our uncertain interpretations. To this extent they not only accept epistemological scepticism but also the distinction between essence and existence. Let us now see whether their analysis can be defended.

IV

Santayana's distinction between immediate experience, in which nonexistent essence appears, and mediate experience, in which existence is cognized, is, as we have seen, a distinction between the intuition of determinate but uninterpreted data and the interpretation of data thus intuited. Santayana does not expressly define the word "interpretation," but he uses it to mean the functioning of memory and expectation in both classification and signification. Classification is the relating up of the datum to other data, whether on the basis of similarity, contiguity, or constant concomitance, etc. Signification occurs when the datum is taken to be the sign of something else.

I do not suggest that these factors are mutually exclusive. I distinguish them at present because they afford a convenient

---

* In a footnote Lewis adds, "Though it would appear that Santayana calls some other things essences also."

way of organizing my criticism of Santayana's doctrine. Before turning to them, however, I should like to make a few remarks about interpretation in general. I shall try to show that a determinate datum cannot be uninterpreted and, therefore, that Santayana's distinction between mediate and immediate experience cannot be upheld.

Santayana admits, and indeed maintains, that our ordinary consciousness is one in which interpretation takes place and in which the distinction between mediate and immediate aspects of experience does not generally occur. Yet, he also maintains that ordinary experience is "really" composed of these two aspects and that the immediate aspect is what a perfect solipsist would experience. But since our ordinary experience is permeated by interpretation, how are we to know that it includes an "aspect" which corresponds to solipsistic experience? On the one hand, the solipsist cannot tell us how his experience is related to ordinary experience, because once he does he ceases to be a solipsist. On the other hand, the ordinary man, acting and interpreting in one way or another, is not aware of any respect in which his experience significantly resembles the solipsist's.

Consequently, the descriptive side of epistemological scepticism is clearly an impossible position. The attempt to reduce consciousness to its core of immediacy seems to be a self-defeating procedure: if we succeed in the attempt, we automatically prevent ourselves from comparing or contrasting our datum with what is ordinarily experienced. Even if there were occasions on which a pure solipsistic experience occurred, one has difficulty imagining how the evidence to this effect could be produced. One likewise wonders what *could* substantiate the belief that rock-bottom but determinate data actually underlie all consciousness and are present to an intuitional aspect of experience that excludes interpretation. Since Santayana does not offer evidence for the existence of this special, but presumably pervasive, kind of intuition, his attempt to distinguish aspects in experience is *prima facie* suspect, and as a descriptive doctrine hardly worth considering.

As a tool of analysis, however, epistemological scepticism might be able to justify its position. In examining this possibility, let us suppose that solipsistic experience actually is an aspect of all experience. What I shall try to show is that the very concept of solipsistic or immediate experience is untenable in its formulation by epistemological scepticism.

Santayana maintains that immediate experience "excludes" interpretation. To say this can mean that the datum is uninterpreted, that is, not already interpreted, or else that immediate experience is not one of interpreting the datum or deliberating about it. Santayana holds both views. Since the essence is merely intuited, it comes wholly uninterpreted; and since one does not proceed to deliberate about the essence, immediate experience is not one of interpreting.

Now it may be true that to intuit a datum is not the same as to deliberate about the datum. If so, it makes sense to say that immediate experience is not an experience of interpreting. But it does not follow from this that the datum is uninterpreted. If it were, the organism would be wholly passive in its reception of data. If, however, the organism is not wholly passive, the datum must appear as it does *by means of* interpretation. Then, although immediate experience is not one in which further interpretations are made, it may yet be said to include interpretation inasmuch as interpreted data are present to it. That the data in immediate experience are definite and determinate only by means of interpretation, in this sense, is what I propose to argue.

According to Santayana, the solipsist's datum is everything present to immediate experience, and this is everything that remains clear and determinate after all interpretation has been eliminated or discounted. The datum of immediate experience cannot be indefinite or vague in any respect. "There can be no question in the realm of essence of mistaken identity, vagueness, shiftiness, or self-contradiction." [17] Elsewhere Santayana insists that "nothing given in sensation or thought is in the least vague in itself. Vagueness is an adventitious quality, which a given appearance may be said to possess in relation to an object presumed to have other determinations: as the cloud in *Hamlet* is but a vague camel or a vague weasel, but for the landscape painter a perfectly definite cloud. The vague is merely the *too* vague for some assumed purpose." [18]

But how can the landscape painter see a "perfectly definite cloud" if all he intuits is an absolutely unrelated datum or essence, free from all interpretation? On the one hand, we are led to believe that the landscape painter intuits an essence insofar as he lacks judgment about whether the cloud resembles a weasel or a camel. On the other hand, he intuits a perfectly definite *cloud*, which would seem to indicate that what he sees is already interpreted as something. It may not be interpreted as a weasel or a camel but it *is* interpreted as a cloud, and a perfectly definite one at that. Furthermore, in another place Santayana tells us that "in every doubt or equivocation both alternatives are genuine essences; and in groping and making up my mind I merely hesitate between essences, not knowing on which to arrest my attention." [19] From this it would follow that the cloud-as-weasel and the cloud-as-camel are also essences. But then far from excluding interpretation, essence would seem to be precisely that which is interpreted as something or other.

Giving Santayana the benefit of any doubt, however, let us now suppose that the landscape painter does not intuit a "cloud" but only something white, fluffy, and oblong. For if the painter believes that "this" is a "cloud" — Santayana might insist — he must have been intuiting a "this" that he then proceeded to interpret: but the "this" denotes an essence, which therefore has being apart from all interpretation. In this new version, the painter intuits something white, fluffy, and oblong without interpreting it in any way, though as a matter of fact others would take it to be a cloud and perhaps one that resembles a weasel or a camel. Nevertheless, our difficulty remains. Insofar as the essence is determinate and clearcut, it is seen *as something* — something white, fluffy, and oblong. If formerly the painter was understood to intuit a "this" that was taken to be a cloud, now he must be understood to intuit a "this" that is taken to be a white, fluffy, oblong something. For an essence to be determinate it must be determinate as something, and (I suggest) that means that interpretation must have occurred.

"But tell me," Santayana will ask, "what is the 'this' that is interpreted to be white, fluffy, and oblong? If it is not itself a bare essence, what kind of datum can it be?"

In order to answer this kind of question, we must recognize: first, that in consciousness there are degrees of determinateness and degrees of vagueness, and second, that a datum which is more or less determinate in one respect may yet be more or less vague in another respect. Different persons, two painters for instance, looking at what a physicist might consider to be the "same cloud," will see it differently. What one experiences as quite definite, clear-cut, and sharply etched in character another may experience as something far less determinate. Although both painters see something oblong, white, and fluffy, one of them might focus his attention upon the color of the object rather than its shape or texture while the other concentrated upon the shape instead of the texture or color. In this event, we may very well say, the first painter's datum was more determinate with respect to its color than its shape or texture, whereas the second painter's datum was more determinate with respect to shape. However we ultimately conceive of the datum in immediate experience, we must realize that it will not be equally determinate in every respect. It would be absurd to think that the fringes of consciousness appear with the same clarity as those regions upon which attention is directed.

Since the datum is always more or less determinate in some respects and more or less vague in others, it is hard to see just what Santayana means when he speaks of it as being "perfectly definite." Even in any one respect, for instance the color of this white, oblong, and fluffy thing, there will only be some degree of determinateness, however considerable it may be. Consequently, when we say that the painter sees something that is "determinately oblong, white and fluffy," we mean that the datum is more or less determinate, that is, rather determinate, in these respects. To add that what the painter sees resembles only vaguely either a camel or a weasel, is only to say that his datum is more or less indeterminate or vague in these respects.* The painter's datum is determinate inasmuch as it presents determinate characters of whiteness, fluffiness, and oblongness, but it is indeterminate or vague inasmuch as the character of being a cloud or of resembling a weasel or a camel is concerned. It is indeterminate in these respects because the painter has not yet interpreted it as a cloud (or as not a cloud) or as resembling a camel or weasel. Until this process of interpretation is completed, the datum in question is indeterminate in these respects, regardless of how determinate it may be in others.

We may now return to the question I put into Santayana's mouth. It amounts to asking: If every datum is interpreted, what is there before interpretation has occurred? And the answer is: Another datum, an earlier one in time, similar to the present datum in every respect except that this previous datum was vague in some respect(s) in which the present datum is determinate. If the painter had experienced something white and fluffy but not of any (more or less) determinate shape, he would have been having a datum that one might refer to as a "this" which was later interpreted to be oblong as well as white and fluffy. The datum that had only determinate color and texture might itself have resulted from the interpretation of a "this" that had only determinate color *or* determinate texture. But since the datum with only determinate color or only determinate texture might have resulted from the interpretation of a datum that was determinate in some other respect, shape for instance, we need never reach an ultimate, rock-bottom, and wholly uninterpreted datum.

Let us suppose, however, that we could attain a datum that

---

* Accordingly, I shall use the words "determinate," "indeterminate," and "vague" (except when they are modified by terms such as "wholly") to mean "more or less determinate," "more or less indeterminate," and "more or less vague" respectively.

was wholly uninterpreted. It would still not satisfy the needs of epistemological scepticism. For it could only be a datum that was wholly indeterminate, wholly vague; and our experience could then be nothing more than a blur. In a sense we should have reached bottom, since all interpretation would really have been excluded from consciousness. But since nothing definite would appear, it seems unlikely that consciousness would remain. For we would not be perceiving a blur — if we did, we would be experiencing something definite, like the blur that rapidly turning wheels make — but our perception *itself* would be blurred.* The sensing of a colored patch, often taken to be basic, is the experience, through interpretation, of something determinate. If even that were eliminated, one's mind would literally be "a blank." One cannot be dogmatic about such conditions, but it would seem that the elimination of all determinate, interpreted content in consciousness could take place only with the loss of consciousness itself.

Thus, apart from *all* interpretation, there is only total vagueness and the annihilation of consciousness. It is the function of interpretation to make the datum determinate in some respect or other. Nevertheless, within any particular experience of the datum there need not be a deliberate act of interpreting. That occurs once the datum is doubted or questioned or merely reëxamined and what was formerly vague is made more determinate. Then a new datum presents itself, interpreted in some respects, vague in others.

* In this connection it is interesting to note that Santayana's biographer considers C. I. Lewis to be one who believes that the sense impression is a "blur": "Professor C. I. Lewis particularly objects to Santayana's treatment of sense impressions as essences. He maintains that a sense impression is merely a blur, is often completely ignored unless the mind attends to it and judges its character by an active mental process." (George W. Howgate, *George Santayana*, Philadelphia: University of Pennsylvania Press, 1938, p. 253.) Whether or not this refers to data in general and how this account is to be squared with descriptions of the given that occur in *Mind and The World-Order* and *An Analysis of Knowledge and Valuation*, I do not know. In the *Analysis*, cf. pages 26 and 28, for instance, where Lewis says: "what is directly presented has its own specific character. . . . Immediate apprehensions of sense possess certainty — if we are careful to restrict ourselves to just the directly given content and as it is given."

V

What we have thus far said about interpretation in general should become more evident as we turn to the factors previously enumerated — classification of the datum and the occurrence of signification.

According to Santayana, the solipsist experiences the datum, sees it for instance, apart from all external relations and devoid of all classification. That is to say, the solipsist does not associate the datum, on whatever basis, with any other data or consider it to be itself the member of any class. Santayana recognizes that in ordinary experience such association and classification takes place, but he wishes to maintain that a determinate datum *would* be present even if these cognitive processes were eliminated. What I must show, on the other hand, is that data become determinate only by means of processes such as classification.

First, let us consider once more the experience of the solipsist. In what sense could he be said to "see" a datum that was wholly unrelated to other data, one that was not joined to them, in however subtle a fashion, by means of similarity, contiguity, constant concomitance, or other association? Traces of light bombard the retina and activate the brain; and in this sense, perhaps, the solipsist, perfectly transfixed and wholly passive, may be said to "see" the datum. But from this it does not follow that his seeing at all resembles the seeing of ordinary experience or that his datum is anything like the datum whose classification he has sought to eliminate. Indeed, as we have already had reason to suspect, a purely solipsistic state may not be a conscious one at all. In his eagerness to eliminate all interpretation, the perfect sceptic may have eliminated consciousness itself, and therefore, what we generally mean by "seeing."

But even if consciousness remains to the solipsist, there is no reason to believe that his datum will be determinate in the way that Santayana maintains. Without classification we should be unable to distinguish between data or become aware of anything clearly defined. When we see a white patch, in the ordinary sense of "see," we experience something that is determinate by means of its specific class-relations. It is through the association with the class of colors that are similar or dissimilar, remote or contiguous in space or time, etc., that the particular color we are looking at takes on distinctness and clarity. If it were not seen as a member of the class of colors, it could not be distinguished from a sound or a visceral feeling or a tactual impression. If it were not associated with other color data, it could not be seen as a definite and distinguishable whiteness. *What* it is seen as depends upon *how* it is classified. Without this kind of process, ordinary perceptual seeing would be impossible and no sense impression would be distinguishable from any other. Instead, they would all present themselves in an indefinitely vague medley, a blur or confusion.

Finally, although genetic considerations are secondary, it will be interesting to notice how a psychologist like Gardner Murphy describes the perception of infants. For in their consciousness, as is generally assumed, classification is at a minimum. Murphy summarizes as follows the reasons for believing that the perceptual responses of the infant are diffuse:

. . . sensory projection areas being poorly developed, sense impressions are massive, blurred, incompletely differentiated. There is a rough quantitative difference between a big impression and a little impression, but there are probably no clear distinctions between colors or tones, or even, apparently, between color as such and tone as such. The mind as a whole is a blur; there are no sharp outlines within it. A loud sound and a bright light combined may produce an effect something like that produced by a much brighter light or a much louder sound acting alone. . . . Though the sense organs are for the most part active in the newborn and are constantly funneling energy to the central nervous system, the latter is not differentiated enough to register them independently. But differentiation and learning go on rapidly.[20]

In turning to questions about signification, we carry the argument a little further. As in the case of classification, Santayana does not deny that one may use a datum as the sign of something else, or that this is the general practice in ordinary perception. He only wishes to assert that apart from such use the datum may be distinguished as a definite quality, that one may intuit what the datum is without ever using it as a sign. According to Santayana, signification is a "latent reaction" that can hardly be avoided; but, he also thinks, it may be "discounted in reflection."

What we must determine is whether the latent reaction of signification can actually be discounted in reflection. We are not concerned with any overt process of deliberation, since no one wants to suggest that having a datum, seeing a color for instance, is the same as deliberating about it. The question before us is whether a datum could be determinate after the contribution of signification had been eliminated. If the datum that results from such elimination is vague, we shall have to conclude that signification cannot be discounted.

Let us first consider a datum that is determinate in only one respect, a particular whiteness. Since we do not employ this determinate datum as the sign of a cloud or a napkin or a sheet of paper, Santayana would conclude that we are intuiting a datum independently of all signification. For all we have in consciousness is a white patch. We see a clear, determinate, "perfectly definite" color, he would say, but nothing we use as a sign.

Santayana is justified, I think, in holding that a particular color may be experienced without in any way being the sign of something like a cloud, napkin, or sheet of paper. When the painter focusses his attention upon the whiteness of the cloud, he might not take the white patch to signify a cloud. He sees what he sees not as a cloud but as a white patch, or more precisely, just as an instance of whiteness. But this does *not* mean that his datum, if it is determinate, is not used as a sign. For although it is not taken to be a cloud, it *is* taken to be an occurrence of whiteness. In seeing it as something definitely white, the painter classifies the datum with respect to a great variety of colored objects that he has already perceived. In one of these classifications it signifies the color of things that are *similar* to it in color. It is only as one among a class of similarly colored objects, and as a sign of their similar color, that the datum becomes determinately *white*.

It is this kind of datum that would remain after all other sign-relations were eliminated. To the extent that signification of this sort is lacking, the datum diminishes in determinateness. For if it is not taken to be *something*, even if only something white, how can the datum be definite and clearcut? But if it is taken to be something white, then it is already used as a sign: at least, it signifies the color one finds in certain clouds, napkins, sheets of paper, etc. This relevant signification enables the painter to react as he does. He merely looks at the white patch because, as he has learned from experience, that is all one can do with a color. And he takes his datum to be the sign of the similar color shared by a class of similarly colored objects because this is the way to see a particular color as clear-cut and determinate, distinct by means of its resemblance to other members of the class as well as its difference from all else.

As a matter of fact, however, other sign-relations are generally not eliminated, even from the consciousness of painters. What they see as something white, they also see as a cloud or as something that would look red at sunset. It would, however, be a mistake to confuse these different kinds of seeing: for they employ different kinds of signification. Insofar as the painter sees something white, his experience is of the sort we have described. But insofar as he sees something as a cloud or as an object that would appear red at sunset, his experience is somewhat different. His seeing the datum as something that would look red at sunset is based not only on his seeing it as something white but also on the further use of sign-relations involved in seeing it as something whose apparent color would be affected by changing sunlight. It is by means of such additional signification, together with the seeing of some present "sensory-quality," such as whiteness, that the seeing of a cloud or something red at sunset takes place. Signification involved in the experience of some present sensory-quality let us call "primary signification"; by "secondary signification" I refer to the more complex use of sign-relations exemplified by our seeing the datum as a cloud or something red at sunset. It follows from what we have said thus far that every occurrence of secondary signification is based upon primary signification of some sort.

By means of this approach one can distinguish between types of perception without being forced to distinguish between a determinate but uninterpreted datum, on the one hand, and the occurrence of signification, on the other. I am suggesting that whenever we have a datum that is at all determinate we use it as a sign, though we do so in different ways for different types of data. As a result, signification, like classification, cannot be "discounted in reflection." Without these factors of interpretation our consciousness would lack the clarity and definiteness that Santayana finds preëminent in the realm of essence.

VI

On these grounds we may reject the fundamental tenet of epistemological scepticism. Epistemological scepticism sought to distinguish essence from existence by means of a distinction between two aspects of experience: the mediate and the immediate. This distinction was effected for epistemological purposes, in order to detect an absolutely indubitable foundation for knowledge — a determinate and clear-cut datum free of all interpretation. This kind of distinction may be called an "epistemological distinction." My discussion has attempted to show that it cannot be successfully maintained. A datum is determinate in some respect only if it is already interpreted in that respect. And since we are never able to analyze out the rock-bottom kind of datum that Santayana refers to, there is good reason to deny that mediate and immediate experience can be distinguished in the way that his ontology requires. At least with regard to the contents of ordinary experience, his distinction between essence and existence cannot be upheld.

My criticism of Santayana's position enables me to make two distinctions of my own: one between the datum as vague and the datum as determinate; the other between mediate and immediate experience. Both of these distinctions are made on different grounds from those of epistemological scepticism.

First, epistemological scepticism considered the datum to be a determinate and "perfectly definite" character. I have maintained that any datum — that which is present to consciousness — is always (more or less) determinate in some respects and (more or less) vague in others. To the extent that a datum is uninterpreted in some respect, it is in that respect — as we say — "less meaningful, less significant," and something that we are "less conscious of." To this extent it is less determinate, definite, clear-cut, distinctive, or precisely discriminated. And vice versa: the more we focus our attention upon a datum and interpret it to be a certain something, the more does it become determinate. The vagueness of the datum accounts for its capacity to be further interpreted. The determinateness of the datum accounts for its clarity in consciousness, resulting from prior or simultaneous interpretation. And, of course, we need not think of the datum *as* determinate in order for it to *be* determinate, just as we need not think of the datum as vague in order for it to have features that are indeterminately given.

Second, epistemological scepticism distinguished immediate from mediate experience on the basis of two aspects in consciousness, a solipsistic and a nonsolipsistic one. Because the solipsistic aspect was considered to be the intuition of an uninterpreted but determinate datum, it caused us to reject the entire dichotomy. Nevertheless, it will be useful to distinguish a factor of acceptance in experience from one of questioning, doubting, or reappraising. By "immediate experience" let us refer to the process of accepting the given at its face value. The datum is then taken to mean or to be just what it seems to mean or to be. Immediate experience is not passive or unresponsive. Instead, it is just that response (behavioral or otherwise) of accepting the datum and foregoing any doubt or indecision with respect to it. The datum that is taken in this fashion may be highly interpreted, and therefore highly meaningful and determinate, or else it may be more or less uninterpreted, meaningless, and vague. In either event the experience can be one that excludes questioning and is, correspondingly, immediate.

By "mediate experience" let us mean the process of questioning, doubting, and seeking evidence or clarification. Every datum, however determinate, may be halted at the frontiers of belief and asked to show its papers. Mediate experience occurs whenever the given is not accepted at its face value.

Mediate and immediate experience, as I understand them, are not joint aspects in all consciousness. With respect to all experience, epistemological scepticism wished to distinguish an aspect of interpretation from one of mere givenness. Once we reject this kind of distinction, we see that there is no need to separate aspects in experience as a whole. For some experiences are entirely immediate. One might almost say that for the ordinary man consciousness is more often immediate than mediate. We need not seek that rare bird, the solipsist whose experience is devoid of interpretation, in order to find immediate experience. Immediate experience is what we all have in our moments of simple faith and untroubled belief. In those experiences there is no aspect of mediacy because there is, *ex hypothesi*, no questioning of the given. Mediate experience, on the other hand, cannot be dealt with so easily. We cannot reverse the coin and say that in mediate experiences there is no immediacy. For when we doubt or question what is given, there is usually something about it that we also accept. When I wonder whether the painting before me is really a Giotto, I at least accept the fact that it is a painting and not a tapestry. In saying this, however, we are still maintaining something different from epistemological scepticism. Instead of asserting that there are two components in experience, one of which is epistemologically more reliable, we are only saying that what is interpreted in one respect may be accepted as such, although when it is interpreted in another respect it is doubted. Our distinction is not an epistemological one. We may say, then, that sometimes mediate and immediate experience accompany one another, and sometimes they do not. It is hard for us to imagine a purely mediate experience, an act of unmitigated doubt without some presuppositions; but immediate experience often occurs separately. Even if the two modes of experience figured in all consciousness, the distinction between them might still be worth making. The crucial thing is to make the distinction on the basis of describable acts and processes instead of presumed certainties at the core of experience.

My denial that Santayana's distinction between essence and existence can be upheld has followed his argument through only one of the four "approaches to essence." Nevertheless, the sceptical is for Santayana the most fundamental approach. Santayana's essences are "*the whole* of what is actually visible, audible, imaginable, or thinkable," [21] and only the sceptic concerns himself with everything that is given to consciousness. In dialectic one's intuition is limited to abstract ideas and interrelated meanings; in spiritual discipline, to actions envisaged in their totality and in their results; in contemplation, to sensuous patterns. The solipsist, on the other hand, intuits *everything* that is given. Consequently, although our argument has concentrated upon the analysis of experience, it has indirectly dealt with approaches other than the sceptic's and may easily be extended to cover them.

In turning to problems of aesthetics and the philosophy of art, we direct our attention more specifically to the fourth approach, the approach through contemplation. Here we discover issues that are similar, in large part, to the ones we have encountered thus far. Santayana's fundamental distinction pervades his aesthetics as thoroughly as his epistemology. The protagonists cast aside the masks of scepticism and animal faith in order to assume those of detached contemplation and active interest. The play of their conflict resumes the former pattern, but now in a different setting and according to different details. The plot progresses in a way that we could only partially have foreseen. What happens now has happened before, but with a difference that warrants close examination and careful criticism.

PART II

PART II

2

BEAUTY AND THE SENSE OF BEAUTY

In our examination of Santayana's aesthetics, we must remember that the doctrine of essences received its complete
statement many years after Santayana's theories about beauty
and the aesthetic experience were first formulated. There are
those who believe that his later philosophy took a radically
different turn from his earlier. According to critics such as
Vivas, Edman, Munitz, and Schilpp, Santayana's youthful
psychological and mechanistic approach stands in sharp oppo-
sition, if not actual contradiction, to his subsequent emphasis
upon essences. [1] This later phase they take to be an ill-fated
concession to mysticism and Platonic folderol. Santayana himself denied that his basic outlook changed: "I should say that,
during a long life, I have expressed in turn different sides of
my nature, and developed different parts of my innate philosophy." [2] Santayana admitted that the unity of his earlier
and later philosophy was complicated by a shift in philosophical interest — his earlier concern for psychology yielding
to a later concern for ontology — but he denied that he had
ever relinquished the scientific and naturalistic approach.[3]
This is not the place to arbitrate the dispute between Santayana and his critics. On the whole, I think, his claim is justified. There is a unity, albeit a fragile one, between his earlier
and later philosophy. But this is true only because his youthful
works are as thoroughly pervaded by Platonism as his mature
works are by naturalism. On many specific issues a difference
of expression occurs, and sometimes a difference of opinion,
but nothing so extreme as to warrant the belief that Santayana's
writings encompass two different systems of thought. With
respect to his aesthetics, therefore, I shall take Santayana's

word in the matter: I shall regard his various statements as pieces of the same mosaic, designed, according to the author's admission, to form a single pattern. If inconsistencies appear, they will have to be treated as internal contradictions within his total outlook.

I

There are two projects that a naturalistic aesthetics might undertake: first, to explain what beauty is; and second, to explain where or when beauty occurs. In its first endeavor, naturalism seeks to define beauty itself; in its second, it tries to delimit the locus or field of aesthetic experience, to indicate the conditions for the occurrence of beauty.

Unless we realize from the outset that Santayana's aesthetics never undertakes the first task, we shall misconstrue both his earlier and later formulations. Despite an unfortunate misuse of language in his first book, *The Sense of Beauty*, Santayana never attempted to give a definition of beauty. The entire *Sense of Beauty*, like Santayana's subsequent writings in aesthetics, is restricted to an investigation of the *conditions* under which beauty is experienced. After having been (quite understandably) misinterpreted for some forty-five years, Santayana writes in "Apologia Pro Mente Sua": "Nor was my book even about the beautiful, in its dialectical relations, perhaps to the real or to the good; I wrote only about the *sense* for the beautiful." [4]

With this in mind, we see that the title of Santayana's first book could not be paraphrased as "the essence of beauty," or "the meaning of the word 'beauty.'" It must be interpreted as something like "the organic and other conditions under which beauty appears," or "the human faculty of being susceptible to beauty," or simply "the aesthetic experience." Consequently, whenever Santayana uses terms like "the definition of beauty," "the nature of beauty," "the materials of beauty," etc. in *The Sense of Beauty*, he is being unrigorous in a way that he might not have been fifteen years later. What he is really referring to, as indicated by his later writings and by occasional but significant statements in the book itself, is the definition of the sense of beauty, the nature of the sense of beauty, the materials of the sense of beauty, etc. The book was, as the later Santayana admits, an excursion in psychologism — an attempt to describe a kind of human experience: the aesthetic experience. The definition of beauty itself he did not attempt.

This approach appears most clearly in Santayana's criticism of Bertrand Russell's "hypostatic ethics." Russell, like G. E. Moore, had held that the predicate "good" was indefinable. From this he concluded that "good and bad are qualities which belong to objects independently of our opinions." [5] Santayana criticizes this conclusion as a hypostatization of good, which he, like Moore and Russell, also takes to be an unanalyzable, indefinable, simple quality. Moore and Russell had maintained that so-called definitions of "good" — such as its being pleasure or the desired — are really references to things that have been called "good," instead of being definitions of the predicate "good" itself. Their view in this matter Santayana calls a "correct, if somewhat trifling, observation." [6] He defends his charge of hypostatization in the following manner: "That the quality 'good' is indefinable is one assertion, and obvious; but that the presence of this quality is unconditioned is another, and astonishing. . . . Green is an indefinable predicate, and the specific quality of it can be given only in intuition; but it is a quality that things acquire under certain conditions, so much so that the same bit of grass, at the same moment, may have it from one point of view and not from another." [7]

What Santayana says here about the predicates "green" and "good" may easily be extended to the predicate "beautiful." The most complete statement of this extension occurs in *The Realm of Essence*. Having suggested that beautiful things are those we intuit with delight, Santayana makes it clear that to say this is not to give a definition of beauty: "the beautiful is itself an essence, an indefinable quality felt in many things which, however disparate they may be otherwise, receive this name by virtue of a special emotion, half wonder, half love, which is felt in their presence. The essence of the beautiful, when made an object of contemplation by itself, is rather misleading: like the good and like pure Being, it requires much dialectical and spiritual training to discern it in its purity and in its fullness." [8] And he warns against burying the essence of the beautiful under "heavy descriptions of the occasions on which perhaps it appears." [9]

Intimations of this position occur in *The Sense of Beauty*. In the "Introduction" Santayana insists that his analysis will not ignore the insights of the Platonists, but rather explain and justify them. When we consider something good or beautiful, we make a categorical judgment that invokes a standard or ideal which is both "intrinsic and ultimate" for that occasion: "all ideals are absolute . . . for the judgment that involves them." [10] When we revise our earlier judgment and consider the original thing to be bad or ugly instead of good or beautiful, we employ another standard, which is equally absolute, though only for the new judgment. Throughout our experience and as long as we make judgments, *some* absolute ideal always appears before us. But when it comes to definition, we are speechless: "if we try to define that ideal, we shall hardly be able to say of it anything less noble and more definite than that it is the embodiment of an infinite good. For it is that incommunicable and illusive excellence that haunts every beautiful thing. . . ." [11]

Consequently, the first thing we may say about Santayana's aesthetic theory is that it is not wholly naturalistic and does not attempt to be. The "naturalistic fallacy," whether or not it is really a fallacy, does not occur in Santayana's philosophy. He is a naturalist only when he attempts to specify the conditions under which the elusive essence of beauty actually appears. In saying this, I do not wish to minimize the ambiguities of Santayana's first book. He most assuredly does claim to be giving a definition of the word "beauty." * Two pages

* In *The Foundations of Aesthetics* (C. K. Ogden, I. A. Richards, and James Wood, London: Allen & Unwin, Ltd., 1922), where sixteen definitions

after he asserts, as quoted above, that there would be nothing to say if we tried to define an ideal such as the beautiful, he indicates what we *are* to say in a definition of beauty:

A definition that should really define must be nothing less than the exposition of the origin, place, and elements of beauty as an object of human experience. We must learn from it, as far as possible, why, when and how beauty appears, what conditions an object must fulfil to be beautiful, what elements of our nature make us sensible of beauty, and what the relation is between the constitution of the object and the excitement of our susceptibility. Nothing less will really define beauty or make us understand what aesthetic appreciation is. The definition of beauty in this sense will be the task of this whole book. . . .[12]

The contradiction inherent in Santayana's statement is eliminated if we understand him to mean that aesthetic appreciation is what he really wishes to define. But whatever he means, this is what he does: he defines the sense of beauty.

Santayana attains his definition by progressively excluding irrelevant factors. Each exclusion narrows the field of human experience a little further, until Santayana hits the bull's eye at which he is aiming: the experience of an objectified pleasure.

Preparatory to this whittling process, similar in some respects to the paring of experience to its solipsistic core, Santayana points out that he is trying to analyze "the sphere of critical or appreciative perception."[13] But although the words "critical" and "perception" occur in this statement of his purpose, Santayana does not intend to imitate what was formerly known as "criticism" or what was sometimes called "aesthetics." According to Santayana, the philosophy of beauty

---

of beauty are listed, Santayana is referred to as "the most accomplished modern advocate of the theory of Beauty as pleasure" (p. 53). Actually, his theory comes under another of their headings: "anything is beautiful which possesses the simple quality of Beauty," which is equivalent to saying that beauty is indefinable (cf. pp. 20–21). In *The Basis of Criticism in the Arts* (Cambridge: Harvard University Press, 1946), Pepper takes Santayana's aesthetics as the outstanding illustration of mechanism and hedonism, although he shows evident annoyance each time Santayana's position deviates from "the implications of the mechanistic categories."

must be more than a theory of criticism, since the beautiful object is felt and enjoyed rather than being deliberately judged or compared with standards. Neither can it be limited to aesthetics, understood as the theory of perception or susceptibility. For this kind of aesthetics investigates all pleasure and pain and probably all perception; it does not specifically deal with beauty. Santayana offers to combine the two fields, retaining the word "aesthetics" but concerning himself with critical perception. Santayana makes the combination as follows:

> Criticism implies judgment, and aesthetics perception. To get the common ground, that of perceptions which are critical, or judgments which are perceptions, we must widen our notion of deliberate criticism so as to include those judgments of value which are instinctive and immediate, that is, to include pleasures and pains; and at the same time we must narrow our notion of aesthetics so as to exclude all perceptions which are not appreciations, which do not find a value in their objects.[14]

In taking his first step towards the definition of the aesthetic, Santayana delineates the conditions for value in general. He denies that values have existence apart from consciousness. In a mechanical world, devoid of all consciousness, neither purpose nor value could occur. Values come into being only when a sentient creature develops an interest in something. Otherwise, there is not even the "possibility of worth." [15]

But consciousness is not enough. Santayana proceeds to exclude a consciousness that would be solely rational. We can, he says, imagine beings "of a purely intellectual cast." They would have consciousness and perhaps even knowledge, but they could not have valuable experiences. "Every event would then be noted, its relations would be observed, its recurrence might even be expected; but all this would happen without a shadow of desire, of pleasure, of regret." [16] For the existence of good, in any form, consciousness is required, but it must be a specifically "emotional" consciousness.

By insisting that there is no value apart from some felt appreciation, Santayana provides a basis for describing the nature of value-judgments. As a result of habit our linguistic behavior leads us to approve or condemn; but "unless there is in us some trace of passionate reprobation or of sensible delight, there is no moral or aesthetic judgment." [17] Without feeling any emotion at all, we might detect certain characters in a work of art and judge it accordingly. But this could not be a judgment of value, for none of the "immediate and inexplicable reaction of vital impulse" would be involved. Judgments of value spring from our irrational nature and, unlike "intellectual judgments," are wholly unconcerned about matters of fact or relation. "If we approach a work of art or nature scientifically, for the sake of its historical connections or proper classification, we do not approach it aesthetically." [18]

Santayana supports this distinction between intellectual judgments, on the one hand, and value-judgments, on the other, by means of a brief comparison of science with art. In science we desire truthful information; in art we demand entertainment that can be obtained by the stimulation of our senses and imagination. If truth is a factor in art, it is aesthetically relevant only as it subserves our demand for entertainment. Science has value as a practical enterprise and as a possible source of inspiration for the artist, the former a moral value and the latter an aesthetic one; but these values are only derivative from science's preëminent concern for truth. Moral and aesthetic judgments are judgments of value; intellectual judgments are judgments of fact, which in itself is neither good nor bad in any moral or aesthetic sense.

Next, Santayana distinguishes between moral and aesthetic values. He makes this distinction on the basis of two considerations: first, that aesthetic judgments are mainly positive, whereas moral judgments are mainly negative; and second, that aesthetic judgments are "necessarily intrinsic and based on the character of the immediate experience," whereas moral judgments, when they are positive, merely predict that something is instrumental to a desired experience.

On similar grounds Santayana distinguishes work from play

and duty from enjoyment. The difference between work and play he interprets as the difference between slavery and freedom. Duty and work are negative or restrictive, for they deny our natural impulses, which lead to play and enjoyment. Play and enjoyment are positive in being spontaneously undergone for their own sake and without any consideration of further utility.

Thus, on their positive side moral perceptions are justified only as instrumental to aesthetic perceptions, which themselves are immediate and intrinsic. In one sense, Santayana adds, all values must be aesthetic since they all must be "ultimately intrinsic." "The useful is good because of the excellence of its consequences; but these must somewhere cease to be merely useful in their turn, or only excellent as means; somewhere we must reach the good that is good in itself and for its own sake, else the whole process is futile, and the utility of our first object illusory." [19] And that which is "good in itself" is the aesthetic. All values are reducible to immediate aesthetic appreciations: they alone are intrinsically valuable and exist for their own sake.

At the same time, one's adherence to moral principles may also be aesthetic. Not only are the goals towards which these principles lead intrinsically valuable, but also our attitude towards the principles themselves can be aesthetic as long as it is based on "constitutional sensitiveness" rather than "reflection and benevolence." When conscience has been instilled, we *feel* that a course of action is right, and this feeling may itself be aesthetic, despite the fact that the course of action can be justified only by reference to its utility. Similarly, the miser has an aesthetic experience when his eye is fascinated by the glittering, yellow gold, which is an immediate good, instead of figures in a bank account, which only represent possible values. If the gold is also taken to represent further aesthetic values, we have an object that is both aesthetic and representative, like principles of conduct that are both intrinsic, because felt by a constitutional sensitivity, and instrumental, because conducive to further values. The aesthetic and the moral or practical may coöperate in any object, but the distinction between them is one that reason can always effect.

Having excluded intellectual and moral judgments or values from the intrinsic and immediate ones which are alone aesthetic, Santayana next demarcates a still smaller class of perceptions. All pleasures are intrinsically valuable, he now says, but they are not all related to the sense of beauty. Some of them must be eliminated before the aesthetic itself can be discerned.* First to go are the ones that Santayana calls "physical pleasures" or "bodily pleasures." By physical or bodily pleasures Santayana does not mean pleasures that have some bodily or physical condition, for even aesthetic pleasures have that: "they (aesthetic pleasures) depend on the activity of the eye and the ear, of the memory and the other ideational functions of the brain." [20] But whereas the bodily organs and physical conditions for aesthetic pleasures are "transparent" and direct our attention outwards to some external object, the so-called physical pleasures do not. They attract our interest to the bodily organs themselves. Aesthetic pleasures give us the illusion of immateriality and spiritual freedom, but the physical pleasures draw us back to the clay of which we are made.

Now Santayana has reached the inner circle of his analysis. When we perceive beauty, he says, we perceive it as belonging to an object; the projection of our enjoyment out of ourselves and into the object constitutes the sense of beauty. This

* It is important to note that, within seven pages of *The Sense of Beauty*, Santayana presents two inconsistent views about the relation between intrinsic value and aesthetic value. As we have seen, he first maintains that "all values are in a sense aesthetic," by which he means that "all values must be ultimately intrinsic" (p. 28). This is an identification of intrinsic value with aesthetic value. But later, as paraphrased above, Santayana states that "all pleasures are intrinsic and positive values, but all pleasures are not perceptions of beauty" (p. 35). From this it would follow that aesthetic value is not the same as intrinsic value. I fail to see how both of these views can be maintained without inconsistency. Santayana *usually* identifies intrinsic value with aesthetic value, and this is the position I shall continue to ascribe to him.

projection Santayana calls "objectification." In the objectification of pleasure he finds his desired definition.

Identifying the aesthetic experience with the objectification of pleasure, Santayana appeals to the empiricist theory of perception that he was later to reject. Every element of the perceived world is a sensation; sensations are combined by the intelligence to form material objects; these objects differ from their constituent sensations in being taken to be permanent, external, and substantial. In human development all sensations were originally objectified in this way, but soon the distinction between primary and secondary qualities arose and men became increasingly aware of the fact that their experiences were at least partially determined by their own organic conditions. Pleasures and pains were among the first qualities that were considered to be separate from the object in itself, although they were still liable to objectification. Among primitive peoples such objectifications contribute greatly to the variegated world of their experience. With civilized persons the objectification of pleasure occurs only in the perception of beauty.

The sense of beauty is, therefore, a deceptive condition. Beauty is perceived when an element of sensation has been transformed into the quality of a thing. Aside from this process, beauty has no existence. It is not an independent constituent of the object, as extension, for instance, is supposed to be. The sense of beauty is not, fundamentally, different from any other process of enjoyment, for all pleasures exist only in perception. And yet, beauty alone is taken as a quality in things and as having an independent existence. The sense of beauty is a survival of the aboriginal tendency to objectify every effect that anything might have upon us. In these terms Santayana distinguishes the scientific idea of a thing from the aesthetic idea. The former is "a great abstraction from the mass of perceptions and reactions which that thing produces"; the latter is "less abstract, since it retains the emotional reaction, the pleasure of the perception, as an integral part of the conceived thing." [21]

Now Santayana has attained what he calls "the definition of beauty." Beauty is "value positive, intrinsic, and objectified. . . . Beauty is pleasure regarded as the quality of a thing." [22] As a value, beauty is a felt emotion or pleasure rather than the perception of a matter of fact. As positive, it contrasts with ugliness, which is the mere absence of beauty and therefore a positive evil only on moral, not aesthetic, grounds. As intrinsic, it is an ultimate good or satisfaction. As objectified, it is distinguished from the pleasures of sense in the same way that a percept is distinguished from a sensation. And here Santayana adds that the distinction is mainly one of degree. There is no facile means of deciding just when a person will stop saying "It pleases me" and begin to say "It is beautiful."

In his later philosophy Santayana rejects the empiricist theory of perception that underlies this formulation of his aesthetics, substituting for it the kind of critical realism that we examined in the First Part of this study. In accordance with his doctrine of essences, Santayana revises his "definition of beauty," although he maintains that nothing fundamental has been changed. This revision of his early position occurs in a footnote appended to an article entitled "The Mutability of Esthetic Categories," published almost thirty years after *The Sense of Beauty*.[23] In view of its importance for understanding Santayana's aesthetics, I should like to quote the major part of it:

My whole little book *The Sense of Beauty* was written from a subjective point of view, and nothing was further from me than a wish to hypostatize either beauty or pleasure. Even now, when I speak of the terms actually present in intuition as of so many eternal essences, I should not now use the phrase "objectified pleasure," because I see that a term does not become subjective merely because an intuition of it occurs. Nothing is subjective in experience except experience itself, the passing act of intuition or feeling; the terms distinguished during that experience, such as specific qualities of color or pleasure, are neither objective nor subjective, but neutral; at most they might be called, so long as attended to, subjective objects, such objects as subjective idealism would admit. On the other hand the objects of animal faith, assumed in action to exist apart from the agent, are past, future, or remote events, not so much objective as substantial, although they may become on occasion the objects of intent or investigation. *Pleasure therefore does not need to be objectified in order to be fused into an image felt to be beautiful: if felt at all, pleasure is already an object of intuition;* and the beautiful image is never objective in any other sense. Nevertheless I am far from disowning my old view in its import. I was making an honest effort, with the categories then at my command, to express accurately what happened within me whenever I felt that anything was beautiful. Nor was the phrase "objectified pleasure" a definition of beauty, a visionary essence utterly indefinable: it was an indication of the conditions and manner in which the momentary apparition of beauty arose and vanished. If I tried now to give such an indication I might perhaps say that *beauty was a vital harmony felt and fused into an image under the form of eternity.* I add the last five words, which are not strictly requisite, in order to emphasize the fact that *beauty, as I feel it, transports us altogether into the realm of essence, and that no pleasure, interest, or admiration becomes a sense of beauty unless it does so.* Every image, however, if animal faith is suspended in its presence, is an essence seen under the form of eternity.[24]

Thus beauty occurs wherever two essences are combined, one a pleasure or "vital harmony," the other an image. This seems to have been Santayana's final statement in the matter. Whether it is consistent with the major import of his earlier formulation, and the extent to which either is acceptable, is what we shall consider in the rest of this chapter and in the two succeeding ones. Throughout this discussion, and indeed, the remainder of this book, I shall take "beauty" and "beautiful" as terms of general aesthetic commendation. This will save us the trouble of distinguishing between "beautiful" and other aesthetic adjectives, such as "pretty" and "sublime." It will also serve to remind us that in aesthetics we are more interested in explaining a certain way of using language than in analyzing the meaning of particular words.

II

If there are any advantages to a thorough-going naturalism, they must surely consist in the elimination of magical and superstitious entities of thought, such as a "dormitive capacity" used to explain why some things tend to make us sleepy. The naturalist who rejects this kind of explanation does not deny that some things have a dormitive capacity, just as he does not deny that some things tend to make us sleepy. Instead he denies that the capacity is different from the tendency or that one can be understood to be the cause, condition, or circumstance for the occurrence of the other. In short, for the naturalist "dormitive capacity" is *definable* as "tendency to make us sleepy."

In discussing the issue of thorough-going naturalism in aesthetics, it will be instructive to compare Santayana's views first with those of John Dewey, and later with those of C. I. Lewis. The advantages of thorough-going naturalism are recognized by all three, although, as I shall try to point out, they are imperfect naturalists with regard to the distinction between a quality of beauty and the conditions for its appearance.

In his article "Dewey's Naturalistic Metaphysics," Santayana alleged that Dewey's naturalism, unlike his own, was "half-hearted and short-winded." [25] Dewey's philosophy prescribed "the dominance of the foreground," which is to say, the dominance of immediate experience. In bringing forward immediate experience, Santayana claimed, Dewey allowed the external world to recede indefinitely or even to vanish. In addition, Santayana found fault with Dewey's conception of immediate experience, since Dewey denied that it was "specious" and since he limited "consummation," or the enjoyment of immediate experience, to aesthetic contemplation without concern for any other approach to essence. Dewey replied in an article called " 'Half-Hearted Naturalism' " in which he corrected Santayana's misinterpretations and concluded that with respect to fundamental philosophical positions one might say of him and Santayana, that these two men were very much alike, "especially one of them." At the same time, he took umbrage at Santayana's use of the word "specious" and attempted to turn the charge of "half-hearted naturalism" against Santayana himself. For it was Santayana who considered immediate experience to be specious, dreamlike, or nonnatural.

This issue, about the natural or nonnatural status of immediate experience, emanates from the basic distinction between essence and existence, but it has special relevance in aesthetics and theory of value. For there above all, one should think, the naturalist must stiffen his backbone against any nonnaturalistic incursion. As a matter of fact, however, both Dewey and Lewis, as well as Santayana, maintain that immediate experience has a felt character or quality of value (and even, perhaps, of disvalue) which is simple, unanalyzable, and indefinable. This conception is, I suggest, a queer and nonnaturalistic notion, not basically different from the idea of a special dormitive capacity, and a hang-over from an untenable intuitionism. Before criticizing the conception in detail, let us see further how Dewey and Lewis use it.

A year after the article answering Santayana appeared, Dewey published a brief but highly instructive review of *The Realm of Essence*. In the review Dewey summarized Santayana's position, listed the four approaches, and then, without very much argument, rejected three of them as merely "preliminary" to contemplation, an approach that he did accept:

It would appear that not only is sense an organ or apprehension of essence but is its only organ, understanding by "sense" not the desiccated "sensations" of analytic psychology but direct and pregnant realization, in which emotion is also contained. . . . It thus appears that, of the four approaches to genuine and final essence, but one, that of sense, is complete and adequate. The others are preliminary and instrumental, preparing the antecedent machinery which is indispensable to a rich and vital appreciation of the realized potentialities of nature. Which is to say that *they* are *not* essence but means of approach to natural existence alone possessed of essential, that is, final and self-sufficing, quality.[26]

This "final and self-sufficing quality" of experience Dewey had referred to elsewhere as "ultimate, simple, and indefinable." [27] That this variety of naturalism is similar to Santayana's modification of Moorism should be evident from the following passage:

Values are values, things immediately having certain intrinsic qualities. Of them as values there is accordingly nothing to be said; they are what they are. All that can be said of them concerns their generative conditions and the consequences to which they give rise . . . . To take into account the reason for liking and enjoyment concerns the cause of the existence of a value, and has nothing to do with the intrinsicalness or nature of the value-quality, which either does or does not exist.[28]

C. I. Lewis holds a similar view, together with further specifications as follows:

Immediate or directly findable value is not so much one quality as a dimensionlike mode which is pervasive of all experience. . . . Value or disvalue is not like the pitch of middle C or the seen color of median red or the felt hardness of steel. It is not one specific quale of experience but a gamut of such; more like color in general or pitch or hardness in general. It is like seen bigness or apparent littleness of things.[29]

Now, I do not deny that one may experience something *as* good or beautiful. What I do deny is that there is any indefinable quality of beauty (or value or goodness, etc.). My argument runs as follows: a) the experience of something *as* beautiful is not the same as the aesthetic experience (the sense of beauty); b) there is no quality of beauty in aesthetic experience as such; c) in the experience of something as beautiful we never experience an indefinable quality; d) therefore, neither in the experience of something as beautiful nor in the aesthetic experience does one discover an indefinable quality of beauty.

Let us begin by distinguishing between the experience of something as beautiful and the sense of beauty or aesthetic experience. Whenever we experience something *as* beautiful, we not only see or hear or touch the object, but also we accept it as being beautiful. It is such acceptance that determines what we ordinarily call "taste." A person's taste is revealed by what he considers to be beautiful. As such, taste is a disposition to classify in a specific fashion, viz. to accept certain things, and not others, as beautiful. But a person's taste, his classificatory practice in this respect, only indirectly and inexactly manifests his own likes and dislikes. These do sometimes determine what an individual takes to be beautiful, but often his judgment depends on considerations of what the object is, the conditions under which it makes an appearance, what others think about it, and so on: much as a color-blind person who can't tell red from green knows to cross the street when the lower traffic light is burning. To say of a person that he has "good taste" is to say that he knows what is worthy of choice, regardless of what he himself may actually enjoy.

However one characterizes aesthetic experience, it is clearly distinguishable from the experience of something as beautiful. In the former experience what I have called "secondary signification" may be entirely lacking; in the latter it must be present, for otherwise the datum could not be determinate *as* something beautiful. The two kinds of experience frequently coexist, and often we enjoy things *because* we believe them to be beautiful; but also we may undergo an aesthetic experience without making any judgment about the beauty of what we see, hear, or touch. In the latter event, we would have the sense of beauty without any experience of something *as* beautiful.

Thus, insofar as we are merely having an aesthetic experience, we are not making aesthetic commendations. To enjoy an object is one thing; to regard it as something *beautiful* is another, and quite different. And since it is only when we take something to be beautiful that the quality of beauty could occur, it follows that the appearance of this quality cannot be the condition for an aesthetic experience.

But does even the experience of taking something as beautiful disclose an indefinable quality of beauty? There are two questions we must ask: In the experience of something as beautiful, do we perceive a quality? If so, is that quality indefinable?

When we take something to be beautiful, we are not deliberating about its classification. We are not doubting the given and our experience is not mediate. As a result, the object has taken on a determinate character that it did not have before. Shall we say that this determinate character must be a "quality"? To do so would be a mistake, I believe. For it would lead us to think of the determinate character as inevitably being "in" the object, more or less in the way that the whiteness is in the cloud. We might then expect to *perceive* the beauty in all objects that are determinately beautiful. As a matter of fact, however, we do not usually perceive a quality of beauty when we take something to be beautiful. Generally and for the most part, we merely make a judgment, we merely accept an interpretation. It does *sometimes* happen that the interpretation is accepted with so strong a feeling of affirmation that the character is *virtually* perceived in the object. When this occurs, we may possibly wish to claim that a "quality" of beauty is present. This claim is innocent enough — but only as long as we remember that one need not perceive any such "quality" in order to experience something as beautiful; that perceiving a quality of beauty involves the fervid acceptance of an interpretation to the effect that something is beautiful; and, finally, that the quality of beauty is not "in" an object in the same sense in which its colors are.

Furthermore, the experience of beauty involves complex interpretation in a way that the perception of colors, for instance, does not. The quality of beauty has a different *kind* of character from a "simple" quality, such as the green that persons who are not color-blind ordinarily see as green and take to be green. There is no aesthetic sense at all comparable to the visual or auditory sense. The connoisseur who "instinctively" chooses what he considers to be beautiful does not resemble the normal man pointing to green so much as he resembles the color-blind person who unhesitatingly crosses the street.

In this respect Lewis does well to suggest that directly findable value is more like seen bigness or apparent littleness than a "specific quale" like the pitch of middle C or the seen color of median red. But what Lewis and Santayana seem to overlook is the fact that seen bigness or apparent littleness is vague and almost wholly indeterminate unless it has been interpreted even more than the heard pitch of middle C: seen bigness depends upon secondary signification as well as primary, like the painter's white object being seen as something that would look red at sunset. Just what does one perceive when one sees the bigness of a house? Very little of a determinate character, I suggest, unless one has already interpreted bigness to mean bigness in comparison *to* something else or bigness *for* someone and for some *purpose*. For a dog and his occupations, even a doghouse may be big. And when one looks at a house and takes it to have bigness, one might have the needs of a dog in mind. Interpreted with respect to human beings and their requirements, doghouses are not, as a matter of fact, taken to be big. It is this kind of interpretation, extending as it does beyond primary signification, that enables a datum to be determinate with respect to seen bigness. Without interpretation of this sort, the bigness perceived would be indefinitely vague. When the word "big" is used although the speaker has no such interpretation in mind, however tacitly, one may conclude that for him the word is without meaning.

Something similar holds for the quality of beauty. Unless it is indefinitely vague, the quality of beauty involves interpretation beyond that of a simple quality like the seen color of median red. It differs from the quality of bigness in referring specifically to aesthetic experience. I may feel that this house is big for a family of three if I believe, perhaps, that it gives them more than enough space to entertain guests, to maintain privacy, to play their phonograph, etc. I feel that the house is beautiful only if I believe that it tends to participate in someone's aesthetic experience. The quality of beauty becomes more and more determinate when we specify just whose aesthetic experience is authoritative and what is to be taken as aesthetic experience. When we believe that something is beautiful, we may only mean that it tends to participate in our own individual aesthetic experience. Some persons would consider the object to be beautiful only if it had the capacity to enter into *everyone's* aesthetic experience. Generally, we mean that trained and sensitive observers would have aesthetic experiences in the presence of the object. With respect to our conception of just what an aesthetic experience is, a further relativity obtains. The different theories about the nature of aesthetic experience (when they are actually believed in and not merely mouthed) color one's experience of the beautiful each in its own way. The determinate quality of beauty experienced by two persons cannot be the same unless their conception of aesthetic experience is the same. But regardless of what the conception of aesthetic experience may happen to be, the quality of beauty becomes determinate only by means of secondary signification. I conclude, therefore, that the quality of beauty is neither simple nor indispensable to the experience of something as beautiful.

If this is so, can we now define the beautiful? And just what does that involve? When Santayana says that the quality of beauty is indefinable, I presume that he means three things: First, that the predicate "beautiful" is indefinable; second, that the quality itself is unanalyzable; and third, that the predicate is indefinable *because* the quality is unanalyzable. If Santayana does hold this position, as G. E. Moore seems to, there are two good reasons why he is mistaken: First, even if the quality of beauty were unanalyzable, the predicate "beautiful" would still be definable; and second, the quality of beauty is analyzable.

Especially in his article "Hypostatic Ethics" Santayana

seems to accept the view that a word is indefinable unless one can specify the constituents of that which it denotes. Moore expresses this belief in the following way: " 'Good,' then, if we mean by it that quality which we assert to belong to a thing, when we say that the thing is good, is incapable of any definition, in the most important sense of that word. The most important sense of 'definition' is that in which a definition states what are the parts which invariably compose a certain whole; and in this sense 'good' has no definition because it is simple and has no parts." [30]

Still, as others have also pointed out,[31] a "definition," in its most important sense, is different from any statement about the constituent parts of the object denoted. To give a definition of "brother," we need to present an analysis of what we mean by "brother"; and such an analysis does not tell us how a brother is composed, but only how our meaning for "brother" is composed. Brothers are composed of feet, hands, heart, liver, etc.; but "brother" means "male sibling."

Thus, even if the experience of something as beautiful always involved an unanalyzable quality of beauty, we could still define the predicate "beautiful." To say that something is beautiful (or aesthetically good, aesthetically commendable) is to say that it tends to, or has the capacity to, participate in aesthetic experience. The vagueness of the word results from the loose reference to aesthetic experience; just as "big" is vague insofar as it loosely refers to something else with which the object is compared or to some use or function. When "beautiful" is employed without any specification as to what an aesthetic experience is and whose aesthetic experience one has in mind, the word loses whatever definite meaning it ever had.

Furthermore, once we recognize that the quality of beauty depends upon a felt interpretation, we can see how the beautiful is analyzable. Even green, median red, or middle C, "simple" as they may be in comparison to other qualities, are liable to analysis of a sort. Such data in immediate experience are determinate only by means of their respective interpretations on the level of primary signification. Accordingly, an analysis would specify that they have been accepted by the organism (otherwise they could not appear in immediate experience) and that they possess their particular sign- and class-relations (otherwise they could not be determinate in precisely the way they are).

Similarly, analysis would resolve the beautiful into the constituents of organic acceptance and interpretation, but now on the level of secondary signification. Taking something as beautiful is tantamount to accepting a certain judgment: that the object has the capacity to function in an aesthetic experience. It is the unique complex of class- and sign-relations involved in this use of secondary signification, together with the fact that the organism is firmly accepting instead of doubting, that makes the quality of beauty determinate in its own particular fashion. But, once again, let us remember that we need not experience anything like a quality of beauty in order to take something *as* beautiful.

Our discussion leads to two further observations:

First, that "beautiful" is a disposition term, like "soluble." When we call something beautiful, we generally mean that it has a tendency to participate in aesthetic experiences; just as we call objects soluble when we think they have a tendency to dissolve in some fluid or other.

Second, that Santayana is mistaken when he says that in a mechanical world, one from which all consciousness has been removed, the "possibility of worth" is also lacking. The beauty of an object, its capacity to enter into aesthetic experience, is not altered by the fact that currently there are no aesthetic experiences. That famous "gem of purest ray serene which dark unfathomed caves of ocean bear" may be called "beautiful" although hidden from our sight. For the tendency, capacity, or disposition of the beautiful gem assures us that some person who saw it *would* have an aesthetic experience. That no one actually does see it may lead us to wonder how anyone can know whether the gem is beautiful; but if we are told that it *is* beautiful, we understand that it has the relevant relation to a possible aesthetic experience. In this respect too, "beautiful" resembles words like "soluble."

III

I submit, then, that Santayana, Dewey, and Lewis alike are mistaken in thinking that beauty or value is a simple or unanalyzable quality. Nothing in experience is immediately or directly found to be good except by means of a value-judgment, perforce on the level of secondary signification. Such judgments describe a tendency in the object and are as fallible as any other empirical judgments. They mark an interpretation of the object and presuppose a conception of valuable or aesthetic experience that need not be the same for any two persons. In fact Santayana, Dewey, and Lewis all seem to hold somewhat different views about the nature of valuable experience. As a result, their opinions about goodness vary somewhat, although they agree that value is an indefinable quality that simply is what it is.

As a further instance of this mistaken approach, consider the following statement by Lewis:

. . . it is essential for a naturalistic view to maintain that the quality or character by reference to which, ultimately, all things are to be judged valuable or disvaluable, is a quality unmistakably identifiable in the direct apprehension of it when disclosed in experience. It must hold that such immediately apprehensible value-quality or value-character constitutes the criterion by reference to which, eventually, those value-predications which are subject to possible error and need confirmation are to be attested. Thus such a naturalistic view can hardly attain to clarity and cogency unless the distinction be remarked between value-predications which are merely expressive statements of the value-quality immediately discovered, and those which attribute to some existent the objective property of conducing to such realization of the immediately valuable. . . . Immediate prizings of the directly presented as such, are not judgments.*

* *An Analysis of Knowledge and Valuation*, pp. 400 and 457. Lewis does not identify aesthetic value with intrinsic value, of which aesthetic value

In distinguishing between the apprehension of an unmistakably discovered value-quality and a value-judgment about some objective property, Lewis is making a distinction similar to his distinction between the intuition of an irreducible datum and the interpretation imposed upon this datum. In doing so, he ignores the fact that anything determinately given must already have been interpreted, and also that every value-quality depends upon a value-judgment accepted in an immediate (that is, nondoubting) experience.

Accordingly, Lewis confuses the aesthetic or valuable experience with the experience of something taken to be beautiful or good. When we are having a valuable experience, we are enjoying ourselves — seeing green, perhaps, and liking it — but we are not necessarily believing that what we see and like is "valuable." That usually happens afterwards, when we recollect our experience and infer that the object has this capacity to delight. Even when an aesthetic experience occurs simultaneously with an experience of taking something to be beautiful, they are distinguishable — for the analyst, if not the participant — as different kinds of experience that often occur separately. Apart from the value-judgment that occurs in taking something as good or beautiful, there is no quality of value or beauty to be found in experience; if anything is found, it is enjoyment, pleasure, satisfaction, harmony, or whatever turns out to be the defining characteristic of aesthetic experience. This datum is not "unmistakably identifiable" any more than other determinate, and therefore interpreted, data. To be sure, it is "immediately discovered," but this only means that it is accepted by the organism instead of being doubted. And although this defining character of aesthetic experience is not indubitable in any ultimate epistemological sense, we generally assess value or beauty on the basis of its tendency to occur. This assessment is a value-judgment; and it is corrigible, by no means unmistakable.

---

is taken to be a species. Nevertheless, Lewis employs the same approach with respect to aesthetic value as he does here with respect to intrinsic value.

But to have a valuable experience one need never have made a value-judgment.

Santayana's treatment of this issue is, as we have seen, similar to Dewey's and Lewis', though his conception of intrinsic value is somewhat different from theirs. All three wish to construct a naturalistic theory of value; all three hope to do so by reference to an unmistakable but indefinable value-quality in ordinary experience. I have tried to show that there is no value-quality of the sort they describe and that predicates such as "valuable" or "beautiful" can readily be defined. By defining "beautiful" in terms of aesthetic experience, we effectively carry out the naturalist program. For the empirical cash-value of the word does not reside in any special or mysterious quality, but merely in the capacity to enter into aesthetic experiences.

At the same time, however, we must avoid the errors of those traditional naturalists who defined value-predicates in terms of necessary and sufficient conditions. A definition of that sort would either be trivial or a violation of ordinary usage. It is true that I have provided necessary and sufficient conditions for "beautiful" inasmuch as I defined it as "having the capacity to enter into aesthetic experience." But, it will be remembered, I insisted that the meaning of "beautiful" remains indefinitely vague until we define "aesthetic experience" and indicate whose experience is relevant. Consequently, although it is a useful means for showing that "beautiful" can be defined, my definition as it now stands is trivial. And once we render it significant, we shall find that the "open texture" of our language prevents us from giving necessary *and* sufficient conditions.* As the next step in the direction of a non-

* The term "open texture" is Friedrich Waismann's: "Try as we may, no concept is limited in such a way that there is no room for any doubt . . . In short, it is not possible to define a concept like gold with absolute precision, i.e. in such a way that every nook and cranny is blocked against entry of doubt. That is what is meant by the open texture of a concept . . . Open texture, then, is something like *possibility of vagueness*. Vagueness can be remedied by giving more accurate rules, open texture cannot. An alternative way of stating this would be to say that definitions of open

trivial definition, we turn more directly to problems concerning the nature of aesthetic experience. The remainder of this Part will be largely devoted to them.

———

terms are *always* corrigible or emendable." ("Verifiability," in *Essays on Logic and Language*, First Series, p. 120, his italics.) Cf. also Max Black, "Definition, Presupposition, and Assertion," in *Problems of Analysis* (Ithaca: Cornell University Press, 1954).

3

AESTHETIC VALUE

In trying to define "aesthetic experience," in this Chapter
and the next, we must bear in mind clear cases of the use of
the term. We would not be shocked to hear a man say that
he had an aesthetic experience in the presence of a stirring
symphony, a delicate poem, a profound drama, an awesome
thunderstorm, a spectacular sunset, a delectable repast, or a
soothing rubdown. Some of us might wonder whether enjoyment derived from a meal or a rubdown is appropriately
called "aesthetic," but no one would be shocked by such usage. The term is loose. It is used to describe an indefinitely
vague range of different experiences associated with different
kinds of objects or circumstances: everything from the simplicity of a smile to the complexity of sexual intercourse, from
the melancholy drift of summer clouds to the turbulence of
a street scene in a new city, from the somber tones of a plain
chant to the harsh rhythms of jazz, from the directness of an
Elizabethan lyric to the elusiveness of a symbolist novel. At
the same time, however, the aesthetic excludes everything distasteful or irritating. It would be astounding for a man to
speak of an "aesthetic" disgust, loathing, nausea, anxiety, or
frustration. We would suspect a hidden meaning in his words.
His utterance would be perplexing, paradoxical.

However amorphous its use may be, "aesthetic experience"
plays a part in everyday language. The same is not true of
"intrinsically valuable experience." That is a technical term,
a bit of jargon. Philosophers use it to refer to experience that
is good in itself, for its own sake, and not merely as a means
to something else. As such, it is usually contrasted with "in-

strumentally valuable experience" — experience that conduces to the intrinsically valuable but may or may not be good
in itself. Whether an intrinsically valuable experience is actually worthy of choice depends upon a variety of factors
that we shall examine later; but nothing is worthy of choice
unless it is intrinsically valuable either in itself or in its consequences. We discover what is worthy of choice, therefore,
by first discovering what is intrinsically valuable.

Now, in dealing with "aesthetic value," we are concerned
with the aesthetic character of intrinsically valuable experience. Some philosophers have claimed that aesthetic value
is different from intrinsic value. I myself fail to see any justification for this distinction. Like Santayana, I shall identify
aesthetic experience and intrinsically valuable experience, aesthetic value and intrinsic value. I make this identification because I find that the ordinary use of "aesthetic" coincides
with the philosophical use of "intrinsically valuable." The
exact nature of this use is what we must now discover. Let us
begin with an analysis of Santayana's value theory.

I

Santayana is generally said to hold an "interest theory of
value." [1] By this it is meant that he defines intrinsic value in
terms of human impulses or interests. But his use of the terms
"impulse" and "interest" lends itself to various interpretations. He seems to employ the word "impulse" sometimes in
a broader sense and sometimes in a narrower one. Munitz
points out the ambiguity as follows: "In the broader sense of
the term, impulse means not only what it ordinarily con-
notes — the biological expression of some bodily or organic
tension — but also the fact of interest on every level of life.
It then includes not only such things as the drives of hunger
and sex, but various economic, parental, or political interests
of social life, as well as the interests of imagination and reflection as these express themselves in science, art and religion." [2] In his article on Santayana's theory of value Pepper

claims that a literal interpretation would conclude that Santayana considers all of the following to be kinds of interest:
pleasure, discomfort, aversion, dread, anticipation, desire, conation, satisfaction, preference, instinct, and impulse. Pepper
concentrates his attention upon pleasure, desire, and preference, showing them to be irreducible to a single basic, common unit of value and therefore incomparable among themselves. As such, they seem to be antagonistic, and Pepper
wonders just what Santayana's conception of intrinsic value
really is.

In his reply to Pepper Santayana avoids the issue: "Pepper
finds my 'theory of value' ambiguous. It is so ambiguous that,
under that name, I was not aware that I had one. . . . But I
confess that when Pepper goes on to distinguish various literal theories of value, I hardly know what he is talking
about." [3] Without deciding who is to blame for Santayana's
difficulty in this matter and before considering his restatement of his position, I should like to analyze Santayana's
theory of value on somewhat different grounds.

There are, I think, at least six different kinds of value theory
that Santayana might hold. In his adherence to some general
"interest theory," he neglected to distinguish between these
different points of view, with the result that none of them
seems to be more than just one aspect of his thinking. Although they could easily be made to contradict one another,
I have tried to arrange them in a cumulative order so that
the broad strokes of Santayana's approach become more intelligible as we proceed. These are the six theories:

(1) An experience is valuable if it is the completion of a
desire, the attainment of a goal object — for example, the
bread for which one hungered. This version would require
that some definite object was desired or wanted, so that any
attainment that occurred would be influenced by the entire
history of the desire. What matters is "getting what you
want": not the fulfillment of any *need*, but merely the
achievement of your desire. This is the position that Santayana might hold when he says the following:

There is no value apart from some appreciation of it, and no good apart from some preference of it before its absence or its opposite, . . . Or, as Spinoza clearly expresses it, we desire nothing because it is good, but it is good only because we desire it.[4]

No doubt any desire, however capricious, represents some momentary and partial interest, which lends to its objects a certain real and inalienable value.[5]

(2) An experience is valuable if it is the fulfillment of a need. The previous theory excluded the kind of criticism implied by statements like "you don't *really* want that," or "you'll be sorry once you get what you want." According to the previous version, the completion of *any* desire was a sufficient condition for value. On the present theory, however, the object desired is not valuable unless there is some need that its attainment fulfills. It is the fulfillment that makes the experience valuable. And, therefore, one may now deny that the presence of an object, whether or not desired, is essential for value. For if fulfillment is the criterion, what difference does it make whether an object is present and whether the fulfillment occurs after an object is desired?

Santayana, on one occasion at least, presents this theory in surprisingly close proximity to the previous one. The following passage occurs just before the second quotation above:

. . . the words desire and will are often used, in a mythical or transcendental sense, for those material dispositions and instincts by which vital and moral units are constituted. It is in reference to such constitutional interests that things are 'really' good or bad; interests which may not be fairly represented by an incidental conscious desire.[6]

In another place the fulfillment theory appears as follows:

A need is not a good. It denotes a condition to be fulfilled before some natural virtue can be exercised and some true good thereby attained.[7]

(3) An experience is valuable if it is the achievement of pleasure, taken to be an hedonic tone that serves as the ob-

ject of some desire. As an object of desire, pleasure does not differ from other desired "objects" except in being sought for the sake of its own hedonic feeling. In this version what primarily matters is completing a desire for pleasure. Desire of this sort is usually accompanied by the association between pleasure and some other object. This theory finds expression as follows:

The desire for an object logically precedes and conditions whatever pleasures are enjoyed in its attainment.[8] . . . it is hard to recall or estimate a feeling with which no definite and complex object is conjoined. The first step in making pleasure intelligible and capable of being pursued is to make it pleasure in something. The object it suffuses acquires a value, and gives the pleasure itself a place in rational life.[9]

(4) An experience is valuable if it is pleasurable, whether or not the pleasure has resulted from desire. Here it is merely the hedonic tone, the quality of enjoyment, that is taken to be valuable. It is this version that most hedonists really accept. Santayana's reduction of value to "immediate pleasure" in *The Sense of Beauty* was directed towards this conception of pleasure as it is actually felt and independent of any desire. Elsewhere he describes it in the following way:

. . . but pleasure, in its absolute essence, is certainly simple and indefinable. If instead of enjoying it on the wing, and as an earnest of the soul's momentary harmony, we attempt to arrest and observe it, we find it strangely dumb; we are not informed by it concerning its occasion, nor carried from it by any logical implication to the natural object in which it might be found. A pure hedonist ought therefore to be rather relieved if all images lapsed from his consciousness and he could luxuriate in sheer pleasure, dark and overwhelming.[10]

(5) An experience is valuable if it is an instance of satisfaction. Santayana does not frequently use the term "satisfaction" and he never claims to hold a "satisfaction theory." Nevertheless, his theory of value often resembles some of the views that are currently receiving attention under that name.

Giving him the benefit of several doubts, one might consider this version, more than any of the previous ones, to be representative of Santayana's general approach. At least, it gives his theory the broad scope that he desires.

Like the second and fourth theories above, the satisfaction theory refuses to define intrinsic value in terms of desire. While satisfactions may result from a prior interest in an object, they may also come unbidden, gratuitously and even fortuitously. At the same time, the satisfaction theory denies that value can be limited to occurrences of either pleasure or need fulfillment. Every pleasurable experience, and every experience of fulfillment, is a satisfying one; but not all satisfying experiences are pleasurable or fulfilling. An experience is pleasurable only if it includes an hedonic tone, a definite *quality*, like the quality that comes when you drink something cool in summer. An experience is a fulfillment when it involves reduction of a need like thirst. To be *satisfying*, however, an experience need only be acceptable, engaging, attractive, intriguing, gratifying, or enjoyable — provided these words do not connote a *quality* of enjoyment. Any kind of consummation or well-being would serve as an instance of satisfaction. Similarly, any kind of annoyance, anxiety, frustration, or uneasiness would count as a dis-satisfaction.

Since the present theory considers desire to be an inessential condition, it does not define value by reference to effort or the search for an object. Any satisfying experience is valuable, regardless of how it comes into being. The realization of a desire, like the fulfillment of a need or the feeling of pleasure, may be satisfying; but no satisfaction is more distinctively valuable than any other.

Most of my quotations under the earlier headings could be used to illustrate Santayana's adherence to a satisfaction theory. The following passage contributes further evidence:

Value is something relative, a dignity which anything may acquire in view of the benefit or satisfaction which it brings to some living being. If God or the Ideas were mere values, as are pleasure or health, they would be unsubstantial, and only a desired or achieved perfection in something else.[11]

As relative to satisfaction, value is understood by Santayana to be "absolute" in three different senses of that word. First, value is absolute in being constant as long as the organism and its environment remain constant. Second, value is absolute in being based upon "objective conditions" of some organism: it is "rooted in the unconscious and fatal nature of living beings."[12] (Consequently, the moralist speaks with authority about persons whom he knows better than they know themselves. For then he has greater knowledge than they do about their needs and impulses and about what would really satisfy.) Third, value is absolute in the sense of being "intrinsic, final, and all-sufficient."

Neither the first nor the third of these senses poses any special problems here. The second sense, however, presents relevant and particular difficulties. For when Santayana refers to the "nature" of an individual or his "real needs,"[13] just what does he mean? In the passage where he distinguishes "constitutional interests" from capricious desires, he concludes that "passing fancies and passions may indeed have bad objects, and be bad themselves, in that they thwart the more comprehensive interests of the soul that entertains them."[14] And elsewhere: "The true needs of a psyche would be those that, if satisfied, would free that psyche from moral contradiction." * But now we seem to be leaving an interest theory of value. References to *comprehensive* interests make us wonder whether Santayana may not be defining intrinsic value, and hence aesthetic enjoyment, in terms of a criterion other than mere interest. We are thus led to the sixth, and final, aspect of Santayana's value-theory. It represents the view that is most characteristic of Santayana's philosophy. After examining it in detail, I shall try to show that a modified version of the satisfaction theory would have been preferable.

* *Dominations and Powers*, p. 43. By "psyche" Santayana means the structure or self-sustaining pattern of an organism. Cf. *The Realm of Spirit*, in *Realms of Being*, p. 569.

(6) An experience is valuable if it is a felt harmony or integration. In Santayana's later philosophy intrinsic value is referred to as vital or felt harmony more frequently than in his earlier writing. But Santayana nowhere tells us exactly what "harmony" is, and, as it eventually appears, he uses the word in two different ways. Sometimes he uses it to mean the coördination or reconciliation of interests, and sometimes a condition of integration within a particular interest. One might think that the first use of "harmony" is more relevant to moral philosophy than to theory of value, since it gives a criterion for choosing among interests which have already and independently been considered intrinsically valuable. Still, Santayana's position is ambiguous; and, as we have seen, he does occasionally seem to say that no interest could even be intrinsically valuable unless it harmonized with other interests. On this view, which closely resembles Dewey's theory of value, "real" goods would differ from "specious" ones in being able to contribute to an harmonious system of interests.

In its first use harmony is identified with the assessive or appraisive operation of intelligence, which is supposed to institute the life of reason through the coördination of various goods. Harmony is thus interpreted as the "formal and intrinsic demand of reason," and "reason as such represents or rather constitutes a single formal interest, the interest in harmony." [15] The materials that mate with this formal interest "are such at each point as nature and accident have made them." [16]

Serving to distinguish real from specious goods, harmony (in the first sense of the word) is envisaged differently by the earlier and later Santayana. As a young man, Santayana emphasized the importance of harmonizing a large class of goods, with special attention to intellectual values. He also thought that most goods could be harmonized. As an older and more experienced man, Santayana concluded that harmony and the life of reason need not be "architectural" or highly intellectual — "it might be simple and like disillusioned Christian Charity, alms for the moment." [17] Furthermore, he came to believe that it is "simply impossible" to harmonize some intense interests: in the life of reason one can aspire only "to separate, to alternate, or partially to sacrifice all the passions, or some of them, so that they may collide as little as possible and that each may not fanatically call evil that which another finds good." [18]

These changes in Santayana's conception of harmony result from the emphasis upon contemplation that manifests itself most strongly in his later philosophy. The changes also reflect a less optimistic attitude towards the efficacy of intelligence in a world of unreason; and on this account, the later Santayana has been subjected to a great deal of criticism, some of it what he called "pragmatist propaganda" and much of it ungrounded. In this place, however, there are two other problems that need concern us more directly:

The first problem is presented by Pepper when he wonders how the demand for harmony can have any sanction in an interest theory. Santayana says that only harmonious interests have intrinsic value, but the interest in harmony is itself only one among many interests, some of which are not harmonious with *it*. If *all* interests are intrinsically valuable, then even those that are not harmonious must be; if only harmonious interests are valuable, then Santayana's doctrine is not specifically an interest theory.

The second problem is a continuation of the first and serves to drive home the difficulty. If an interest is valuable as long as it is harmonized with other interests, should we not conclude that all interests are intrinsically valuable? For every interest can be harmonized with *some* other interests and usually with a great many of them. If Santayana denies that all possible coördinations are "really" harmonious, how would he decide that "real" harmony has or has not occurred? In making this decision, would he not manifest an interest in a certain *kind* of harmony, antagonistic perhaps to other types of harmony to which the original interest may also have lent itself? And then how would he show that one kind of harmony is preferable to every other?

An argument not too remote from this one is developed by Vivas when he takes issue with Santayana's early remark that philosophy cannot "accuse a barbarian of loving a wrong life, except insofar as the barbarian is supposed capable of accusing himself of barbarism. If he is a perfect barbarian he will be inwardly, and therefore morally, justified." [19] Noting that *The Life of Reason* is a condemnation of barbarism, Vivas wonders what "perfection" and "harmony" can mean if a barbarian can be perfect after his own kind: "If it is in the nature of the barbarian to be disrupted by mutually contradictory impulses, he could plead that perfection in the barbarian consists in being so disrupted, and the more disrupted the more perfect the barbarian would be after his kind. The disrupted barbarian could then look down on the harmonious barbarian, who is imperfect after his kind and perfect only after Santayana's kind, and accuse him of being imperfect." [20]

Santayana does not reply to Vivas' *reductio* but he might have done so by admitting that on this occasion he was not using the term "barbarian" in the way that he usually did. Santayana generally used "barbarian" to refer to one who was disrupted by mutually contradictory impulses: here he is using it to mean someone who is not *guided* by an interest in harmony, although his life might not actually be disrupted. But even so, the necessity for giving criteria for "perfection," "harmony," etc. would still remain, and until Santayana does provide them he cannot distinguish real goods from specious goods on the basis of harmony, nor justify his identification of intrinsic value with the fulfillment of "true needs" or "inherent nature." In the last Chapter of this study we shall examine the same difficulty from the point of view of Santayana's theories of moral and aesthetic criticism. I drop the problem here in order to consider the second use of "harmony," which takes us further into Santayana's conception of intrinsic value.

The second use occurs in Santayana's reply to Pepper. In his reply, Santayana agrees that an interest in harmony is just another interest. He appeals to what he calls "the relativity of morals": the value of rationality or harmony, he says, is only that of a "natural or relative value." An interest in harmony is valuable but only in the way that all interests are. From this it would follow that Santayana does hold an interest theory. But then he goes on in the following vein:

It (harmony or rationality) is the condition of any specific perfection, but not the totality of all good. Even the most narrow and rebellious passion may find its chosen good perfect, if that passion is inwardly integrated and harmonious. Harmony turns out, in this way, to be a prerequisite of precision in interest or passion itself: a physical prerequisite, not an inevitably chosen end for the world at large or for each individual. We may prefer discord, if none of our passions consents to surrender anything; or we may love harmony, and prefer that our natural hopes should enter halt and blind into the kingdom of heaven rather than that they should, all but one, perish in mortal combat.[21]

It may be in this fashion that Santayana would also answer Vivas' *reductio*: by saying that the barbarian is perfect if his dominant passion is inwardly integrated, although he is a barbarian none the less for having "mutually contradictory" impulses. But this imaginary reply to Vivas, like the actual one to Pepper, does not alleviate the difficulty; it merely passes it on to a different part of Santayana's philosophy and introduces new complications. For one thing, Santayana would have to give up his former assertion that nothing could be really good if it thwarted the "comprehensive interests of the soul." If we relied entirely on Santayana's answer to Pepper, we would have to conclude that Santayana's philosophy supported a relativity of values in a way that Dewey's, for instance, does not. For now Santayana is saying that interests may be intrinsically valuable even if they cannot be harmonized with one another. They only have to be harmonized within themselves, that is, inwardly integrated. But still we would not have eliminated our difficulty, for we must ask the same kind of question about inward integration as we did about the coördination of interests. Just how does a passion that is "inwardly integrated" differ from one that is not? In one way or another *every* interest is inwardly integrated, yet Santayana would seem to be saying that not all interests are *truly* harmonious within themselves. But how is this decided? We lack the criteria for detecting a perfect or harmonious passion just as formerly we lacked the criteria for detecting a perfect or harmonious organization of interests. Finally, if he says that some interests are not inwardly integrated but that harmony in the sense of inward integration is "the condition of any specific perfection," how can Santayana claim to hold an interest theory of value?

To get some leverage upon this problem, let us now examine Santayana's distinction between contemplation and action. In studying this distinction, we should get a better idea of what Santayana means by "harmony" and "intrinsic value."

II

Although Santayana does not specifically give the criteria for harmony, it may be that he implicitly defines harmonious, and so aesthetic or intrinsically valuable, experience in terms of interest in a contemplated essence. This supposition seems likely in view of his later definition of the sense of beauty: a vital harmony felt and fused in an image or essential object.

That Santayana does maintain a position similar to this is indicated by the way in which he effects the distinction between contemplation and spiritual discipline (spirituality), on the one hand, and belief or practical intelligence, on the other. To understand this distinction, we must realize that Santayana uses the words "spirit" and "spirituality" to mean entirely different things. Spirit, which inhabits a realm all its own, does not enter into the above distinction. For it includes both of the terms. Spirit is "roughly the same thing as feeling or thought; it might be called consciousness; it might be identified with the *pensée* or *cogitatio* of Descartes and Spinoza." [22] As such, it includes both contemplation and belief, both spirituality and practical intelligence. A kind of belief also belongs to a lower stage of the organism's development — to the "psyche" or self-maintaining and reproducing structure. Spirit comes to improve the work of the psyche, to make it more resourceful and more intelligent. This it accomplishes by discovering essences, to the contemplation of which spirit would devote its entire energy if only it were pure. It is at this point that Santayana distinguishes between spiritual discipline and practical belief. *Pure* spirit is the goal of spirituality; but for the most part, spirit is not pure: it is usually bound by the psyche's need for intelligent action. Instead of merely intuiting essences, as spirituality would prefer, spirit interprets and uses them, as action requires.

In making this distinction, Santayana points out the difference between two kinds of feeling. Both are intuitions and, like everything that occurs in consciousness, effects of spirit; but their occurrence constitutes different kinds of feeling. Hereafter I shall call them different "modes of intuition," since Santayana often uses the term "feeling" to refer just to one of them. The mode other than "feeling" is that of contemplation or "pure feeling."

According to Santayana, action and animal faith biologically precede contemplation. Once the organism has consciousness, however, even its most rudimentary actions will be accompanied by intuition of a sort — namely, feeling. Feelings are "balked intuitions," and the essences they disclose are "generic and inarticulate." [23] These essences vary widely but, it would appear, they fall into two classes. One class includes essences of shock or brute contact with substance — loudness, dazzlingness, pain, terror, lust, impatience, or effort; the other class includes visceral, kinaesthetic, tactual, gustatory, and olfactory qualities. For Santayana both of these classes represent the intrusion of the psyche into consciousness or spirit. The psyche cannot evoke graphic and articulate essences but only those that are suitable, on however rudimentary a level, for the purposes of survival. Smell, for instance, "can teach animals to react suitably on things without any . . . graphic creations, which are the first toys that nature makes for the mind." [24]

These "graphic creations" would seem to be articulate essences that contemplation singles out, particularly qualities of sight and hearing. They further the intelligent adaptation of organism to environment; but pure spirit clings to them, not because they are useful in action, but "for their own sake." Contemplation occurs whenever "sense itself, without any dialectical analysis, distinguishes essences from facts, and recognizes them in their ideal sphere. . . . The stimulus that calls animal attention to some external fact, in provoking an act of the body, also presents some image to the mind." [25] Contemplation is "pure feeling." What does Santayana mean by "purity" in this connection? Passages such as the following give us some idea: "Anything is enough if it be pure; but purity itself comes to things from the simplicity of the spirit which regards them, not indeed with indifference, rather with joy, but without any *ulterior* interest: in other words, purity comes of detaching the thing seen and loved from the world that besets and threatens it and attaching it to the spirit to which it is an eternal possession." [26]

Santayana's distinction between feeling and contemplation (pure feeling) is a distinction between two classes of essences and two kinds of attitudes or interests. At this point Santayana seems to contradict himself: he has already told us that data are never vague; but here he speaks of "inarticulate" essences. However, he is probably using "inarticulate" in contrast to "describable," and he primarily wishes to show that the psyche's interest in action prevents some essences from being suitable for contemplation. "Thus attention to the not-given, anxiety, suspense, precipitation dominate the spirit in the beginning; and the element of clear intuition, the sense of what is happening in reality even within the mind, though always present, remains inarticulate." [27]

Santayana's distinction between classes of essences we shall return to when we consider the aesthetic object. Here we need only remember that he is also distinguishing between two kinds of attitudes or interests, each with a different structure: one is balked intuition, "frustrated in its function, and tells itself nothing;" [28] the other is a purified intuition, fixed upon the appearance before it and straining for nothing ulterior. Feeling is an intuition of the inarticulate; contemplation is an intuition of the graphic and describable. The one is an effect of the psyche; the other, of spirit itself.

It is, I believe, on the basis of this distinction between the two modes of intuition that Santayana distinguishes intrinsically valuable experience from instrumentally valuable experience. Both types of experience include the two modes of intuition; but whereas intrinsically valuable experience occurs when feeling is subordinated to contemplation, instrumentally valuable experience occurs when contemplation is subordinated to feeling.

According to Santayana, all values, all interests, are "irrational preferences," and to this extent they are all intuited by means of feeling. But when feeling is accompanied by, and subservient to, contemplation, intuitions of intrinsic value take place. Thus, Santayana describes the "intuition of the good" in terms of both feeling and contemplation, the former enabling it to meet the conditions for value, and the latter, the conditions for purity: "(the intuition of the good) is a pure feeling, and however delicately its quality may be felt in each of its instances, it always remains a direct transcript of the will, that is to say, of the total direction of life at that moment in the psyche." [29] Intrinsically valuable experience is directed towards things as they are in themselves (essences), without any concern for their ulterior use or significance, and therefore it is an instance of contemplation as well as feeling. Feeling without contemplation, or feeling that is not subordinated to contemplation, is neither pure nor intrinsically valuable; contemplation without feeling is not valuable at all.

Hence, intrinsically valuable experience occurs when the feelings of the psyche are submerged in a contemplated essence, while instrumentally valuable experience occurs when these feelings overwhelm contemplation in keeping with the psyche's bent towards action. These are two different kinds of experience, Santayana would maintain, and the difference between them is grounded in a difference of intuition.

It was toward this position that Santayana was groping when, in *The Sense of Beauty*, he said that every instrumental or practical value is directed towards a felt appreciation that is "good in itself and for its own sake." I conclude, therefore, that Santayana's theory of value is not an interest theory after all. In its major import his philosophy does not consider all and every interest to be intrinsically valuable. Intrinsic value is limited to a special kind of interest — an interest in a contemplated essence. For only that kind of interest — it would now appear — is "inwardly integrated" and "harmonious" within itself.

III

We may also conclude that Santayana's treatment of aesthetic value is based upon, or at least presupposes, the same kind of epistemological distinction as he used for distinguishing between mediate and immediate aspects of experience. But whereas Santayana considers all aesthetic experience to be immediate, he does not think that all immediate experience is aesthetic. All aesthetic experience is contemplation, and all contemplation is immediate experience; but some immediate experience is not contemplation, and some contemplation is not aesthetic experience. Contemplation is only one of four approaches to essence: "intuition of essence is *Anschauung*, but not necessarily sensuous; it may be conceptual or intellectual." [30] Consequently, some immediate experience will not be contemplation.

Contemplation, in turn, is not necessarily aesthetic experience. For it is only "aesthesis," the appearance of a quality in sensation.* Contemplation presents a "formal or ideal" pattern, both intelligible and harmonious, but "it has no exclu-

* ". . . the *aesthetic* character can be attributed to my theory of essence only in the Kantian sense of Aesthetik" ("Apologia Pro Mente Sua," p. 501, his italics).

sive connection with the arts or with the beautiful." [31] Essences discovered in contemplation are not beautiful unless one's nature is attuned to them, unless one takes delight in beholding them. Contemplation becomes aesthetic experience only when its objects are valued as well as intuited.

Thus, Santayana considers aesthetic experience to be a species within the genus contemplation, itself a species within the genus immediate experience. The sense of beauty is a form of intuition. But though he maintains that beauty "transports us altogether into the realm of essence," Santayana has no desire to treat the sense of beauty as an isolated kind of experience. Not only does he hold, as we have seen, that immediate experience may be an aspect of the total conscious experience, but also he goes to some length to show why aesthetic contemplation must not be isolated from the rest of life.

There are two things that Santayana means by this doctrine of, as Dewey would say, the "continuity" of aesthetic experience: First, that aesthetic experience is not to be limited to the perception of *objets d'art* or any other objects that have been removed from the thoroughfare of everyday life. No matter what a thing is or does, and regardless of what instrumental values it may *also* have, it lends itself to an aesthetic experience insofar as it is pleasing to contemplation: "whenever a work, for whatever purposes constructed, happens to have notable intrinsic values for perception, we utter the word 'aesthetic.' " [32] Or, as he says elsewhere, "beauty . . . is not intrinsic to any form." [33] Second, that there is nothing inherently incompatible between contemplation and practical belief necessary for successful action. Whenever action is masterly, it results in the intuition of "a graphic image and a pure emotion," [34] which serves as consummation of the action. This compatibility between contemplation and practical belief reveals the second way in which aesthetic experience is continuous with other experience. Santayana is referring to this kind of continuity when he says that there is "no single agency in nature, no specific organ in sense, and no separable task in spirit, to which the aesthetic quality can be attributed." [35] Santayana's allegiance to both types of continuity is forcefully expressed in statements such as the following: "To attempt, then, to abstract a so-called aesthetic interest from all other interests, and a so-called work of art from whatever ministers, in one way or another, to all human good, is to make the aesthetic sphere contemptible." [36]

Although Santayana insists upon the compatibility of aesthetic and nonaesthetic experience, he nevertheless considers them to be distinct aspects of experience in general. Insofar as an experience is practical, it is not aesthetic; insofar as it is instrumental or even instrumentally valuable, it is not intrinsically valuable; insofar as it is an experience of thought or noncontemplative feeling, it is not an aesthetic experience. Santayana holds that any experience which is aesthetic may *also* be practical, instrumental, etc.; but in saying this, he is merely indicating that ordinary experience can be distinguished into aspects. His entire aesthetic philosophy is an attempt to effect a distinction between compatible, that is, possibly coexistent, but distinct elements such as the aesthetic, on the one hand, and the cognitive or practical, on the other. And just as he prescribed solipsistic detachment for the discovery of an indubitable datum, so too does he prescribe sensory contemplation as the approach to the aesthetic aspect of experience.

It is this kind of distinction that I shall criticize in the following pages. I shall try to show that aesthetic experience can not be defined in the way that Santayana suggests, and that it is not limited to any preferential mode of intuition such as sensory contemplation.

IV

Let us begin by admitting that an interest in a contemplated essence (assuming Santayana's doctrine of essences) is different from an interest in something ulterior. Does this lead us to the conclusion that the former kind of experience is intrinsically valuable while the latter is, at best, only instrumentally valuable? I think not. For if we held — as Santayana does — that an interest is intrinsically valuable whenever it is inwardly integrated and harmoniously constituted, we might very well find that an interest in something *ulterior* can be intrinsically valuable. We are given no reason to believe that an action must be accompanied by a "graphic image and a pure emotion" in order to be inwardly integrated and harmoniously constituted (as these words are commonly used). If, as I have suggested, *every* interest is inwardly integrated in one way or another, they might all be intrinsically valuable. An interest in a contemplated essence would be different from an interest in something ulterior; but why think that one type of inward integration must be intrinsically valuable while the other can only be instrumental?

Unless Santayana can establish the reasonableness of this position, he cannot defend his aesthetic theory. He must show why "impure emotions," those that subordinate contemplation to the feeling of a kinaesthetic quality, for instance, are inherently less desirable than emotions that lose themselves in a contemplated essence. Or, to transfer the problem to another phase of his value theory, Santayana must show why the satisfaction of one kind of interest is to be preferred over the satisfaction of another kind of interest.

I submit that Santayana's approach cannot meet this challenge and that it is based upon a mistaken conception of immediate experience. Aesthetic experience has traditionally been subsumed under immediate experience; and immediate experience, in turn, has generally been understood to be the confrontation with some bare and uninterpreted datum. From this initial epistemological error two erroneous beliefs in aesthetics have resulted:

First, that aesthetic experience must be defined in terms of a special or unique kind of entity, an uninterpreted image or quality determinately present to consciousness and specifically "sensible," or rather given to senses such as vision and hearing.

Second, that insofar as the individual is concerned with the use or significance of this presentation, instead of engrossing himself in its "given character," he is not undergoing a distinctively aesthetic experience.

Santayana inherits this tradition and complicates it with a naturalistic theory of satisfaction. But satisfaction is not defined in terms of any particular object or image. The "pure hedonist," as Santayana calls him, undergoes an experience entirely free of contemplation; for him there are no "images," only the feeling of pleasure. Moreover, the activist who does not pause to contemplate may nevertheless enjoy his action. The satisfaction provided by the movement of one's body is as real a satisfaction as any provided by the sight of shape or color. They are different *kinds* of satisfaction, the former deriving from a kinaesthetic quality, and the latter from a visual one. But if one is to define aesthetic experience in terms of satisfaction, both kinds of satisfying experiences must qualify equally.

Furthermore, as a criterion of aesthetic experience, satisfaction undermines Santayana's usual distinction between instrumentally and intrinsically valuable experience. For an intrinsically valuable experience is one that satisfies, and an instrumentally valuable experience is one that leads to further satisfaction. Now Santayana would maintain that *insofar as* an experience is instrumental or even instrumentally valuable, it is not intrinsically valuable — though he would also hold that an intrinsically valuable experience may be instrumentally valuable as well. But what if an instrumental experience gives satisfaction simply because it is believed to be instrumentally valuable? Might not the instrumental experience then be *intrinsically* valuable? For whether or not our belief about its instrumental value is correct, this instrumental experience has satisfied.*

Like Santayana, we can say that any experience may be both instrumentally and intrinsically valuable: for it may lead

* An instrumental or practical experience is *instrumentally valuable* only when it actually leads to an experience that is intrinsically valuable.

to satisfaction at the same time as it provides satisfaction it-self. But unlike Santayana, we should also insist that a prac-tical experience may be intrinsically valuable insofar as one appreciates its utility and delights in it as something instru-mentally valuable. According to Santayana, an experience is not intrinsically valuable unless it is enjoyed independently of all conception of its relations to anything ulterior, viz. the effects to which it leads, the causes from which it sprang, and so on. An experience is aesthetically rather than instru-mentally valuable, he would say, only when it is undergone and enjoyed apart from any consideration of its external rela-tions. I am suggesting, however, that if we enjoy an expe-rience *because* it is instrumentally valuable, or is thought to be, it is precisely our awareness of the relations between the experience and something else that enables us to have this particular satisfaction. Consequently, an experience that was instrumentally valuable could also be intrinsically valuable if only one delighted in its instrumentality.

Thus, when I swim across the pool, my experience is in-strumental if swimming is the way that I have chosen to get from one end to the other. It is merely instrumental if I do not enjoy the activity. But it may also be intrinsically valu-able if swimming, *for this purpose*, gives me satisfaction. If I swam "just for the sake of swimming," I *might* enjoy the experience; alternatively, I might be bored. I might find that I didn't like aimless swimming as much as I thought. But if I entered a race or gave myself some goal to reach, I would be swimming with an ulterior purpose in mind and *possibly* enjoying the experience more than before. In that event, the instrumental experience could be itself intrinsically valuable. Conversely, experiences that are *not* undergone as instru-mental for something else might or might not be aesthetic, depending on whether they satisfied.

Santayana's distinction between work and play is related to the present issue. Santayana claims that only play is spon-taneous, experienced for its own sake and without consider-ation of further utility. But this cannot be right. It neglects the role of satisfaction in what is ordinarily called "play." No matter how spontaneous an experience may be and no matter how much we may ignore its ultimate utility, the experience will not be *play* unless it also satisfies. Likewise, an experience is work if it does not satisfy, but it does not become work merely because it is undergone as a means to a further end. For instance, when a baseball player steals a base, his action is not done for its own sake or apart from a useful context. He steals the base because that is the way to win the game, and he is interested in winning. If he does not enjoy winning the game in this fashion, if he takes no delight in making a score or getting to the base before the fielder can tag him, his action cannot be play. Playful experience must be enjoyable, but the fact that an experience is practical or instrumental does not prevent it from being play. And the same is true of the aesthetic.

Consequently, Santayana is not justified in maintaining that "the useful is good because of the excellence of its consequences; but these must somewhere cease to be merely useful in their turn . . . somewhere we must reach the good that is good in itself and for its own sake, else the whole process is futile." If he means that an experience must be satisfying in order to be good in itself and for its own sake, then he is right, I believe. But he is mistaken if he thinks —as he seems to — that a useful experience is good only because of its consequences and that these consequences are intrinsically valuable only insofar as they are not useful for anything else. On the one hand, an instrumentally valuable experience may be intrinsically valuable *as* an instrumentality. On the other hand, an experience that is not instrumentally valuable is not intrinsically valuable either unless it satisfies.

v

Thus far, I have used Santayana's satisfaction theory for the sake of criticizing the intuitionistic views he also holds. As I have already mentioned, I subscribe to a satisfaction theory of aesthetic value myself. In doing so, however, I have no desire to *reduce* the aesthetic to the satisfying. "Aesthetic" and "satisfying" bear a close logical relation to one another; they may be defined in terms of each other; but neither provides necessary and sufficient conditions for the other. An experience must be satisfying in order for it to be aesthetic. Satisfaction is, therefore, a necessary condition for the occurrence of aesthetic value. But it is not a sufficient condition. In saying that an experience is satisfying, we are not *thereby* saying that it is aesthetic. In saying that an experience is aesthetic, however, we do imply (although we do not explicitly *assert*) that the experience is, or would be, satisfying. In ordinary language, the following kind of utterance would be logically absurd: "Looking at that painting, I had an experience that was aesthetic but completely devoid of satisfaction." The word "pleasure" or "enjoyment" would probably be used instead of "satisfaction" — but I think the reader will see the point of the example. The point is that our evaluative use of language is such as to make it logically impossible for an experience to be considered aesthetic, or intrinsically worth-while, unless it is satisfying. The example given is not self-contradictory in the same way as "No paintings are paintings." It is more like: "That painting is red, but no one under any conceivable circumstances could ever see it as red." In each case, a necessary condition for something to be called "red" or "aesthetic" has been violated. The explicit assertions contradict what must be implied in order for words like "red" and "aesthetic" to be used in the way that they ordinarily are.

Although our use of "aesthetic" presupposes one, and only one, invariable condition — namely, that the aesthetic is always satisfying — the conventions of ordinary language are not firm enough for us to *identify* the aesthetic with the satisfying. By incorporating sufficient as well as necessary conditions into their definitions, the traditional naturalists, Santayana included, rendered their analyses inevitably artificial. They ignored the fact that satisfactions are not always taken to be aesthetic. No satisfaction is inherently nonaesthetic, as

I shall go on to argue; but neither is any satisfaction guaranteed to be aesthetic. Although it is logically absurd to say, "This, or that, experience is aesthetic but not satisfying," it always makes sense to say, "This, or that, experience is satisfying but not aesthetic." Nor can aesthetic experience be defined in terms of any other sufficient condition.

By means of this approach, we end up with an interesting reversal of Santayana's position. Santayana thought that the beautiful was indefinable; I have suggested that it can be defined as the capacity for entering into aesthetic experience and that this is both a necessary and a sufficient condition. Santayana tried to define aesthetic experience in terms of necessary and sufficient conditions; I have claimed that, by the nature of the case, this cannot be done. Still, as it stands, my definition of the beautiful is not complete. As yet, I have not specified whose aesthetic experience is particularly relevant. It has sometimes been held that when we make that specification the open texture of the term "aesthetic experience" can be definitively closed. For in limiting ourselves to a circumscribed group of observers, it is thought, we shall discover satisfactions whose occurrence would be a sufficient condition for aesthetic value. Actually we shall find that these hopes cannot be realized. However complete our definition, it can never be exhaustive. In Part III we shall see just how and why this is so. After examining related problems in the philosophy of art, we shall be in a more favorable position for dealing with questions about the aesthetic observer.

VI

In this place, let us next consider whether satisfaction must be determinate in consciousness in order for an experience to be aesthetic. It seems to me that such determinateness is not at all necessary for the occurrence of aesthetic value. Although every aesthetic or intrinsically valuable experience is satisfying, the person undergoing the experience need not be determinately aware of it *as* a satisfying experience. While a man enjoys himself, it need never occur to him that he *is* enjoying himself. Very often the realization that we are experiencing satisfaction intensifies our enjoyment, but the enjoyment often appears independently of such realization.

On this issue Santayana is particularly unclear. In the first formulation of his aesthetics he says that beauty differs from most pleasures in being objectified in a manner similar to the objectifications of a sensation. In aesthetic experience we do not assign the quality of delight to some area of the body but feel it *in* the object. This means that aesthetic experience occurs only when the pleasure is taken to be a quality of the object in the same sense in which its color or extension is. Not only would this require a belief about the pleasure, far from being a mere intuition of an essence, but also it would involve the awareness of enjoyment actually being undergone. For we could not objectify our pleasure, instead of subjectifying it like most pleasures, unless we were cognizant of an object and also aware of its hedonic effect upon us.*

In the second formulation, Santayana says that pleasure need not be objectified: "if felt at all, pleasure is already an object of intuition." This too would seem to indicate that we are aware of the hedonic tone in an aesthetic experience at the same time as we are having the experience. Aesthetic experience would then be envisaged as the joint awareness of two essences, one of them related to the object and the other

---

* It is interesting to note that Pepper interprets Santayana's doctrine of objectification in an entirely different way. He summarizes it as follows: "When, however, a situation is such that pleasures are objectified and appear to be incorporated in an external object along with the colors and textures of the object, then this object is aesthetically perceived. What this limitation means in practice is that the spectator is so absorbed in the object that he forgets himself or loses himself in it, and all of his experience is merged into one pleasant or even ecstatic whole. There is no split then in his perception setting this much of it on one side as due to him and that much of it as due to the object. Santayana thus virtually describes the aesthetic field as that of completely absorbed pleasant experiences." (*The Basis of Criticism in the Arts*, p. 42.) But if there is "no split" in aesthetic perception, how can the pleasure be said to be "objectified" rather than "subjectified"?

to the pleasure of vital harmony. Thus, as we have already surmised, aesthetic experience would include the two modes of intuition: contemplation and feeling.

Both of these formulations seem extravagant. Aesthetic experience involves the having of a satisfaction, but it need not be had as a determinate content in consciousness. On the one hand, there is no intuition of an essence of satisfaction; on the other hand, a judgment about the relationship between the satisfaction and the object need never occur. But over and above all this, the datum may not even be determinate with respect to satisfaction.

That Santayana recognizes something like this would seem to be indicated by his definition of aesthetic experience as a *submerged* feeling, an emotion or enjoyment *subordinated* to contemplation. In *Scepticism and Animal Faith* he mentions that "the purest aesthetic or logical contemplation hardly goes on without a throbbing accompaniment of interest, haste, reversals, and satisfactions; but these dramatic notes are merged in the counterpoint of the themes surveyed, and I think, prove, and enjoy without noticing that I do so." [37] But then why consider aesthetic enjoyment as either objectified or an object of intuition? In a remarkable passage Santayana describes the solipsist enjoying the scene before him, never conceiving of himself as a separate entity, nor "his enjoyment as anything but its (the scene's) beauty." [38] But surely a solipsist that cannot distinguish himself from the object of his intuition will not be able to ascribe his enjoyment either to himself or to his object. As a solipsist, he cannot make the needed objectification; and if his enjoyment has been merged in the contemplated essence, how could one say that the enjoyment itself is an object of his intuition?

Santayana's difficulty arises from the assumption that everything in consciousness occurs in intuition. This necessitates his distinction between feeling and contemplation, only the latter of which is an intuition of the articulate or describable. But even this compromise is inadequate: for aesthetic enjoyment is not *intuited*, and it is not merely inarticulate. It is part of the aesthetic experience, but it need not be determinate.* It *becomes* determinate once we pass judgment and conclude that our experience was (or is) aesthetic. As long as our experience was merely aesthetic, the satisfaction felt may only have been vague. As such, it is not an inarticulate *quality*, since it is not a respect in which the datum is even determinate. Although aesthetic experiences are often accompanied by an awareness of their satisfying character, this is what does not happen on the occasions of complete absorption: afterwards we recall that we were "unconscious" of having as good a time as we actually did. There is no denying that we were experiencing an enjoyment, and in this sense our satisfaction was a part of the total datum, but it was not a determinate part.

Furthermore, Santayana is mistaken in his distinction between physical or bodily pleasures and the aesthetic ones. Santayana makes this distinction on the ground that bodily pleasures direct our attention to the very organs that condition them instead of elevating us and giving us the illusion of immateriality. If we review some of our earlier conclusions, we see why he cannot be right.

"Bodily pleasures" are those that accompany tastes, smells, kinaesthetic qualities, organic fulfillments, etc. These data are sometimes determinate, but often highly indeterminate — just vague qualities or feelings. Whether or not they are determinate in consciousness, and whether or not we are determinately aware that they satisfy, these feelings may be aesthetic. Indeed, the same is true of conation itself, even when it hungers for something it knows not what. I do not wish to imply that undirected impulse is always satisfying. On the contrary, it is usually a painful and distressing anxiety, assuredly not aesthetic. What I am referring to is the vague feeling of love or joyful aspiration of which the happy man who is undergoing

---

* I hope the reader will remember that vagueness and determinateness are arranged in a continuum. I call something "determinate" if it is "rather determinate" or "more or less determinate." If anything were *wholly* indeterminate, it would not be in consciousness at all.

it is not always fully aware. It may not be determinate in consciousness and it may not have an object or goal; it may be sheer free-floating affection, as yet unattached, *just* a feeling, an "emotional *uplift*," a blind soaring of the soul, or pleasant surprise, shock, or quickening of the heartbeat. Insofar as any of this is satisfying and an actual enjoyment, it can be as aesthetic as anything else.

Finally, we may conclude that aesthetic experience cannot be limited to "immediate experience" — either as Santayana uses those words or as I do. Aesthetic experience cannot be defined in terms of the contemplation of essences but neither can it be defined in terms of accepting the given without doubt or indecision. Immediate experience (in my usage) cannot be aesthetic unless it satisfies, and aesthetic experience need not be wholly immediate. The procedure of inquiry, the process of doubting or questioning the given, may also be aesthetic. As long as they satisfy, mediate and immediate experiences are equally eligible. Since all mediate experience includes immediacy of some sort, aesthetic experience will always have an immediate component. Some aesthetic experiences may be entirely immediate; but there is nothing in our ordinary habits of language and behavior to prevent the mediate from also being considered "aesthetic."

In offering this modified version of a satisfaction theory, I wish to avoid an error that satisfaction theories sometimes make. Because the criterion of value is taken to be a final consummation or quiescence pattern, satisfaction theories occasionally refer to aesthetic value as a result or culmination. Actually, however, we often find it impossible to separate means and end, tension and quiescence, search and attainment. The organism generally accepts the entire situation, the whole interrelated pattern of bitterness, pain, strife, and struggle together with the pleasure, comprehension, or sense of mastery that may eventuate or even occur simultaneously. In order to be aesthetic, a strident development need not result in happy endings — it need only satisfy in *itself*. And although an experience causes dissatisfaction in some respects or in some of its integral parts, it may be aesthetic in its totality if only it satisfies as a whole.

My treatment of aesthetic value has emphasized the close logical relation between satisfaction and aesthetic or intrinsically valuable experience. Under some circumstance or other, every satisfying experience *may* be called "aesthetic"; and no experience will ever be distinctively aesthetic unless it satisfies. Satisfaction has been analyzed out because it is the only thing shared in common by all those diverse experiences which are ordinarily taken to be aesthetic. Most aesthetic experience is more significant, exciting, and vivid than the words "satisfaction" or "enjoyment" might indicate. But in these terms I hope to specify the fundamentals of what certainly is more complex. The next step towards this actual complexity brings us to the aesthetic object.

4

AESTHETIC EFFECTS

When philosophers talk about "the aesthetic object," they sometimes mean the object which enters into aesthetic experience, and sometimes the datum in aesthetic experience — the object *as* it is actually given. I shall limit "aesthetic object" to the object itself, and I shall use the term "aesthetic effect" to refer to any vague or determinate datum given to aesthetic experience. Thus, the beautiful object has the *capacity* to become an aesthetic object and so to provide aesthetic effects.

With regard to aesthetic effects, there are three problems, closely related to Santayana's conception of intrinsic value, that I should like to examine: (a) Can facts or the objects of an intellectual attitude be distinguished from aesthetic effects (values)? (b) Can moral values be distinguished from aesthetic values? (c) Is there any one kind of object or effect that is specifically aesthetic?

I

Santayana's distinction between intellectual and aesthetic values resolves itself into three related propositions, which we shall take up in turn.

(1) Since values spring from vital impulse, a judgment of worth, particularly an aesthetic judgment, is always accompanied by "some trace of passionate reprobation or of sensible delight." Judgments not accompanied by a felt enjoyment are merely intellectual judgments, even if they purport to be judgments of worth.

Santayana's use of the word "judgment" creates difficulties here. In explaining how he proposes to combine "criticism" with "aesthetics," Santayana points out that his subject is the field of "instinctive and immediate" judgments which are also appreciations and enjoyments. In attempting to make this combination, however, Santayana seems to confuse the aesthetic experience with the experience of taking something as beautiful. For a judgment about the beauty of something need not be enjoyable. We do not always have aesthetic experiences when we judge that an object is conducive to aesthetic experience. And conversely, an appreciation or enjoyment can be aesthetic, whether or not it accompanies a judgment about the beauty of the presented object.

Santayana's confusion in this matter is reflected in his distinction between judgments of worth and intellectual judgments. He claims that a proper judgment of aesthetic value is always accompanied by an actual enjoyment in the object judged. Without this enjoyment our judgment is only intellectual and evinces an insensitivity usually coupled with a reliance on other people's opinions about what is good or bad. A real judgment of worth, he maintains, occurs when we actually delight in what we hold to be good.

Now, I entirely sympathize with Santayana's desire to distinguish between "appreciations" and "intellectual judgments." When we say that something has the capacity to satisfy, we are making a judgment that may or may not reflect our own satisfaction. But this does not mean that an intellectual judgment cannot be a judgment of worth or that a judgment of worth must be accompanied by aesthetic enjoyment. Only rarely do the judgments we make in an aesthetic experience pertain to the aesthetic character of the experience itself. Value-judgments need not be aesthetic; and aesthetic experiences need not include value-judgments.

(2) Intellectual judgments may report the circumstances under which an object has come into being, but it is the "direct effect" of the object upon someone, and not his knowledge of its conditions, that makes the object aesthetic. Santayana insists that when we approach an object for the sake of its historical relations or its classification as an art form or natural product, we are not approaching it aesthetically.

Part of what Santayana here suggests is worth retaining, though not the whole of it. It seems to me that Santayana is justified in distinguishing between the experience *of* an object and knowledge *about* that object. Looking at a painting is not the same as reading that it was painted in a certain year and under certain conditions. Knowledge about an object, such as its date or the name of its author, often contributes to our enjoyment of the work, but interaction with an object is distinguishable from any interaction with source materials that provide facts about the object.

Nevertheless, Santayana is mistaken if he thinks that objects are aesthetic only in their "direct effect," so that the knowledge of facts about the object cannot also be aesthetic. The distinction between an experience in which we look at a painting and an experience in which we study the historical connections of the painting is not a distinction between aesthetic and non-aesthetic experience. If the painting bores us although we enjoy learning about the conditions under which it was done, it is precisely the "direct effect" that is *not* aesthetic.

Santayana might reply that if the experience of studying history is aesthetic, it must also have its direct effect, so that a distinction between aesthetic value and intellectual judgment may still be defended. And yet, where does this direct effect lie? It is true that thinking has its own characteristic feel; but this is not what Santayana means by "direct effect," which he reserves for *sensory* experience. But what if the sensory constituents of my experience are not the enjoyable ones? I might not enjoy the sound of the prose or the imagery of the style; I might only enjoy the act of learning, the experience of gathering a fact and approaching truth in some aspect of art history. The network of meanings involved is a kind of aesthetic effect that differs from aesthetic effects like seen colors or heard sounds, but it is an aesthetic effect nonetheless. We must not confuse historical interests with an interest in objects apart from their historical connections; but neither can we rule out the possibility of either experience being aesthetic.

(3) An aesthetic object is sought for its own sake and en-

joyed apart from *any* concern about its relations; an object of
science fits into a wider network of generalization and is sought
not for its own sake but for its ability to give information.

In a sense, this concluding proposition sums up the preceding
ones. It differs from the second proposition in extending the
ban on historical connections to cover all relations whatsoever.
The aesthetic object is to be apprehended in its bare givenness,
freed of all interpretation. As such, it is contrasted with the
"scientific object," about which intellectual judgments, judgments of fact, are made.

There are several arguments that I should like to advance
against this view. I derive them from what has gone before,
both in this Part and in the preceding one:

First, no aesthetic object is apprehended in its bare givenness.
Nothing can enter into aesthetic, or other, experience unless it
has *some* determinateness, which means that it must already
have been interpreted.

Next, aesthetic objects sometimes appear in immediate experience, but sometimes they do not. To question and doubt
an object is not necessarily to be dissatisfied. In one respect, we
reject the object; we are not content with its classification and
therefore subject it to inquiry. But this mediate experience may
nevertheless be satisfying; we might derive considerable enjoyment from doubting and reinterpreting the object. This entire
procedure resembles nothing so much as a kind of variation on
a theme in music. We begin with something that is at first
accepted, then doubted, questioned, put into a variety of different relations, and finally restored to immediate experience,
often in a determination different from the original one. And
how are we to lay our finger on the aesthetic effects? Do they
belong to the theme as it was first presented, or the theme in
each of its variations and contrived relations, or the last appearance of the theme, whether in restatement or final variation? Surely, the aesthetic effects include everything that contributed to making the process a satisfying whole. Mediate
experience may not only be instrumental to aesthetic experience, but also an integral part of it.

Furthermore, Santayana begs the question when he defines science as the "response to the demand for information" and art as the "response to the demand for entertainment, for the stimulation of our senses and imagination." Santayana does not deny that "facts have a value of their own"[1] and that the perception of truth is often enjoyable; nor does he deny that science enlarges our vision and intrigues the imagination. He merely insists that these (aesthetic) functions of science are subordinate to, or derivative from, its principal and, one might add, *essential* purpose.

And yet, there are scientific treatises that could very well be classified as works of art. In their "elegance" and simplicity of expression, mathematical systems often resemble abstract paintings. Biographies are both historical and imaginative. Modern novels read like treatises in psychology — and if the result is sometimes unfortunate, it is generally because the author did not understand human nature and could not have written a good psychological treatise either. As we shall see more clearly in the Third Part, a work of "fine" art may be as much concerned with truth as a work of philosophy or science.

In any event, the distinction between a cognitive, scientific, "abstract" approach to experience and one that is contemplative, "concrete," and aesthetic makes a false demarcation between two areas of life that are closely interrelated. In saying this, I do not deny that distinctions can, and should, be drawn between different kinds of intellectual practice. The man who works at a mathematical formula is not doing exactly the same thing as one who traces the symbolism in a poem. But it would be erroneous to suggest that one or the other of these acts is simply abstract or unemotional or incapable of being aesthetic. The enjoyment of science need not be subordinated to any demand for information. On the other hand, the enjoyment of poetry usually requires an explicit manipulation of ideas based on some conception of what the world is like.

Of course, intellectual activities often take us through intricate mazes and problematic situations. And when our experience is largely mediate, it frequently taxes the furthest powers of our intellect, patience, and stamina. How then could anyone consider such experience aesthetic, and all the brain-searing conceptions aesthetic effects? Indeed, these experiences are often frustrating, dissatisfying. To *that* extent, they are not aesthetic. Let us remember, however, that some works of art accredited by many to be beautiful, stimulating, and worthy of the most serious and detailed attention, are likewise difficult and trying. But if *their* game is worth the candle, the same is true of the intellectual operations that Santayana distinguishes from the aesthetic. With respect to both alike, we must deny that a work ceases to be distinctively aesthetic insofar as it requires discursive reasoning. A work ceases to be aesthetic when it ceases to satisfy. But to say that a scientific, or other, treatise is predominantly concerned with intricate meanings is *not* necessarily to say that it fails to be aesthetic. For it may provide its own kind of satisfaction.

This leads us to a crucial distinction between different types of aesthetic effects. We have already distinguished between primary and secondary signification and have already concluded that a datum cannot be determinate without the occurrence of primary signification. Secondary signification is based on primary signification of some sort, supplementing it with additional class- and sign-relations. By means of secondary signification, the painter's white patch is seen as a cloud, or something that will appear red at sunset, and so on. As something *white*, the painter's datum does not necessarily become more determinate through the operation of secondary signification. But the datum as a whole becomes more determinate, since it has been interpreted with respect to a greater system of sign-relations. It is now seen to be much more than just a white patch, and it is, correspondingly, much more "significant."

On these grounds let us distinguish between highly determinate data and less determinate ones, between highly meaningful experiences and those that are less significant. To the former class belongs what I shall call "cognitive" experience; to the latter, "sensible" experience. Since both types of datum are determinate, and therefore interpreted, in some respect or other, the difference between them is only a difference of degree. In cognitive experience the datum is more interpreted than in sensible experience, inasmuch as it is determinate in more respects. A datum may be said to be "more cognitive" to the extent that it becomes determinate in more respects and/or more determinate in each of the respects in which it is determinate. In sensible experience the datum is limited to determinateness in only those respects that result from primary signification. This datum approximates the datum in cognitive experience partially to the extent that it becomes more determinate in these limited respects, but more specifically to the extent that it becomes determinate in additional respects.

Although there is only a difference of degree (of interpretation) between sensible and cognitive experience, we may specify the kind of datum that ordinarily belongs to each. All "sensory qualities," such as colors, outlines, textures, etc., may belong to either sensible or cognitive experience, but usually, and for the most part, they are not determinate enough to be considered cognitive. Except when they *become* cognitive, when, for instance, the physicist or psychologist examines a presented color with respect to a broad context of class- and sign-relations, sensory data generally appear within sensible experience. Let us refer to these sensory qualities, in their usual appearance, as "sensible effects." Sensible effects result from the operation of primary signification. Secondary signification, on the other hand, provides data that are highly determinate. Let us call these data "cognitive effects." Because secondary signification is always based on some primary signification or other, cognitive effects occur whenever sensible effects are interpreted with respect to a wider context of class- and sign-relations. When an idea is vague and fails to have a definite meaning, the datum is often just a sensible effect. Cognitive effects are always highly determinate, meaningful data. They are not objects of a queer sort (they are not "meanings"), and their nature can be understood only in terms of the process of interpretation itself.

Because sensible and cognitive effects occur at different places along the continuum of greater interpretation and greater determinateness (of the total datum), it is possible for one or the other to predominate. Although they generally appear together in consciousness, one kind of effect may attract our attention more than the other. In some experiences we see the cloud and see that it is white, but are more conscious of its being a cloud (and therefore a certain mass of condensed watery vapor in the sky) than we are conscious of its being a *white* something. The continuum of interpretation, we would then say, is more heavily weighted in the cognitive area than in the sensible one. And such is probably the case in most practical experience. Nevertheless, it often happens that sensible and cognitive effects are equally attended to at the same time. When the painter looks at the whiteness of a cloud, he may see a definite light gray color at the same time as he knows that it, like other light grays, would result from a mixture of certain pigments on his pallette.

Sensible effects and cognitive effects, when they satisfy, may be aesthetic effects. That they are different kinds of aesthetic effect follows from our discussion thus far. But as long as they are both satisfying, it also follows that neither is more distinctively aesthetic than the other. In order to discover a third kind of aesthetic effect, we must next consider Santayana's distinction between aesthetic and moral values.

II

Santayana's distinction between aesthetic and moral values follows a familiar pattern. Santayana maintains that aesthetic judgments are "necessarily intrinsic and immediate" whereas moral judgments are, whenever positive, based on an idea of eventual utility in the object. From this he concludes that aesthetic objects are never "practical or representative" (insofar as they are *aesthetic* objects) and that moral values, which are both practical and representative, are merely instrumental to some aesthetic value.

Here, as before, Santayana's way of confusing aesthetic experience with judgments about the beauty of something must give us pause. If an "aesthetic judgment" is a belief that something is beautiful, it is as much based on considerations of eventual utility as any moral judgment. What we are judging in either case is the capacity for an object to participate in a specific kind of experience; that is, we are making a judgment about its usefulness in this respect.

If, however, Santayana means that aesthetic experience is "necessarily intrinsic and immediate" in a way that moral experience is not, we may both agree and disagree with him. Aesthetic experience is intrinsically valuable whereas an experience that is merely moral may only be instrumentally valuable. But, on the one hand, aesthetic experience is not limited to immediate experience, and, on the other hand, moral experience may itself be satisfying and therefore aesthetically or intrinsically valuable.

In combining the practical with the representative as opposed to the given and aesthetic object, Santayana seems to be introducing an intellectual factor into moral values. An object that is merely representative, like figures in the miser's bankbook, is cognitive and not especially practical. The figures in a bankbook are not instrumental to the achievement of anything, although they represent the "glittering gold," which itself may be useful in the attainment of other goods. Still, Santayana's combination of the practical with the representative is, I think, a fortunate one. For it emphasizes the fact that the practical object is closely related to the representative one, since, actually, both provide cognitive effects. Objects that are instrumental to further ends are often symbolic of them, and a judgment about the usefulness of something is not fundamentally different from a judgment about its representative function.

Thus, we may think of practical and useful objects in terms of their cognitive effects. Like other objects, they can become aesthetic if one's experience of them in their relations — in this case, the means-end continuum — itself gives satisfaction.

But over and above these cognitive effects there are other aesthetic effects that occur in the midst of action and practical adaptation by the organism. These effects are vital feelings, the emotional concomitants of active behavior. They are not in the datum in the same sense in which sensible and cognitive effects are; but they are given to aesthetic experience and have as good a right to be called "aesthetic effects." We discover them when we direct our attention to the yearning of all endeavor and the forward tension of choice and conscience.

With this in mind, let us first take issue with Santayana's remarks about moral principles, such as honor, truthfulness, and cleanliness. Our reaction to these virtues can be aesthetic, Santayana says, but only if it is based on "constitutional sensitiveness," rather than reflection or benevolence. Leaving aside the fact that a reaction based on reflection is no less aesthetic for having a cognitive effect, we may ask: precisely what is constitutional sensitiveness? It is not reflection, and surely it is not the perception of a quality like green or middle C; it is neither an intellectual disposition nor a contemplative one. Instead, I suggest, it is a feeling. The man who has constitutional sensitiveness feels emotions of sympathy, affection, or communion in the presence of the moral virtues Santayana mentions, and emotions of revulsion, disgust, or shame when they are flagrantly absent. Constitutional sensitiveness is an effect of "adaptation by the psyche" — to use Santayana's term. As such, Santayana could not consider it to be aesthetic, since it subordinates contemplated images to felt emotions and the ulterior purposes of an active organism. But having refused to limit aesthetic experience to mere contemplation, we may now consider these feelings as possibly aesthetic, just like everything else that satisfies.

In general, these and other emotions tend to be less determinate than sensible effects. Emotional effects, as I shall call them, are usually less interpreted than most sensible, and all cognitive, effects. When more highly interpreted, emotional effects may become cognitive; but otherwise, and in their usual occurrence, they are just strong feelings, emotions felt and partially recognized, not wholly vague but still not articulate or especially determinate. Emotional effects that satisfy may be aesthetic effects.*

Consider now two of Santayana's illustrations: one about the miser's passion and the other about the mother who discovers a fine bull pup in her child's cradle. According to Santayana, the miser's passion is rendered "a little normal" when his eye is fascinated by the glitter of the yellow gold. His enjoyment is aesthetic, Santayana implies, if it is occasioned by the sensible image of gold; otherwise, the coins have only practical and instrumental value. But this seems to ignore the most important feature of the miser's passion — his emotion. What the miser savors is a feeling of power, security, pride, etc., and these are emotional expressions of an active psyche. Feelings of lust, enthusiasm, anticipation, and excitement are often emotional effects. The "shock of surprise" felt by the mother when she finds the bull pup is an emotional effect. In her experience the emotional effect is not aesthetic, since it does not please; but the feelings of the miser were probably enjoyable, and all feelings may, under some circumstances, become aesthetic.

Santayana uses the illustration of the mother and the bull pup to prove that ugliness is never an aesthetic evil but only a moral or practical one. The absence of beauty, he holds, is not an aesthetic evil except in relation to some aesthetic value expected in its place; and that, the frustrating of an expectation, is a moral evil. Thus the mother's displeasure is moral, not aesthetic, and "no form in itself gives pain, although some forms give pain by causing a shock of surprise even when they are really beautiful." [2] But the fact that the bull pup is beautiful, as bull pups go, has nothing to do with the mother's distress. She would feel pain whether or not the dog was beautiful.

* Cp. William James: "A glow, a pang in the breast, a fulness of the breathing, a flutter of the heart, a shiver down the back, a moistening of the eyes, a stirring in the hypogastrium, and a thousand unnamable symptoms besides, may be felt the moment the beauty *excites* us. And these symptoms also result when we are excited by moral perceptions, as of pathos, magnanimity, or courage." (*Principles of Psychology*, New York, Henry Holt & Co., 1890, Vol. II, p. 470, his italics.)

Her experience is negatively aesthetic because the emotional effect, her shock of surprise, does not satisfy. To say that it is a moral evil is only to overlook the fact that sensible effects are not the only kind that can be aesthetic. The mother's experience was strongly dissatisfying and therefore not aesthetic, as it might have been if her shock of surprise had proved enjoyable.

We may say, then, that aesthetic effects can be sensible, cognitive, and emotional effects.

III

We have reached the point where it becomes clear that Santayana limits aesthetic experience to a preferred kind of effect. This effect or "object" is an essence intuited by means of contemplation. It is a sensible essence and describable. It is an image, rather than a cognitive effect or an inarticulate feeling. Santayana does not define the word "image," but he probably means an essence discovered through the visual, and possibly the auditory, sense. It is this kind of essence that interests Santayana most, as indicated by the fact that he often refers to essences in general as "pictures," "scenes," "landscapes," "vistas." Aesthetic effects are reduced to visual and auditory qualities, and among them the former are given preference. In order to enjoy aesthetically we have to *see*. This bit of significant advice, similar to Henry James' concern for the scenic art, Santayana elaborates into a doctrine that serves to exclude the rest of life from the distinctively aesthetic.

In criticizing Santayana, I have tried to show that there is no special aesthetic object, other than the object of any satisfaction. Any satisfying effect may be aesthetic. The images found in sense experience can be aesthetic effects, but they are not the only kind. They are sensible effects, but even among sensible aesthetic effects there are many that are not images of sight or hearing: for example, visceral, kinaesthetic, tactual, gustatory, and olfactory qualities. Santayana is right to consider these qualities effects of an adapting organism, but why he thinks that they are thereby distinguished from the qualities disclosed in vision and hearing, I fail to understand. Furthermore, these effects are capable of the same degree of determinateness as sights and sounds, although it may be more difficult to describe them. In any event, the distinction between the inarticulate and the describable, like the distinction between the types of aesthetic effects, is only one of degree; so that instead of demarcating two classes of sensible data, we may say that there is only a single continuum stretching from the inarticulate to the describable. All members of the continuum are more or less determinate, and all are capable of being aesthetic.

Because all three types of aesthetic effects belong to a continuum of inarticulate-describable and vague-determinate, they are not distinguishable as ultimate epistemological or ontological categories. It is precisely Santayana's kind of distinction that I am trying to avoid. Thus in distinguishing between a sensible effect and a cognitive one, I do not distinguish between a passively intuited quality and a mere object of interpretation. Without interpretation, the former would not be determinate; and as an effect of secondary signification, the latter must be based on the sensible qualities of some primary signification or other. In distinguishing the emotional effect from the cognitive effect, I am not separating a meaningless emotion from an emotionless meaning. The former would be a wholly indeterminate feeling, which could not appear in consciousness; the latter would be an interpretation that was not accepted by the organism, which would indicate that the datum was not actually meaningful. In distinguishing between a sensible effect and an emotional one, I am not distinguishing between the passive object of contemplation and the object of a mere feeling. If it were not accepted, the former could not be determinate; if it were merely felt, the latter would not be in consciousness. The interpenetration between these different types of aesthetic effects illustrates, and results from, the integral coöperation of action and receptivity, of doing and undergoing, interpreting and accepting, that pervades every moment of the organism's experience. The three kinds of "effects" are singled out as points of reference in an extensive continuum. I have no desire to perpetuate traditional tripartitism. The trichotomy of emotional-sensible-cognitive is heuristic and tentative, by no means hard and fast. At the same time, it gives us a basis for analyzing aesthetic experience — as we shall see later, when we get to the aesthetic elements in the work of art.

Corresponding to the three kinds of aesthetic effects, there are three kinds of aesthetic experiences, interests, and "attitudes" — in a loose sense of that word. No one type of aesthetic effect or attitude is more distinctively aesthetic than any other; an effect or attitude is aesthetic if only it belongs to one or another of the three types. As a matter of fact, however, the types often co-exist. Whenever an object provides satisfaction, it participates in experience that may be aesthetic in one, two, or three of the modes. A single painting, for instance, may institute sensible, cognitive, and emotional aesthetic effects. The way in which aesthetic effects interact to form a total unit of enjoyment, together with problems about the choice of satisfactions, forms the subject matter of Part III.

IV

Santayana never explains his use of the phrase "aesthetic attitude," but he evidently agrees with recent writers who have tried to define the aesthetic in terms of a unique, distinctive attitude. Like many of them, not all, Santayana tends to treat aesthetic experience as an "aspect" in ordinary experience that is usually joined with other, nonaesthetic, aspects. To believe in the aesthetic attitude is not to deny that what is experienced with a practical or cognitive attitude may also be experienced aesthetically. All three atttitudes are generally understood to be combined in everyday life. Theorists like Santayana only insist upon the possibility of making a distinction of reason between the different attitudes. Once that is accomplished, they can discover what makes art and nature beautiful, and, having isolated the essential germ, they can help us to increase our appreciation. My criticism has been designed to show that although three "attitudes" may be discerned, no one of them is distinctively aesthetic. Consequently, as the following Part will indicate more thoroughly, the analysis of art and the definition of artistic excellence cannot proceed through the isolation of an essential aesthetic attitude or unique aesthetic object, but only through an understanding of the nature and function of the various aesthetic effects and the ways in which they coöperate.

Like Santayana, many philosophers who believe that there is an aesthetic attitude have singled out the "contemplative attitude" as the aesthetic one. Regardless of whether they identify the contemplative object with an essence, they generally maintain that only "sense-quality" contemplated in itself and apart from all relations is intrinsically aesthetic. The following kind of illustration is often employed: Three men look at a field of corn. One man, seeing how large the field is, wonders what its yield will be — his attitude is cognitive or intellectual. The second man, seeing that the corn is ripe, feels that he ought to start getting it in — his attitude is practical or moral. The third man just *sees*; he intuits patterned lines, colors, shapes — his attitude is contemplative *or* aesthetic. For only his attitude is directed towards the sense-quality as it is barely given and not as it is related to ulterior ends.

As in this illustration, the visual sense is especially emphasized, and reference is often made to the pictorial arts, where active participation on the part of the spectator is presumed to be at a minimum and cognition of only slight importance. The ideal aesthetic observer, we are often told, merely absorbs the pleasing effect produced by the contrasting lines and colors that arrange themselves into a striking pattern. He sees what is "immediately given"; he is not concerned with the meaning of the scene but only with its presented quality apart from all relationships. As Dewey says, describing the aesthetic attitude without naming it: "Finally the scene formed by the buildings may be looked at as colored and lighted volumes in relation to one another, to the sky and to the river. He (a man on the ferry) is seeing aesthetically, as a painter might see." *

Dewey's belief in the aesthetic attitude is complicated by the fact that he also *seems* to deny that there is any uniqueness in aesthetic experience. On the one hand, he maintains the following, which would indicate a rejection, somewhat like mine, of all aesthetic attitude theories:

> It is not possible to divide in a vital experience the practical, emotional, and intellectual from one another and to set the properties of one over against the characteristics of the others. The emotional phase binds parts together into a single whole; "intellectual" simply names the fact that the experience has meaning; "practical" indicates that the organism is interacting with events and objects which surround it. The most elaborate philosophic or scientific inquiry and the most ambitious industrial or political enterprise has, when its different ingredients constitute an integral experience, esthetic quality.[3]

But in the very next paragraph Dewey goes on to distinguish the intellectual and the practical from the "distinctively esthetic," and this is precisely what Santayana and others who believe in the aesthetic attitude wish to do:

> Nevertheless, the experiences in question are dominantly intellectual or practical, rather than *distinctively* esthetic, because of the interest and purpose that initiate and control them. . . . In a distinctively esthetic experience, characteristics that are subdued in other experiences are dominant; those that are subordinate are controlling — namely, the characteristics in virtue of which the experience is an integrated complete experience on its own accord.[4]

---

* John Dewey, *Art as Experience* (New York: Minton, Balch and Co., 1934), p. 135; in *Experience and Nature*, Dewey says: "Immediate things may be *pointed* to by words, but not described or defined. . . . Reflected upon, this phase of experience manifests objects which are final. The attitude involved in their appreciation is esthetic." (Pp. 86 and 81, transposed, his italics.)

I fail to understand how Dewey can say first that the most elaborate scientific inquiry and the most ambitious political enterprise have "esthetic quality" when their ingredients constitute an integral experience, and then maintain that a *distinctively* aesthetic experience is not preëminently intellectual or practical because in them the characteristics that make for an integrated complete experience are not dominant. Either there is an "integral experience" or there is not. If there is, the ingredients of the scientific inquiry or political enterprise are able to bestow "esthetic quality" upon these activities, and the fact that one experience is intellectual and the other practical is not at all to the point. Or, as I would prefer to say: as long as they satisfy, intellectual and practical experiences are inherently no less aesthetic than any other. No one denies that a philosophical treatise is intellectual in a way that a nonobjective painting or light novel is not, and certainly we may have different interests in approaching these different productions; but to say that this difference of interest makes some experiences dominantly intellectual or practical and *therefore* not distinctively aesthetic serves only to beg the question.

Lewis, too, begins with the recognition that all satisfying experience is, or may be, aesthetic and then limits his definition to the objects of sensory contemplation. Despite his belief that "in a broad and literal sense, all direct apprehensions are esthetic," Lewis distinguishes the goods of action and thought from *distinctively* aesthetic values, those that are "grasped by absorption in the presented in its own inherent quality and for the sake of the value so realizable in immediate experience."[5] He thus distinguishes the broad from the narrow sense of "esthetic," with the result that: "Although all experience is esthetic in the broad sense of being presentation of some quality-complex in which value or disvalue is directly findable, it becomes esthetic in the narrower sense, which is more appropriate, only if it becomes object of the esthetic attitude; only if the experience is marked by absorption in the presented content on its own account."[6] But in this manner, I believe, Lewis negates the importance of the "broad sense" of the aesthetic.

Even more obviously than Dewey, Lewis seems to agree with Santayana's definition of aesthetic contemplation as the intuition of sensory essences. But not only does this approach fail to account for the aesthetic enjoyment of novels, tragedies, and philosophical poetry, but it even prevents an adequate treatment of nonrepresentational arts such as abstract painting, sculpture, architecture, and music. As Aiken points out in criticizing Lewis for restricting the aesthetic object to epistemologically given data: "But even in such nonrepresentational arts as music, it is clear that what we enjoy is not simply a sequence of individual sounds, but also a complex system of expectations, surprises, and fulfillments which are fundamentally cognitive in nature. Apart from such responses the essentially musical and aesthetic devices of development, variation, and recapitulation simply would not exist, and our sense of form would be limited to impressions of clang tints and immediate juxtapositions of pitch."[7] The expectations, surprises, and fulfillments that one experiences in listening to music are not always what I mean by "cognitive." Sometimes they are, but at other times they are merely vague emotions. When we hunger for the first entrance of the solo instrument in a concerto, our expectation may be said to be cognitive, insofar as we are anticipating something definite, the first notes of the piano, for instance. But when our excited anticipation is more or less indeterminate and we do not foresee anything in particular, it is usually an emotional effect that the music has aroused. In any event, I agree with Aiken that aesthetic experience cannot be limited to the intuition of sensory data.

I conclude that Santayana's adherence to the doctrine of essences leads him to an unacceptable aesthetic philosophy. On the one hand, he considers beauty itself to be a simple, unanalyzable, and indefinable quality or essence; thus ignoring the fact that when we consider anything to be beautiful and are not merely emoting, we are making a value-judgment. On the other hand, he defines aesthetic experience as an interest in a contemplated image, or specifically describable essence; thus ignoring the fact that aesthetic experience cannot be defined in terms of either images or essences.

If Santayana's epistemology finds its application in the aesthetics that we have examined, his aesthetics finds its application in the philosophy of art to which we now turn. In the role of moralist and literary critic, as well as analyst, Santayana brings his philosophy to the focus of practical evaluation. Analyzing the work of art, and assessing several examples of it, he manifests the implications of both his aesthetics and his theory of essences. The protagonists exchange the masks of contemplation and action for those of formal and expressive elements, but once again the play of their conflict follows the recognizable pattern, now carrying it to a resolution on the level of practice.

PART III

PART III

5

THE CREATIVE PROCESS

Like his aesthetics, Santayana's philosophy of art received its most complete formulation some years before the doctrine of essences was fully developed. It was the work of a young poet and critic whose interests were more literary or humane than analytical or ontological. Nevertheless, the continuity that binds the doctrine of essences to Santayana's aesthetics also binds it to his philosophy of art. Because his thought progressed crabwise, from the application to its derivation, Santayana occasionally entangled himself in what he later took to be irrelevancies that had to be rectified; but the earlier views were not considerably different from the later ones. As Santayana himself insisted, his eventual statement of the doctrine of essences merely formulated a position that was latent in even his earliest writings.

Consequently, our examination of Santayana's epistemological approach serves to elucidate his philosophy of art no less than his aesthetics. In conformance with his distinctions between essence and existence, immediate and mediate experience, and the aesthetic and nonaesthetic, Santayana makes epistemological distinctions between fine and servile art, aesthetic and nonaesthetic elements in the work of fine art, and, with some ambiguity, great and inferior art. The next four chapters will be devoted to these issues.

I

The creative process, the process of art, as Santayana conceives of it, originates with the instinctive manipulation of matter. "All art has an instinctive source and a material embodiment."[1] But although art is *based* on instinct, its nature and its value are to be found elsewhere. Instinct is blind, ignorant of its own end; art is purposive, conscious of its aim, and directed by a reasoned insight however momentary or occasional. This conception of art, which resembles the classical theory of *technē*, Santayana summarizes in the following definitions: "Art is plastic instinct conscious of its aim. . . . Any operation which humanises and rationalises objects is called art."[2]

Santayana's belief that art is specifically purposive manifests itself in passages such as the following:

> Action . . . becomes art (when) foresight begins to accompany practice and, as we say, to guide it. Purpose thus supervenes on useful impulse, and conscious expression on self-sustaining automatism.[3]

> If the birds in building nests felt the utility of what they do, they would be practicing an art; and for the instinct to be called rational it would even suffice that their traditional purpose and method should become conscious occasionally. Thus weaving is an art, although the weaver may not be at every moment conscious of its purpose, but be carried along, like any other workman, by the routine of his art; and language is a rational product, not because it always has a use or meaning, but because it is sometimes felt to have one.*

The creative process is practical and active. By means of it, the purposive organism, "moulding outer things into sympathy with inner values,"[4] is able to make a lasting and significant impression upon the environment. The work of art thus produced may or may not possess aesthetic value. No inherent

---

* *The Life of Reason*, vol. IV, p. 4. This statement is followed by a long passage in which Santayana tries to show that art is no less "automatic" for being purposive. He points out that conscious aims or ends in view cannot bring themselves, or anything else, into existence. Consequently, he says, foresight cannot be thought to guide action in the sense of having a causal effect upon it. But this assertion, that purposes are noncausative, must not be taken to mean that Santayana is denying the purposive nature of art. He consistently maintains that a process of art does not occur until the individual is conscious of the purpose that underlies whatever he happens to be doing. Santayana's further belief that such purpose is lacking in causal power introduces an issue with which we need not here concern ourselves.

separation between the aesthetic and the practical prevents an object of utility from also being an object of beauty. All the same, Santayana distinguishes the useful object from the aesthetic one, and accordingly distinguishes between two types of artistic process. As practical operations, each conscious of its aim or goal, these types of artistic process are alike; they differ to the extent that one creates productions in which aesthetic value is prominent (works of fine art), while the other mainly produces nonaesthetic values. The two processes are different, but they coöperate. Moreover, works of fine art almost always have nonaesthetic, as well as aesthetic, values. These nonaesthetic values derive from the occurrence of the object in the realm of matter. Since it provides material conditions for the existence of the work of fine art, the nonaesthetic process is, in one sense, more fundamental than the aesthetic one.

The nonaesthetic process of art Santayana calls "servile art" or "industry"; the aesthetic process of art he calls "liberal art" or "fine art." Servile art is any operation which one does not undertake for its own sake, as its own end, but only as an instrumentality for some ulterior purpose. Speaking of servile art, Santayana maintains that "in so far as a man's occupation is merely instrumental and justified only externally, he is obviously a slave and his art at best an evil necessity." [5] Instrumental and remedial arts may be indispensable, but they are nonetheless "pure burdens," and ought to be eliminated wherever possible, short of distorting our material human nature. In order for servile art to become at all valuable, it must be instrumental to an occupation or activity that is intrinsically valuable; and that operation is the aesthetic one: liberal or fine art.

The relationship between servile and fine art Santayana describes in terms of the relationship between "matter" and "form." Matter or "mere material" he refers to as the primary substance of things, their first cause, their lowest instrument, etc. Matter underlies everything and brings everything into existence, but only in the realm of spirit can values occur: "while values derive existence only from their causes, causes derive value only from their results."[6] Santayana was later to identify aesthetic values as contemplated essences which, although they appear through the agency of matter, are good in themselves and for their own sake. Throughout *Reason in Art*, however, and in most of his philosophy of art, Santayana sometimes uses the word "form" as synonymous with "essence," and sometimes not. At times he seems to consider form to be any qualitative appearance. All forms would then be essences, and vice versa. At other times he takes the form to be a rationally conceived end or goal, a purpose and an ideal. This would mean that all forms are essences, but not all essences are forms. Santayana points out that ideals always emanate from a prior material embodiment; they are qualities that are abstracted from some actual occurrence and then sought as an end-in-view. The same could happen to any essence, but since essences are not inherently ideals, they are not all "forms," as the word is now used.

This ambiguity makes Santayana's entire discussion highly confusing. On the one hand, he says that all matter has form and that art differs from nature only in giving matter "a more propitious form."[7] On the other hand, he says that it is the business of art to mold "a material relatively formless," and he considers "initial formlessness in matter" to be a requisite for the very existence of art. The latter use of the word "form" represents Santayana's more Platonic side. The Platonist would say that the ideal is that which has the *most* form, that which is purified of all material contagion. Santayana is Aristotelean enough to insist that pure form cannot be attained; but he would insist that it can be envisaged as a norm, devoid of all formlessness. On his less Platonic side, Santayana would not identify forms with norms and would interpret them as essences that become ideals only by virtue of being sought by purposive beings. Ideals would not have any more form than unsought qualities; they would only be "more propitious," that is, more serviceable for some human interest.

In either event, however the word "form" is used, Santayana's distinction between matter and form involves the distinction between substance and essence. For even if essences were not the same as forms, all forms would nevertheless be essences. They would be essences which were also ideals.

It is in terms of the distinction between the ideal (whether a more propitious form or a more exclusively formal form) and the material, between the conscious end or purpose and the substance that is only potential with respect to it, that Santayana distinguishes between liberal arts and servile arts. Art in general imposes a new form, an ideal, upon matter: Santayana now clarifies his earlier definitions by referring to art as an operation in which "the ideal is a possible and more excellent form to be given to some external substance or medium."[8] The ideal, then, is the conscious aim that must be combined with instinct; through the pursuit of the ideal, objects are specifically humanized and rationalized. The distinctively formal aspect of the process constitutes fine art; the distinctively material aspect, servile art. They are to be understood as two different stages, hierarchically arranged: "Art has accordingly two stages: one mechanical or industrial, in which untoward matter is better prepared, or impeding media are overcome; the other liberal, in which perfectly fit matter is appropriated to ideal uses and endowed with a spiritual function."[9] Industrial art often occurs without ministering to liberal art; but liberal art cannot exist without suitable materials, which are usually attained through industrial art. Once matter has been prepared, fine art carries it through to a "spiritual fruition." At the same time, all industrial art may itself be accompanied by an element of fine art. Fine art is predominantly the use of material for an ideal end, but the preliminary work with this material, which is the function of servile art, need not exclude an appreciation of the aesthetic values attained at each level of preparation. This is the element of fine art, distinct from industrial art, but not necessarily incompatible.

As a conscious and purposive activity that is an end in itself, fine art mediates between two extremes. On the one hand, it transcends the instinctive and purely spontaneous adaptation by an organism reacting upon its environment; on the other hand, it differs from any utilitarian or dependent activity. Fine art combines freedom with foresight and reflective intention, intrinsically valuable experience with instrumental experience: "utility leads to art when its vehicle acquires intrinsic value. . . . On the other hand, spontaneous action leads to art when it acquires a rational function." Thus, a servile art such as war may give rise to the fine arts of music, armory, heraldry, and eloquence; and an art like the dance originates when automatic and spontaneous "self-expression" gives way to conscious and rationally disciplined actions.*

Santayana's distinction between fine and servile art is paralleled by distinctions between the imagination and the understanding, and between literary psychology and scientific psychology. In *Reason in Art* Santayana states that between sensation and abstract discourse there lies "a region of deployed sensibility or synthetic representation."[10] This "region" is the imagination, the locus of aesthetic values and the fine arts. The distinction between sensation and the imagination remains constant in Santayana's thinking, although he later dropped the category of sensation from his epistemology. But the distinction between the imagination and the understanding, which is the region of intelligence, analysis, and all abstract discourse, did not remain constant: at different times it was formulated in different ways.

In the more common version imagination and the understanding are said to have the same origin, viz., as fictions and convenient distortions that accord with the human bias. The imagination, however, is "prior" to the understanding, which emerges with the growth of knowledge and practical techniques: "Poetic, creative, original fancy is not a secondary form of sensibility, but its first and only form. . . . Fine art is thus older than servile labour, and the poetic quality of experience is more fundamental than its scientific value."[11] The imagination and the understanding are also distinguished in

---

* Self-expression, the uncontrolled venting of emotion, must not be confused with the element of meaning or association in a work of art that Santayana calls "expression." (Cf. Chapter 6.)

terms of their respective functions. Ideas that are useful in action and liable to verification are relegated to the understanding; the rest remain in the imagination. He sums up this conception as follows:

A religion . . . simply offers a system of faith different from the vulgar one, or extending beyond it. The question is which imaginative system you will trust. My matured conclusion has been that no system is to be trusted, not even that of science in any literal or pictorial sense; but all systems may be used and, up to a certain point, trusted as symbols. Science expresses in human terms our dynamic relation to surrounding reality. Philosophies and religions, where they do not misrepresent these same dynamic relations and do not contradict science, express destiny in moral dimensions, in obviously mythical and poetical images. . . .[12]

All discourse, then, is imaginative, and no system of thought can be a literal representation. Only the acquaintance with essences is direct and nonsymbolic, but the intuition of essence is speechless, by no means informative. Science alone gives us reliable, though never indubitable, information about the world; and, therefore, scientific method is the exemplar of intelligence or the understanding. Nonscientific statements, incapable of being verified, are *merely* imaginative, and even their mythological function becomes suspect once they contradict the science they ought to be symbolizing poetically.

In other words, according to Santayana, science, religion, and poetry are all imaginative systems of discourse, but science differs from religion and poetry in being able to supply empirical knowledge. They all originate in the imagination, but their eventual functions suggest a significant distinction between that which belongs to the understanding — science — and that which belongs to the imagination — religion, metaphysics, and poetry.

One of the specialized functions of the imagination Santayana calls "literary psychology," as distinct from "scientific psychology," which pertains to the understanding. Scientific psychology is the study of how organisms act and react. It is a part of physics, carving out, for special attention, a local domain in the realm of matter. Literary psychology, on the other hand, is an art and not at all a science. It is the art of imagining how and what certain animals feel and think. Its field of activity is immediate consciousness and, in general, the realm of essences.

Scientific psychology and literary psychology usually co-operate, like the belief in substance and the intuition of essences. Although scientific psychology concerns itself with material events and systems of behavior, it must begin with immediate experiences that are later to be interpreted. The experimenter must himself have intuited essences before he could formulate any conclusions, and these conclusions are likely to be based on a supposition that others feel and think alike. This supposition manifests the implicit operation of literary psychology: it is a flight of imagination that both underlies and transcends the strictly scientific part of the investigation.

As a description of what occurs in immediacy, literary psychology is distinguished from scientific psychology as poetry and the imagination were distinguished from science and the understanding: "Even in the simplest perceptions on which scientific psychology, or natural science, can be based, there is an essence present, which only poetry can describe or sympathy conceive."[13] Science cannot bother with essences as they appear; it must probe for their significance and uncover the conditions for their occurrence. Only the fine arts can depict or symbolically reproduce the immediate scene in consciousness. Since the understanding is fundamentally imaginative and science basically poetic, Santayana denies that scientific psychology could occur without literary psychology; but the distinction between literary and scientific psychology, and between the two modes of discourse to which they correspond, structures Santayana's entire conception of art.

Finally, it is interesting to notice how Santayana's analysis resembles the views of Dewey and Lewis. Dewey, for instance, makes statements such as the following:

Immediate things may be *pointed* to by words, but not described or defined. Description when it occurs is but a part of a circuitous method of pointing or denoting; index to a starting point and road which if taken may lead to a direct and ineffable presence. . . Reflected upon, this phase of experience manifests objects which are final. The attitude involved in their appreciation is esthetic. The operations entering into their production is fine art, distinguished from useful art.[14]

Lewis effects similar distinctions on the basis of his belief in "expressive language, the terms of which denote appearances as such": [15]

. . . the line of division between *belles lettres* and literature of the more prosaic kind, probably is to be drawn with some reference to the predominance, or the importance in it, of expressive meanings which convey something for the imagination rather than for the intellectual kind of understanding.[16]

In many ways Santayana's philosophy of art differs from those of Dewey and Lewis; but all three are alike in distinguishing between fine and useful art and between the imagination and the understanding.

II

Despite its ambiguities, Santayana's definition of art, like the theory of *technē*, is admirable in at least two respects. As opposed to any distinction between art and craft, as Collingwood, for instance, makes, it insists upon the continuity between useful and fine art. Likewise commendable is its denial that the process of art can be identified with any uncontrolled venting of emotion. On both of these points, however, Santayana's analysis is subject to criticism. For his distinction between art and instinct or spontaneous self-expression, as well as his distinction between fine art and servile art, is based on the mistaken distinctions between form and matter, essence and substance. I shall deal first with the distinction between art and self-expression, and then with the distinction between fine and servile art.

Instinctive adaptation, and all automatic or spontaneous action, Santayana considers the material source and condition for the existence of art. Art itself arises when self-expression is molded in a specific direction and for the purpose of attaining some form or other. The particular form that art seeks as its conscious end is an essence taken as an ideal. Art molds substance in the pursuit of ideal essences; instinct or spontaneous self-expression molds substance without any conscious purpose.

Santayana does well, I think, to separate the process of art from instinct and sheer venting of emotion. These activities, like other occurrences in nature — the rushing of water or the blowing of the wind — might result in the production of aesthetic objects, but still the process would not be artistic. All unknowing, the bird might build a nest that we would pronounce beautiful, and the stamping child might fascinate us as the epitome of uncontrolled irritability. But neither the bird nor the child could be called "artists," any more than the water that eventually carves out a lovely hollow or the wind that bends the trees into a graceful shape. Something more than the capacity to produce aesthetic objects, and certainly more than the capacity to produce nonaesthetic ones, must belong to a process in order for it to be a process of art. Consequently, neither instinctive nor merely self-expressive action is an artistic operation.

The creative process, I suggest, cannot occur until the agent is capable of criticizing his own production. The building bird would be an artist if it were able to foresee that the nest it has made cannot, for instance, last out the season and has to be reinforced; and the child's behavior would become artistic if he were able to realize that his outburst makes him appear ridiculous, whereas a controlled and properly timed display of irritability could lead to more desirable results. Loosely speaking, therefore, Santayana is right when he says that art is a "rational" function. The artist must be able to see meanings and implications of what he has done, its relation to other effects he has already achieved or may want to achieve, and its consequences in a variety of circumstances. He must envisage the response of an audience that matters to him; and he must decide whether his production is likely to give them aesthetic experiences. On the basis of these interpretations, the artist will be satisfied or dissatisfied with his achievement. Although this feeling of satisfaction or dissatisfaction may be the most prominent feature in the artist's mind as he scrutinizes his painting, for instance, one must not overlook the fact that a judgment has been made. The artist may say: "This color doesn't *feel* right." What he "feels" is the acceptance of a judgment together with the resultant dissatisfaction, in this case. His judgment may have been made quickly and without much deliberation, but unless he saw his work in relation to an extensive context, he could not have criticized it. The evaluation by an agent of what he has himself done, plus the satisfaction or dissatisfaction that results, I shall refer to as "artistic criticism." The notion of artistic criticism, I submit, is inherent in the very definition of art. An operation that does not include it may be instinctive or effusive, but it will not be a process of art.

Still, if Santayana is right in speaking of art as "rational," he is nonetheless mistaken, I think, to conceive of it as either the embodiment of an "ideal" or the imposition of form upon matter.

Consider the sculptor facing an unhewn block of marble. According to Santayana, this marble is the material in which the sculptor will then proceed to embody some ideal. The ideal is, for the marble, a new form; but it has already been embodied elsewhere. It may have been a quality or character that the artist has observed or else one that he has imagined. In either event, the sculptor keeps this ideal before his mind's eye as a conscious end and chisels the marble accordingly.

But this conception of the creative process is not adequate, I suggest, to describe what the sculptor, or any other artist, usually does. With respect to representational and nonrepresentational art alike, it is only rarely that exact similarity between the production and some model or ideal is desired or attained. Something seen or heard may have given the artist his original inspiration, but only rarely does he wish to retain this initial quality as a conscious end to be embodied or reproduced. Often he works out something that can hardly be recognized as having any distinct resemblance to what was originally experienced. Having observed or conceived of something, the artist then employs artistic criticism in order to achieve, with the materials at hand, a new and satisfying effect. The artist's production is not the material embodiment of any prior ideal, purpose, or conscious end. It is the culmination of an experimental process in which judgment and satisfaction or dissatisfaction lead to further experimentation, which is judged and modified, and then judged again, and then modified again, and so on until the artist stops working.

In this connection, it is interesting to notice that Boas criticizes Santayana for not carrying his definition of art far enough. Boas thinks that Santayana has done well to recognize that the process of art is rational and purposive, the material embodiment of an explicit intention. But then, he says, Santayana proceeds to classify the arts on the basis of their materials instead of their purpose. Boas himself believes that knowing about the specific purpose which motivates the creation of a work of art is more important than knowing about its materials.

He supports his position as follows: "It is unlikely that any artist ever said to himself, I will make a statue, or a poem, or a dance. His task is always more specific. It is always — at a minimum — to achieve a certain effect in sculpture or painting or dancing." [17] And yet, what is this "certain effect" to be achieved? The artist creates in order to attain a determinate object or effect, but just *what* it is he does not know until it has been attained. The artist begins with a vague conception of what he wants: his conception *becomes* determinate as he critically works over it. If the effect were fully conceived, the process of art would already have been completed, and only transcription would remain — as when a poet composes in his head and only later, after he is entirely finished, writes down his lines. The artistic process occurred while the poet was actually working on his poem and while it was still subject to criticism. For then he was still clarifying his intention and making it definite.

It is, of course, true that an artist sometimes begins with a specific idea of what he wants, as when he works from a blueprint. But since he can only work *from* a blueprint, his intention is still more or less vague with respect to his production, which must occur in a new material. Every beginner in an art soon learns how easily the best laid plans go askew. If he attempts merely to transfer his model from one material to another, without criticizing the effects that are now being attained in the new material, the novice is sure to blunder. Like the raging child, he is unaware of the circumstances under which he acts. The experienced artist, on the other hand, realizes that his representation is something new, depending upon different materials and capable of producing effects that could not have occurred in another context. As a result, he will treat his ideal or blueprint as something to be molded by the new material, instead of vice versa, and as something to be made more determinate by means of artistic criticism.

The concept of artistic criticism also enables us to by-pass Santayana's distinction between form and matter. According to Santayana, the artist works with matter in order to impose a new form or essence upon it. Although the artist's operation amounts to the substitution of one essence for another, it is always some hidden substance that he works with and whose adjudged properties control his labor. On Santayana's view, the sculptor does not chisel the *essence* of the block of marble he intuits. As given forms or essences, both the block and the completed statue are merely images; only the underlying substance can be chiseled.

Santayana's distinction between form and matter, and, at this level, between essence and substance, demarcates two aspects or moments in the artistic process. On the one hand, the artist must contemplate the essence of his presented material, the essence of his eventual product, and the essences that appear at each stage of his process, as well as the essence of the object that he is using as his model; on the other hand, the artist must have warranted beliefs about his material, as a navigator must know about a sunken coral reef that he cannot see, he must interpret each stage of his production with respect to his ultimate goal, and he must manipulate substance accordingly. Neither of these two moments in the artistic process is thought to be dispensable. Art, as Santayana defines it, could not exist if one or the other were lacking. The artist must step back from his work as well as pitch into it. Step by step, he must force matter into its eventual mold; on each step, however, he must pause and savor his approximation. But although the two aspects or moments are interdependent, Santayana wishes to distinguish them from one another. His attempt is an unfortunate one, I suggest, not only because essence cannot be distinguished from substance, but also for the following reasons:

When the sculptor approaches his block of marble, there are two things that might happen: He might have an aesthetic experience, perhaps delighting in the colored expanse as a sensible aesthetic effect; or else he might see the marble as something he could use for a statue. In the former instance, he is enjoying himself and not being particularly artistic. In the latter, he is seeing the marble professionally, as an artist, and therefore in a variety of relations that would escape a mere observer having an aesthetic experience. Even if he could intuit the essence of the marble, he would not wish to do so: for it is only by conceiving of its possible utility, its adequacy for developing relevant ideas of his, that the sculptor treats the marble artistically. At every stage of his operation he is always at liberty to enjoy his handiwork, but that has nothing to do with his activity as an artist. As an artist, his enjoyment is limited to the satisfaction that is involved in artistic criticism. He delights in his work because it is developing in a desirable fashion, or because he feels that it will conduce to future aesthetic experiences. At each stage the artist thinks of what is to come and whether more is to come. He has to see his work as a determinate object, but also as one that may need further elaboration. When he has reached the final stage, he will not intuit a culminating essence as the symbol of his completion. Instead, he will have to decide whether he is really finished, whether he has made a mistake on the way, and whether he ought to start all over. If he decides that his work is finished, he does so because it says just what he wants it to or because he cannot find anything else to improve. Far from intuiting an essence, the artist will make a judgment and feel a relevant satisfaction.

On the other hand, the substance that the artist works with does not belong to any realm of hidden matter or remote external world. The sculptor chisels the marble that appears in his experience as a determinate object which he can see as well as touch. It is only by perceiving its quality or character that he can know what to do with it, or how to deal with it as a particular substance. Since essence and substance cannot be distinguished, there is no reason to believe that the artist intuits the surface of things but labors underground. The marble that the sculptor cuts, and that he interprets to have certain material potentialities, is the same marble that he experiences at each stage and considers to be in need of further chiseling. The creative process cannot be envisaged as either the embodiment of an ideal or the imposition of form upon matter.

In suggesting artistic criticism as the criterion or necessary condition of art, I wish to combine the advantages of Santayana's theory with those of one that defines art as self-expression. The latter is mistaken because, *tout bref*, the artist must know what he's doing; the former is wrong because the artist is not purposive in the way that Santayana supposes. On the one hand, the artist is trying to express himself, to formulate and make determinate a more or less vague inspiration. The less controlled his effusion and the more that it approximates sheer venting of emotion, the less determinate will his production be (for him). It is by criticizing his own activity that the artist adequately expresses his initial impulse: the process of art is a mode of intelligent behavior. On the other hand, action is not intelligent when it is controlled by a pre-arranged ideal, conscious end, or "more propitious form." When an artist has succeeded in expressing himself, in carrying his original vague impression to its satisfactory determination, he will stop and say that he has finally attained the appropriate "form." But just what his final product would be like, he could not have foreseen. He first had to work with his materials and see what satisfied him at the time and under the circumstances.

These reflections give us a basis for criticizing Santayana's distinction between fine and servile art. This distinction resolves into the following propositions, which I shall examine in turn:

First, that since the process of servile art is merely instrumental, it cannot have intrinsic value; only fine art can be intrinsically valuable, only fine art is done for its own sake.

Second, that servile art prepares refractory material, while fine art uses perfectly fit matter for an ideal or spiritual employment.

When Santayana says that an operation is undertaken "for its own sake," he might mean that it is not useful for anything, or else that it is useful only as a means to satisfaction. We may eliminate the first possibility, since an activity that is not satisfying cannot be intrinsically valuable. Therefore, I shall take Santayana to mean that the process of fine art, unlike the process of servile art, is itself enjoyable and has no other utility.

We have already seen, in the previous Part, that any satisfying experience may be intrinsically valuable. An operation, like the process of servile art, that was instrumental could have intrinsic value if only it satisfied by virtue of its function as an instrument. Santayana does specify that servile art is "merely instrumental and justified only externally." If he means that, by definition, it cannot be satisfying even as an instrumental-

III

ity, then I would agree with him that it cannot be intrinsically valuable. Nevertheless, when Santayana usually refers to servile art as, for instance, any industry that prepares matter, he by no means precludes the possibility of its being enjoyable. He likens it to the functions of nutrition and reproduction, which presumably prepare the species for more ideal occupations. But surely he would not characterize nutrition and reproduction as instruments whose instrumentality one could not appreciate. Since any satisfying experience can be intrinsically valuable, I should think that what Santayana usually means by servile art may also be intrinsically valuable.

On the other hand, the process of fine art is not *always* intrinsically valuable. Creation tends to be enjoyable, but even the most consummate workmanship can be accompanied by pain and distaste for what has to be done. Furthermore, and of greater importance, fine art is only rarely autotelic. The artist works not only because he likes to work, which he may or may not, but also because (like Mozart) he knows of no other way to support himself, because he wishes to spread happiness, because he wishes to be adored, because he wishes to express himself or purge his soul, etc. Whether or not it is intrinsically valuable, the process of fine art may always be pursued because of its instrumental value.

As instrumental, the process of fine art, like that of servile art, may be intrinsically valuable at least to the extent that it satisfies by virtue of its utility. But in any event, fine and servile art both have attributes other than their utility that enable them to be intrinsically valuable. These are the intellectual, emotional, and sensory satisfactions inherent in the activities themselves, and regardless of whether they belong to one type of art process or another. Consequently, a distinction between the operations of fine art and servile art on the basis of the intrinsic value of the former and the merely instrumental value of the latter cannot be effected.

Santayana also distinguishes between fine art and servile art by reference to the objects they produce. Servile art makes things that are useful, it prepares matter; fine art makes things that serve some "ideal function," it uses perfectly fit material but does not prepare it.

From the very outset, this formulation of the distinction should be surprising. For Santayana has already told us that *all* artistic effort involves the imposition of ideal form upon matter. One might think, therefore, that Santayana contradicts himself in asserting that only fine art appropriates matter for "ideal uses." Still, he also says that by means of fine art matter is "endowed with a direct spiritual function." This may be taken to mean that fine art, unlike servile art, creates aesthetic objects. When servile art occurs alone, a mere instrumentality is produced; when it is accompanied by fine art, the product is of the sort that enters into aesthetic experience. The object that fine art produces may also be useful, but this aspect is independent of its aesthetic function; the object that servile art produces may become aesthetic, but this aspect is independent of its utility. It is something like this, I think, that Santayana wishes to hold.

Without repeating earlier arguments, we may readily see why Santayana must be mistaken:

In the operation of an artist like the sculptor one cannot distinguish a phase in which he prepares his material from one in which he uses it for an ideal function. For Santayana the "ideal function" would be, let us say, the chiseling of facial features in the marble. What could be the industrial or servile aspect? Cutting the marble down to a manageable size, polishing it, or cleaning it? But these operations do not *merely* provide the fine artist with "perfectly fit matter." They are also the operations of a fine artist. Features chiseled in a block of marble that is too large or that has an ugly texture and an unattractive surface do not give the same effect as features in marble that has been properly cut, polished, and cleaned. It is because the artist requires one effect and not another, in each of these respects, that his work with the marble includes the operations Santayana calls "servile" as well as those he considers "fine." The artist wishes to produce an object that will satisfy in *every* respect. He realizes that the finished texture of the marble, and the rightness of its size, may have an aesthetic effect as much as the shape and outline of the features. Marble with a certain texture is not instrumental to marble with a certain outline. Both are equally instrumental to a total effect that the artist desires. The achievement of each of the subordinate effects may require different operations, polishing for one and chiseling for the other, but there is no ground for calling the first operation servile or merely instrumental and the second operation fine, liberal, or intrinsically valuable.

Because he identifies aesthetic experience with the enjoyed contemplation of an essence, Santayana would insist that something could be a work of fine art only if it lent itself to contemplative experience. For only that kind of object could be aesthetic. Consequently, the products of industrial art — commodities like shoes, chairs, prepared food, etc. — could not have the character of fine art unless they happened to present articulate essences that could be contemplated in an enjoyable intuition. Thus, a chair would be a work of fine art only if its shape or color could be seen as an interesting essence or form. If it merely gives comfort, Santayana would say, the chair is a work of servile art, however valuable it may be as an instrumentality.

Once again we must remark that articulate essences, or essences of the visual and auditory senses, do not exhaust the class of aesthetic effects. The enjoyable feel of a comfortable chair is an aesthetic effect no less than a pleasant shape or color. A tactual or kinaesthetic quality is certainly different from an image of the eye, but this does not permit a distinction between works of fine and servile art. What Santayana would consider to be a work of servile art *may be* just as aesthetic as one that he considers to be a work of fine art. Although they contribute to different kinds of experience, they may function equally well as aesthetic objects of their own sort. Consequently, the distinction between fine and servile arts cannot be effected in the way that Santayana suggests.

IV

Santayana's distinction between fine and servile art is closely related to the more comprehensive distinctions between poetic and scientific discourse and between the imagination and the understanding. Although there are enormous problems here which warrant a more thorough treatment than the structure of this book allows, the next few pages may illuminate one feasible way of approaching them.

First, I would agree with Santayana that science presents a symbolic and not a literal picture of reality, that scientific statements are only probable and never certain, and that science and the understanding are, in a sense, fundamentally imaginative. But in order to learn what this sense is, we must consider what Santayana would take to be *distinctively* imaginative. On Santayana's approach, the poet, the religious thinker, the metaphysician, the child, and the primitive are all lumped together as being more imaginative than practical or scientific. If we demand the evidence for this amalgamation, we find that the primitive personifies material objects, the child is subject to a pervasive egoism and autism, the metaphysician makes statements for the truth of which there is no universally accepted decision-procedure, the religious thinker refers to a world beyond experience, and the poet concocts fables. I am sure that Santayana would agree to all this. Moreover, he would take these as the paradigmatic activities of the imagination, so that scientific thinking is to be considered basically imaginative only because, like them, it is creative and inventive and not merely duplicative. The ability to devise systems of thought that do not correspond directly or literally to the everyday world would seem to be the definitive capacity of the imagination.

But this, I suggest, is only half the story. For the child, the primitive, the metaphysician, and the religious thinker may very well be making interpretations that *they* consider to be literal and exact. As a result, none of their activities is necessarily imaginative in itself. Imagination begins to function when the individual is able to conceive of more than one frame of reference, more than one universe of discourse, at a time, and when he is able to use one or the other in accordance with his conception of what works best under the circumstances. In other words, there cannot be imagination without intelligence.

For instance, the primitive who personifies material objects without any theoretical qualms, and without questioning his procedure, is not an imaginative person. He is merely adapting to the environment in the only way he can. The same is true of the child who has not yet developed out of the autistic stage in which his own desires control his perceptions and beliefs. Children show imaginative capacity only when they are able to live in two worlds at once: one, the world of the adults around them; the other, the world of their own, which is often a world of greater importance to them. They then subordinate those features of the adult world that do not agree with the requirements of their own world. As they become adults themselves, their two worlds gradually coalesce. But for the religious thinker, the metaphysician, and the poet, there remains the possibility of constructing a new world — too often, a world *all* their own, like the world of the schizophrenic. Their activities, like those of the primitive or child, can be considered imaginative only to the extent that they live in more than one world at a time, aware that one or another is more desirable under the circumstances. It is precisely this talent that the schizophrenic lacks. Religious thinkers, metaphysicians, and poets approximate the schizophrenic's condition insofar as the world of their construction is incapable of intelligent coördination with any other worlds, especially the everyday world of the ordinary adult.

In depending upon intelligence and the ability to choose among alternatives, imagination requires the faculty of artistic criticism. To be an artist a producer must evaluate his own production, even when it is a different world in which to live. The artist is, by definition, imaginative, and any system of thought becomes imaginative when it is artistically conceived. But there is no *special* construction, like that of the primitive or the metaphysician or the poet, that is distinctively artistic or distinctively imaginative.

Consequently, science may be imaginative only in the sense of being an intelligent re-interpretation of the everyday world. The imaginative scientist is aware of the relations between his theories and the intimate workings of the common-sense world in which the adult usually lives. The hunches of the scientist, his working hypotheses and ultimate suppositions, are fictional constructions that often resemble a poet's dreams and are sometimes inseparable from the metaphysician's beliefs. They cannot become imaginative unless they are used intelligently.

Since the imagination depends upon the intelligent co-ordination of different conceptions, it cannot be contrasted with the understanding in the way that Santayana suggests. Nor can science be distinguished from poetry because it concerns itself with the world of practice. Both poetry and science originate in the common-sense world and depart from it: both are imaginative to the extent that they can utilize the continuities between the common-sense world and the worlds of their own construction. Science is not necessarily less imaginative than poetry, and poetry is not necessarily less concerned with the everyday world than science. The descriptions of science may sometimes help us adapt to the world in a way that the descriptions of poetry do not; but the converse also holds: and the fictions of poetry often have a more educative and formative effect than any scientific theory. Each, in its own way, deals with the world of ordinary experience, and neither is imaginative unless it is based on the intelligence or understanding.

Nor can a distinction be drawn on the grounds that scientific discourse employs verifiable statements, whereas poetic discourse does not. For even the most imaginative effects of poetry are based on *a kind of* verifiability. When Hamlet says that the dead Polonius is at supper, not where he eats but

where he is eaten, his statement is both imaginative and verifiable. It is imaginative because its import can be appreciated
only by a critical comparison between the fictional world that
Shakespeare has created, including the murder of the older
man by the younger one, with the everyday world in which
corpses decay and are eaten by maggots. Once we realize
the "continuity of experience" between the world of *Hamlet*
and the world of most adults, we are able to verify Hamlet's
statement by reference to previous occurrences in the plot
and to common knowledge about corpses. Unless it were
based on such knowledge and liable to such verification, Hamlet's allusion would be neither imaginative nor significant.
And the same may be said about the verifiability of statements
in science. Scientific hypotheses generally appear within the
framework of an imaginative system of thought and are verifiable by reference to common observation and other parts
of the conceptual scheme. Of course, the scientific function
of verifiability is quite different from the poetic, and the two
must not be confused; but it would be a mistake to think that
no kind of verification was relevant to poetry. This would be
as much of an error as thinking that poetry was *inherently*
more imaginative than science.

Santayana's distinction between the imagination and the
understanding is reflected in his distinction between fine and
servile art, which is itself merely a continuation of his definition of art. Fine art is presumed to be a purified version of art
in general, since it concentrates upon form instead of matter.
We emancipate ourselves from this unsound approach once
we realize that what Santayana means by "form" cannot be
distinguished from what he means by "matter," any more than
essence could be distinguished from substance. As a result, the
artistic process cannot be defined as the imposition of form
upon matter. Similarly, an operation of perfecting material
cannot be distinguished from an operation of attaining aesthetic
value. Arts may be distinguished from one another in the conventional way in which rug-weaving is distinguished from the

writing of a play. In this sense, the cook who makes a soufflé is a different kind of artist from the sculptor who makes a statue. Their tools, their materials, their specific goals, their techniques, and their finished products are different and clearly distinguishable. Such distinctions are commonly made and have their obvious utility; but they do not correspond to Santayana's epistemological distinction between fine and servile art. *Every* art is "fine" if it is suitable for the production of highly aesthetic objects. Music, painting, sculpture, literature, and the dance are often called "the fine arts"; and it may be true that these arts are better suited for the presentation of aesthetic effects. This is a question to which we shall return. Here it need only be said that there is no reason to think that other arts, the industrial ones for instance, cannot also be fine. And in any event, there is no basis for distinguishing between fine and servile aspects within a particular art in the way that Santayana does.

6

AESTHETIC ELEMENTS IN THE WORK OF ART

In pursuing his so-called definition of beauty, Santayana lists three "elements of our consciousness" that contribute to beauty: materials, form, and expression. Although he does not make it too clear, what he actually does is to describe three elements in the work of (fine) art, only two of which contribute directly to beauty. These two elements are those of materials and form — which, as we shall see, correspond to two different kinds of essences; the element of expression contributes to beauty only indirectly, contingent upon its combination with the other elements. Since expression involves interpretation and the understanding, we may expect to find Santayana's epistemological distinction at the base of his analysis here as elsewhere.

I

Searching for the materials of beauty, Santayana turns to objects that can be enjoyably experienced and definitely imagined. He excludes the senses of touch, taste, and smell — the "lower" or "unaesthetic" senses. Though he recognizes their *associational* importance for arts such as sensuous poetry, he denies that tastes, odors, and tactual sensations can themselves be made into works of art. Smell and taste, for instance, are unsuitable for the representation of nature because they are not intrinsically spatial, and "nature . . . allows herself to be accurately conceived only in spatial terms." [1] The same disadvantage applies to the sense of hearing, but sounds can be organized, classified, and precisely distinguished from one another. Since qualities of the three lower senses cannot be organized, except in a loose and tentative fashion, an attempt to achieve desired effects by means of them can only be servile, rather than fine, art.

Thus, sights and sounds alone provide the materials of beauty and the fine arts. After considering how auditory qualities such as a particular pitch, timbre, or intensity contribute to artistic productions, Santayana describes an important conflict of aesthetic principles. One of them is the "principle of purity"; the other is the "principle of interest." The principle of interest really belongs to expression. It is the principle of interpretation, meaningfulness, discursive comprehension. It explains why solitary musical notes, for instance, are uninteresting to human beings who desire something more than mere sensory excitement. The principle of purity accounts for the enjoyment that we do feel in the presence of an elemental sound, a mere musical note, or the tone of a tuning fork.

In distinguishing between purity and interest, Santayana points out that only the former provides beauty directly and by itself. Purity without interest would result in a "tedious beauty," but beauty nonetheless. Interest without purity, however, would not have aesthetic effect. It would lack the sensuous appeal, the basic material of beauty, which the purity principle takes into account. The sound of a child's rattle or trumpet will soon bore an adult, who requires greater variety and significance, but it provides the child with an aesthetic enjoyment, "of however rude a kind." [2] On the other hand, the master of technique who devotes himself solely to interest and gives a performance without sensuous charm is not a musician but a gymnast, and "the author whose novels and poems should be merely expressive, and interesting only by their meaning and moral, would be a writer of history or philosophy, but not an artist." [3]

Santayana admits that this distinction is not absolute. He points out that the simple sensation is often interesting in itself and that an enjoyable discourse could be artistic even though it lacked gracious or euphonious materials. But then he virtually reinstates the original distinction by insisting that the merely interesting object can be aesthetic only "if it is appreciable by sense and does not require discursive thought to grasp it." [4]

The visual sense is, for Santayana, the preëminently artistic one. Beauty, he says, is "derived mainly from the pleasures of sight." [5] The visible is spatial and easy to organize and classify; it is also particularly definite and clear-cut. Anticipating the second element of beauty, Santayana suggests that form, "which is almost a synonym of beauty, is for us usually something visible; it is a synthesis of the seen." [6] But prior to visual form comes the effect of color, which is "purely sensuous" and a readier material for beauty than other qualities.

The materials of beauty and fine art are not the only elements, and they do not provide the most important effects; but, according to Santayana, they are the most primitive, fundamental, and universal. The delight of children and savages who love brilliant colors may have to be subordinated to some more significant enjoyment that form and meaningful expression offer; but primitive delight is spontaneous and desirable as a first step towards the maximum appreciation. Sensuous beauty is not only an innocent and sure delight, but also the foundation for all other beauty, whose effects can generally be enhanced by the artful use of materials. That (we are told) is why the Parthenon is made of marble, the king's crown of gold, and the stars of fire. Largely through their use of sensuous materials pure decorations, abstract designs in color and outline, attain aesthetic distinction. Santayana concludes that "the beauty of material is thus the groundwork of all higher beauty, both in the object, whose form and meaning have to be lodged in something sensible, and in the mind, where sensuous ideas, being the first to emerge, are the first that can arouse delight." [7]

The beauty of form Santayana takes to be the most important aesthetic element, the element in a work of art that most distinctively gives it an aesthetic character. Although it depends upon materials, and is usually combined with expression, form has its own unique quality, different from the effects of either materials or expression. Form is the pattern, the arrangement, of materials that molds them into something more than primitive sensuous elements; and it differs from expression in having aesthetic value apart from any association or extraneous reference.

Form is defined as "the unity of a manifold"; it is neither an absolute unity nor an absolute manifold. It is not an absolute unity since it has material constituents, which must be recognized as distinct, though coördinate, parts. An effect that was not seen to have interrelated constituents would be a mere sensation, and not a form at all. Thus, only in the presentation of materials could an absolute unity occur. Neither is form an absolute manifold, for then it would be indistinguishable from a succession of sensuous stimuli or discursive associations. As the unity of a manifold, form is an aggregation or synthesis of sensuous qualities, each appearing as a distinct constituent, and all contributing to a pattern that has its own unique quality and provides its own kind of beauty.

At times, especially in his early philosophy, Santayana seems to identify all imaginative values with those of form. He then treats form as the principle by which sheer matter or sensation takes on aesthetic relevance. In one place he refers to aesthetic values as those that are "inherent in imagination, in instant intuition, in sense endowed with form." [8] This would seem to agree with his way of distinguishing between fine and servile art on the basis of the difference between form and matter; but it would contradict his previous assertion that sensuous materials can have an aesthetic value of their own.

In order to solve this difficulty, we must recognize Santayana's ambiguous use of the word "matter," as well as the word "form." When he is discussing the process of art and distinguishing between industry, which prepares matter, and liberal art, which imposes an ideal form upon it, Santayana is using "matter" to mean substance. When he refers to the sensuous materials of beauty, however, he is using "matter" to mean a certain kind of essence. In preparing matter, the industrial artist deals with facts and events. Like the scientist, he interprets the external world for the sake of reconstructing it; his material is substantial. But the fine artist, having received perfectly fit material from the industrial artist, works with a filigree of essences. For him, substantial material is only the springboard for an adventure with qualities that in themselves have no relation to existence. One kind of quality is to be termed "sensuous" or "material," but this "matter" is not substantial: it is that kind of essence which serves as a component of form.

With respect to the word "form," we have already seen that Santayana sometimes uses it to mean ideal or norm, but often to mean *any* essence, quality, or character. Now we must note that he also uses it to mean pattern, arrangement, aggregation, or synthesis. It is with this meaning in mind that he discovers a formal element in beauty and defines it as the unity of a manifold. The manifold is composed of the essences known as "sensuous materials," which are not material in any substantial sense but only as constituents of the formal essence which coördinates them.

This interpretation gives Santayana the benefit of several doubts and it ignores the confusions that resulted from his substituting the doctrine of essences for the empiricist theory of perception. Nevertheless, it enables us to see how Santayana can base his distinction between fine and servile art on the difference between form and matter at the same time as he recognizes an element of beauty that is not specifically "formal."

Accordingly, we find that in *The Realm of Essence* Santayana refers to two different kinds of essences: simple and complex. A simple essence is a quality like the pitch of middle C or the color green or goodness; it is both indivisible and unanalyzable. A complex essence is also indivisible and unanalyzable in its totality, *as* a complex essence, but it still contains parts (themselves either complex or simple essences) in a certain "system, order or form." [9] Describing the nature of complex essences, Santayana distinguishes between three kinds of unity: qualitative, quantitative, and formal. Pure unity is qualitative, "like that of a scent or a note, or like that of pure Being." [10] This is the kind of unity that simple essences also have. It is the same as the "absolute unity" that the early Santayana ascribed to sensations, as opposed to forms. When pure unity pervades a continuum, the scent being diffused, the note prolonged, etc., the unity of this continuum is said to be quantitative. If the continuum is elaborated through variation, interrelation of qualities, and the ordering of constituent essences, it takes on formal unity. This formal unity is presupposed in any complex essence. Santayana defines it as "the essential complexity of a form, in which the relations of the parts are internal relations in the whole; so that both the total unity and the contrasting parts are pure essences." [11]

As a result, the contrast between sensuous materials and form, both of them elements in beauty and fine art, must not be taken as a distinction between substance and essence. It is a distinction between two types of essences, between simple essences that have a qualitative unity and complex essences that have a formal unity.

In dealing with form itself, Santayana singles out two kinds that are especially unsuited for aesthetic enjoyment: "indeterminate organization" and "overly-determinate organization." The first is incomplete, the second too discursive. The first relies too heavily on materials, the second overemphasizes expression.

By indeterminate objects, objects that are indeterminately organized, Santayana means those that are vague, incoherent, suggestive, or variously interpretable. [12] The incomplete artist employs an indeterminate form because he is unable to articulate, in some clear and precise way, a theme that he has not himself fully mastered. Such an artist "sketches and never paints; he hints and never expresses; he stimulates and never informs." [13] As a consequence, the observer or reader is forced to use his own powers of interpretation in order to understand what is being so tentatively and elusively suggested.

The work of most landscape painters, and of the impressionists in particular, Santayana believes to be inferior because it is usually dominated by an indeterminate form. The natural landscape, as well as representations of it, contains so many diverse perspectives as to allow the eye to roam indiscriminately. Because it is an indeterminate object, the landscape cannot focus our interest, but rather stimulates revery and fanciful selection. The elements do not cohere aesthetically; they need a synthesizing activity on the part of the observer in order to make a determinate unity. Extreme impressionists carry this disintegration of form into material components even further. They try to present "one absolute momentary view" of the scene portrayed. By shocking the observer with a detached impression, they make him complete the picture himself; in order to see clearly, he must regroup the presented materials and formulate a unity that resembles something he has previously experienced. When the impression is one that the observer has actually had, the effect can be forceful and vivid. But too often the impression is unrecognizable and confusing. And in any event, "such a work is empty and trivial in the extreme; it is the photograph of a detached impression, not followed, as it would be in nature, by many variations of itself." [14]

Santayana has little to say about the second kind of inferior form. He refers to it as the effect of "discursive landscape painting," which makes each scene unnecessarily determinate. Unlike indeterminate form, overly-determinate organization is lacking even in the merit of sensuous appeal. By collecting various glimpses and giving fully "the sum of our positive observations of a particular scene," its portrayal is "perfectly intelligible and plain." [15] Discursive representation is sure to be dull, and Santayana finds it even less aesthetic than indeterminate form, which at least stimulates the imagination and pleases the senses.

In contrast to both indeterminate and overly-determinate organization, Santayana finds beauty of form in a harmonious unification of diverse components: a single and specific pattern in which the parts "suggest inevitably the scheme of their unity." [16] Presented with a definite and determinate object of this sort, the observer need not contribute personal interpretation. He need not refer beyond the given, for what is given appears already organized and unified. The spectator may now intuit a complex essence that alone provides the beauty of form. The cloud that may be seen as a camel or a whale is used as illustration. Once we take it as a whale, an essence seen and recognized without any ulterior reference to the sea or fishermen's yarns or the class of mammals, we intuit a determinate form. "We speak simply of the intrinsic value of the form of the whale, of its lines, its movement, its proportion. This is a more or less individual set of images which are revived in the act of recognition; this revival constitutes the recognition, and the beauty of the form is the pleasure of that revival." [17]

Santayana's treatment of determinate form is not unambiguous. For the most part, however, he identifies aesthetic form, the *truly* determinate one, with some "ideal" or "typical" form. The realistic representation of a particular whale cannot be as beautiful, he says, as the portrayal of common or typical features of whales in general. With typical form, which is more or less purified of unessential details, we get two advantages of considerable importance in art. First, the form takes on universal relevance and may easily be recognized by people with different backgrounds. And second, typical form may depict ideal or supremely desirable characteristics more easily than a detailed figure could. In general, typical form has all the merits of simplicity; it is direct and precise, rather than suggestive or discursive.

This emphasis upon idealized types, especially common in Santayana's early philosophy, elucidates his preference for a strong and explicit unity in artistic form as well as purity and elegant sparsity in the materials that contribute to it. He claims that the best works of art, such as the refined perfections of Greek sculpture, have always embodied idealization and determinate simplicity. It is only the beauty of typical form that can raise expression or meaningful interpretation to its highest aesthetic level. Yet typical form is quite different from expression itself.

Even in his earliest formulations, Santayana sharply distinguishes the element of expression from the beauty of materials and form, which he sometimes treats as modes of "direct" or "bare" perception. The word "perception" is differently employed in the doctrine of essences, but the emphasis upon the directness of given experience — the "sensuous surface," as it is sometimes called — remains constant in Santayana's outlook. Expression, on the other hand, is neither direct nor specifically sensuous. It belongs to the cognitive aspect of experience, the aspect of belief and interpretation. Since memory is closely related to belief, Santayana lays great stress upon the process of association. Association carries us into extraneous and external relations, into the world of facts and events, and hence into the realm of matter. Expression is defined as the character that objects acquire by means of interpretation in all its manifestations, from deliberate and discursive judgment to casual revery and reminiscence.

In order to emphasize the fact that expression is only indirectly and conditionally an element in beauty, Santayana distinguishes between "expressiveness" and "expression" proper. Expressiveness is the "power given by experience to any image to call up others in the mind." [18] It is, in short, the property of being meaningful that may belong to any object. But this property is not an aesthetic value until it is incorporated in, and subordinated to, the bare perception or intuition of the material and formal characteristics of the object. When expressiveness takes on aesthetic value, it becomes "expression."

Santayana next points out that two terms participate in any expressive situation. The first term is the word, image, or physical object that is actually present. This is the "expressive thing." The second term is "the object suggested, the further thought, emotion, or image evoked." [19] This is "the thing expressed." Expression, as opposed to expressiveness, occurs only when the two terms "lie together in the mind" and the second term contributes to the added enjoyment of the first term. Expressiveness is not an element of beauty because, unlike expression, it does not involve a particular interest in the expressive thing itself. However enjoyable an object may be in its meaningfulness, it is not aesthetic unless it also possesses material or formal beauty. Santayana uses the following example to illustrate his view: "I may receive a letter full of the most joyous news, but neither the paper, nor the writing, nor the style, need seem beautiful to me. Not until I confound the impressions, and suffuse the symbols themselves with the emotions they arouse, and find joy and sweetness in the very words I hear, will the expressiveness constitute a beauty." [20]

Although he is not entirely unambiguous in this respect, Santayana does not ordinarily limit the beauty of expression to the formal and material beauty of sights and sounds. For instance, in the passage just quoted he refers to style. The style in "the very words" one hears or reads is not the same as their pattern of sound or written outline. And yet, I think, Santayana wishes to maintain that the style of discourse is capable of having a formal beauty all its own. This effect of formal beauty depends upon the organization of the linguistic vehicle through which expressiveness operates, but it is distinct from the expressiveness itself. Likewise, Santayana would probably say that highly colored and emotive terms provide material beauty which does not result from the mere sound or look of the words. Vagueness and rich suggestiveness of this sort occur by means of expressiveness, but it is an indeterminate expressiveness, an expressiveness in which the second term cannot predominate since it is too indefinite.

Within the element of expression, as in the other two elements, Santayana detects the conflict between a kind of purity and interest. If our experience were *exclusively* aesthetic, all expression would be suggestive of things good, pleasant, or beautiful. In a purified expression the second term would be itself intrinsically aesthetic. Still, Santayana realizes that this kind of expression would lack interest or appeal for mature persons aware that life is really not so sweet and innocent.

For the sake of interest, therefore, art must limit its purity by expressing unpleasant truths. Such unattractive second terms are aesthetic insofar as they appear in an enjoyable presentation, and through the mediation of formal and material elements that are themselves aesthetic. The result is "that while we are saddened by the truth we are delighted by the vehicle that conveys it to us." [21] There seems to be only one kind of expressiveness that cannot become expression. That is the expressiveness of evil. It cannot have aesthetic value; and tragedy and comedy do have aesthetic value, Santayana maintains, only in spite of it, never because of it.

II

Santayana's distinction between the materials, form, and expression in a work of art has been criticized in an interesting fashion by two writers who interpret his message differently, and both of them, I think, incorrectly. On the one hand, Boas complains that Santayana overlooks the effects that significant association contributes to an aesthetic appreciation. Santayana, he says, is too exclusive in choosing the elements of beauty:

> The exclusion of all associated experiences from the aesthetic experience would remove the meaning of words, the subject-matter of paintings, the fitness of buildings from the field of aesthetics. One would arrive at what Mr. Prall has called "the aesthetic surface." It has, however, yet to be demonstrated (1) that the aesthetic surface has any emotional force in and by itself, and (2) that anyone ever has enjoyed a work of art for its aesthetic surface alone.[22]

On the other hand, Mrs. Gilbert understands Santayana to mean that "expression may be absent from beauty as well as constitute its total presence and intent." [23] She criticizes him for maintaining that the elements are "separable" and each of them capable of functioning independently.

Both of these criticisms contain some truth, which I shall try to exploit in examining the three elements of beauty. Furthermore, they both derive from unclear statements that Santayana occasionally made. Nevertheless, they both misinterpret Santayana's doctrine and will have to be answered before we can proceed.

Boas and Mrs. Gilbert both forget that Santayana's distinctions, in his philosophy of art as well as in his other thinking, are distinctions of reason that serve to demarcate aspects or elements that generally occur together. It is true that *occasionally* he seems to contradict himself with respect to the possibility of intuiting essences without also interpreting them, and with respect to having aesthetic contemplation apart from all practical concern. His vague and difficult statements in these important matters are certainly worthy of criticism. Still, it would be disastrous to lose sight of the theses that are most fundamental to Santayana's approach. With regard to the elements in a work of art, they are as follows: first, that the three elements occur together in most works of art, but the uniquely aesthetic quality results from the direct effect of materials and form, as opposed to the indirect effect of expression; second, that the three elements, when they occur together, coöperate as a single unity. Boas overlooks the first of these theses; Mrs. Gilbert, the second, as well as the first.

Thus, when Boas wonders how the aesthetic surface could provide the full enjoyment that a work of art normally supplies, he forgets that Santayana places considerable emphasis, for instance in his literary criticism, upon the function of reason and expression in art. Santayana does not wish to effect "the exclusion of all associated experiences from the aesthetic experience"; he only claims that association does not make an experience distinctively aesthetic, that beauty occurs even when it is not present, and that when it *is* present, beauty results from its fusion with, and dependence upon, the direct effects of materials and form. Santayana wishes to *subordinate* expressiveness to form and materials; he does not try to exclude it from aesthetic experience. And with this kind of approach Boas does not seem to have any quarrel, as it later appears.[24]

Mrs. Gilbert's criticism is composed of two mistakes. First, she misconstrues Santayana's distinction between expression and expressiveness. She does not seem to realize that, according to Santayana, there is no beauty of expressiveness and that the beauty of expression occurs only when the other two elements, or at least one of them, I suppose, is also present. As a result, when she reports Santayana's belief that expression may constitute the "total presence and intent" of beauty, she is not at all showing that Santayana thinks beauty of expression can occur independently of the other two elements. Mrs. Gilbert is right when she says that, according to Santayana, "expression may be absent from beauty," but that is only because he defines aesthetic experience in terms of the material and formal elements. Second, Mrs. Gilbert does not give sufficient attention to Santayana's firm insistence that his analysis is merely heuristic and experimental. In distinguishing the elements that usually contribute to a work of art, he does not wish to deny that, when they do occur together, these elements constitute a unified whole. Pointing out that aesthetic feeling has no parts, Santayana defends his procedure as follows: "By appealing to experiment and memory we can show that this feeling varies as certain things vary in the objective conditions; that it varies with the frequency, for instance, with which a form has been presented, or with the associates which the form has had in the past." [25] Mrs. Gilbert realizes that Santayana holds this position, which she calls "the doctrine of the unity of artistic effect," but she takes it as an admission of guilt and employs it as an argument against his own alleged "doctrine of the separability of functions." [26]

Actually, Santayana's philosophy of art tends to avoid the "doctrine of separability" at the same time as it maintains a commendable attitude towards the function of analysis. As long as we realize that a work of art is a unified totality, we are justified, I think, in analyzing it for heuristic purposes. Without an analysis of some sort we could not define the work of art or discover grounds for evaluation. At the same time, an adequate analysis must recognize that its task is not to *reduce* the original totality into its elemental parts, but only to describe factors that would become elemental parts if they actually belonged to the original totality. A totality, a unity of any sort, is equivalent to its parts in their relations — nothing more and nothing less. It is not an "organic whole" or "emergent quality." Yet, as a totality, it is different from its parts taken separately or else together but in a different relationship. Out of their original context, the parts themselves are no longer the same. Insofar as they can be taken separately, they are not even parts but totalities in their own right. It is the function of analysis to attain these new totalities, realizing all the while that it is no longer dealing with the parts of the old totality. The analyst provides information about the original totality by describing the new units and by specifying relationships that would make them into parts that constitute the original totality. Since Santayana seems to be aware of this proper function for analysis, I would not criticize his procedure in this respect. Instead, I shall attempt to question the particular totalities that he brings forth, and I shall try to show that neither they nor the relationship that is presumed to hold between them would be suitable for reconstituting the unity of a work of art.

III

At first glance Santayana's elements — materials, form, and expression — seem reasonable enough. He would appear to be saying that works of art have materials, such as sound or color, which are organized into a pattern, and that nothing more is needed for an aesthetic experience, although, to be sure, organized material is often expressive as well. Finally he specifies the relationship between the elements by pointing out that they attain an aesthetic unity when the expressive element is subordinated to the two more fundamental ones.

At closer examination, however, we begin to see flaws in the picture. Although he contradicts himself in more than one place, Santayana generally asserts that only visual and auditory arts can be fine rather than servile. Even "the art of combining dishes and wines" can only be instrumental, since qualities of the "lower senses" cannot be aesthetic. And among the beauties of sight he tends to ignore visual effects other than color. Whether Santayana would put seen lustre, iridescence, texture, etc., within the class of aesthetic materials I cannot say.

Furthermore, there are serious structural defects:

(a) Santayana's analysis is not actually an analysis of the *aesthetic* elements in a work of art; (b) Santayana's analysis is based upon his distinction between essence and existence and is equally indefensible; (c) the relationship between Santayana's three elements does not reconstitute them into the unity that correctly defines the nature of a work of art. Let us examine each of these points.

In saying that Santayana's analysis is not actually an analysis of the aesthetic elements in a work of art, I have not forgotten that Santayana *claims* that it is. After defining beauty as objectified pleasure, he proceeds to consider ways in which something may provide objectified pleasure. A painting, for instance, may have delightful colors although they are not well organized; or else it may have an exciting organization of unattractive colors. In the first instance, we would have an object whose beauty was material; and in the second, one whose beauty was formal.

The distinction between the colors of a painting and the pattern into which those colors are organized is a distinction that I do not care to deny. But I wish to point out that color and pattern are not elements of beauty, but rather elements in the painting taken as a kind of physical object. When we say that something is beautiful, for instance a specific color in a specific painting, we mean that this color has the capacity to participate in aesthetic experiences. If we wish to analyze the elements of beauty, we must inquire into the aesthetic effects that this particular color may become or give rise to. This means that we must learn the different ways in which the color is experienced and interpreted. It might be a sensible aesthetic effect on some occasions, a cognitive aesthetic effect on other occasions, and in either event the direct cause of relevant emotional aesthetic effects. Colors belong to pigments on a canvas; the elements of beauty are the three types of aesthetic effects, under the aspect of which colors are variously interpreted and enjoyed.

Consequently, in examining Santayana's three categories, we shall have to keep two classifications in mind: one relating to the components of the object; and the other to the three types of aesthetic effects. Like Santayana we may say that an object can be analyzed into at least three components: its materials, the organization of these materials, and the expressive function that the organized materials may have. For instance, a statue may be constructed of marble, cut to form a particular shape, and capable of representing a certain person. In order to discover the elements of beauty with respect to the statue, the elements of aesthetic experiences in which it participates, we should have to discern exactly how its materials, pattern, and expressive function are interpreted and enjoyed. And this means that we must analyze the work of art in terms of emotional, sensible, and cognitive aesthetic effects. In doing so, we shall also see how Santayana's epistemological distinctions pervade and, I think, vitiate his analysis. Let us begin with materials.

A material like color might be a sensible or cognitive aesthetic effect, and it might occasion any number of emotional aesthetic effects. Needless to say, when we experience three different kinds of aesthetic effects with respect to a color, we are reacting towards it in more than one way. But this often happens, and even simultaneously. For instance, colors in paintings by Titian and El Greco often arouse a vague emotion — a sense of awe, of mystery or grandeur, and sometimes an indefinite feeling of wonder about the function that these colors have in the present painting, the latter emotion resulting perhaps from the fact that we are too greatly engrossed to see just how the colors are being used; at the same time, they stand out clearly as just the colors that they are, distinct from the

colors one sees elsewhere and containing a characteristic quality that we could describe if we had tongues as talented as a
master's brush; finally, we may also see these colors in a greater
context of relations — as contrasting with other colors in the
composition, as symbolizing a person's rank or status, as the
result of a particular mixture of pigments or a particular brush-
stroke, or simply as the way of filling a certain space.

In each of these respects we experience a different kind of
aesthetic effect (provided all this is enjoyable, of course), despite the fact that it is the same color at which we are looking.
To the extent that the color excites vague feelings of excitement, apprehension, surprise, etc., it provides emotional aesthetic effects; to the extent that the color is seen as something
in particular, similar to some colors and distinct from others, it
becomes a sensible aesthetic effect; to the extent that the color
is experienced as highly determinate or meaningful, and perceived in a great variety of relations, it becomes a cognitive
aesthetic effect. Nor is there anything strange about the fact
that one color can be related to three kinds of aesthetic effects
at once. One often has vague feelings of wonder, expectation,
and even foreboding with respect to a particular color at the
same time as one is able to perceive it as something highly determinate. We may see clearly how the color serves to fill up
space and still *feel* that it has a further significance, one that
will appear to us after we have sufficiently trained ourselves
for the understanding and appreciation of the work. This
mingled feeling of apprehension and assurance, mystery and
certitude, is not a fortuitous thing. It is something every great
artist, in every medium, provokes. The feeling of indiscrimi-
nate expectation does not exclude the possibility of knowing
the colors very closely, of seeing them as highly determinate
and meaningful; and it is likewise compatible with enjoying
them as sensible effects.

As the aesthetic elements in a work of art, the three kinds of
aesthetic effects also participate in our experience of what
Santayana calls "form." We have already seen that in this connection he is referring to a complex essence, a unity that per-

vades a manifold of variation and diversity. The colors are now seen to belong to a larger pattern. They are organized into a particular unity which must include everything that is actually there in the painting. It is on the basis of this "thereness" of the formed materials that Santayana feels that he can exclude expression from the "direct effect" of beauty. Expression, he maintains, goes beyond the presented content and is consequently extraneous to the distinctively aesthetic.

But just as every aesthetic element in the experience of a material such as color was more or less interpretative, so too, with regard to form, there is no room for a barely given or uninterpreted essence. Instead, there are different kinds of aesthetic effects, none of which is wholly uninterpreted, since none of them is wholly vague. And here too we may illustrate the three kinds of aesthetic effects by showing how they can occur simultaneously. For instance, imagine a form that excites vague feelings and emotions, some of which result from an indefinite understanding of the total organization, as often happens in first hearings of music. Aroused by what has gone before, we may have a vague though excited anticipation of the form in some of its future developments. To this extent, the form provides an emotional aesthetic effect. But also it may itself be a sensible aesthetic effect; for as it comes before us, the present part of the form may stand out clearly and we may even discern the musical components within it as it passes. Finally, the form would be a cognitive aesthetic effect if the current part were experienced as highly determinate in relation to something that has gone before or is yet to come, or as an instance of a style or convention that is being followed. We might then perceive with perfect clarity just how the preceding parts have led to this bit of the total organization, and we might look forward to some particular detail that has not yet occurred.

Still, if the form organizes the materials, it must not be thought, as Santayana often seems to think, that the form is *composed* of the materials. The materials of sound compose a piece of music, as the materials of color and related effects compose a painting. The sonata form, however, is not composed of sounds but rather of the three movements, themselves composed of smaller formal units. The pattern *according* to which the sounds make up a piece of music known as a sonata is the sonata form. Thus, when we speak of components in the form or pattern, we do not mean particular sounds or colors; we mean particular *organizations* of sounds and colors that contribute, in a certain manner of their own, to the total organization. In this way we avoid difficulties that Santayana would have to overcome in order to clarify his distinction between simple and complex essences.

Furthermore, Santayana's attempt to distinguish the form or complex essence of diversified unity from any interpretative element leads him to treat the form as if it were completely given in a single intuition. Since Santayana rejects temporal atomism, he would not say that the total organization can be intuited in a pregnant moment, as Mozart is alleged to have done with still unwritten works of his. Santayana wisely avoids this atomistic position: his distinction is between an intuition that might last as long as the work of art itself and the interpretation that relates the intuited form with other entities or uses it as a symbol. Consequently, we may have to take issue with Hartshorne when he criticizes Santayana as follows: "A mind that experienced music all at once, without any contrast between expectation and its fulfillment (such as would exist even with perfect memory of the past) would . . . experience less than music." [27] If Hartshorne means that Santayana thinks a complex essence, such as musical form, can be intuited all at once, then he has surely misunderstood the doctrine of essences. By way of correction, we might quote Santayana, who says in one place that "music, which is ethereal in its being and, in the objective direction, terminates in pure essence, nevertheless in its play with pure essence is full of trepidation, haste, terror, potentiality, and sweetness." [28] Hartshorne would be clearly mistaken, therefore, if he thought that Santayana was expounding the possibility of momentary intuition.

Nevertheless, Hartshorne is right if he wishes to argue that Santayana's doctrine of essences excludes the possibility of expectation and fulfillment in music. In music the form manifests itself by its development, by the very process of repetition, variation, suggestion, and novelty. Themes are stated, worked at, and then somehow resolved. The form is what it does in the course of its development; it is the succession of sounds in their particular organization. But this succession can be appreciated, it can have aesthetic significance, only to the degree that memory and expectation are employed. We cannot enjoy musical form without remembering what has gone before and expecting what is yet to come. This interpretative process involves the association of each present part of the form with past and future parts, the association of each of these parts with the total form as it works itself out, and the association of the total form with similar forms that we have already experienced. When the critic is told that a work he is about to hear is in the sonata form, he expects a certain organization of sounds. The actual organization is the one that develops as he listens (each time), and the music becomes meaningful to the extent that the critic interprets it. If he does not make the necessary associations, the form is for him less determinate and less significant. If it were only a vague excitement to indefinite expectation and muddled memory, it might provide an emotional aesthetic effect but it would not be cognitive. If there were *no* interpretation, the critic would not be hearing the music, or at least, he would not be conscious of it, and for him no form would be present *at all*.

Consequently, one may well wonder what Santayana is talking about when he says that music terminates in pure essence although its play is "full of trepidation." When the music ends, we do not intuit an image that recapitulates the form in its development. The form ends with the music and has no being apart from the sounds that it organizes. Neither is the form a complex quality to be distinguished from the qualitative simplicity of materials. Form is more complex than materials inasmuch as it is perceived by means of secondary, instead of primary, signification; but form is not a *quality*. Form is pattern or design. As such, it may be distinguished from materials in the way that the shape of a statue is distinguished from its texture or consistency. These are quite different effects, each requiring a special sort of response. If we could use our hands on statues (a gesture that might increase our appreciation, and, incidentally, one that relies on tactual — not visual or auditory — qualities), we would pat them in order to feel the texture, but we would trace their contours with the tips of our fingers. This is the kind of behavior we might go through if we were teaching someone the difference between material and formal components. But neither form nor materials can be understood in terms of essences. However they may differ from one other, they are alike in being experienced by means of interpretation. In this respect at least, they cannot be distinguished from expression.

In the category of expression itself, Santayana's denial that interpretation can be intrinsically valuable shows up in his refusal to admit a beauty of expressiveness. Expressiveness cannot be an element of beauty, he says, because it takes us beyond the "given" object. Only when the second term, the "thing expressed," is subordinated to the first term, the object whose form and matter are directly presented, can beauty of expression occur.

Santayana's insistence upon the aesthetic priority of the first term is designed, in part at least, to forestall the possibility of an object being considered aesthetic simply because it induces pleasant revery. If this were all that Santayana meant, I would entirely agree with him (although he ignores the fact that a pleasant revery may itself be aesthetic and even a work of art). I would agree with Santayana because the object, a piece of music for instance, cannot be considered aesthetic just because it provokes daydreams. From the information provided, that the music stimulated a pleasant revery, we are unable to reach any conclusions about the intrinsic value of listening to it. The music may have had instrumental value, but we cannot call it aesthetic until we learn whether it was *itself* satisfying.

To deny that a work of art is a mere stimulus to random association is not, however, to deny that it can be aesthetic by virtue of its expressiveness. An aesthetic object may be appreciated for its expressive function as well as its materials and form. When the object, the first term or expressive thing, suggests or symbolizes something else, the second term or thing expressed, they both become elements within a larger context. The two terms become materials that are organized by the particular sign-relationship that now holds them together. The function of expressiveness may be aesthetic if its own pattern or form, the relationship between the two material terms, is satisfying in itself. Although the intrinsic value of encountering the first or second term may possibly add an extra glow to the total experience, the expressive function can be aesthetic independently of such additional effects.

In this fashion we are able to side-step two difficulties, only one of which Santayana's theory avoids. Like him we prevent the expressive relationship from making the aesthetic object into a random stimulus. When that happens, as in the case of revery or irrelevant association, expressiveness distintegrates and we are faced with a new object, the second term, which may or may not be aesthetic in itself. But unlike Santayana we must not analyze the aesthetic object into nothing but material and formal components. For the object might also have the function of being expressive in a certain fashion, and that provides aesthetic effects over and above those of form and matter. An interest in the given object often requires us to ignore its formal and material components and to detect the way in which it becomes a component itself. To subordinate the first term to the second might destroy the expressive relation, but this could also happen if the second term were subordinated to the first. In order to appreciate the expressive function of an object, we must be aware of both the formal and material components in the larger context to which it belongs. The aesthetic effects of expressiveness are the effects of this new form — the mode of organization between the first and second terms.

From this point of vantage we may now take issue with Santayana's assertion that expressiveness cannot become beautiful until we "suffuse the symbols themselves with the emotions they arouse." In the example he employs, if the paper, writing, or style of a letter were not beautiful and were not rendered attractive by the joyous news conveyed, no beauty of expression could occur. The enjoyment of the second term, he wishes to say, cannot count aesthetically until it contributes to the direct effect of the first term. What Santayana forgets is that the direct effect of the first term derives as much from its expressive function as from its material and formal components, and that this function can have its own aesthetic character. Although the symbols were never suffused with the emotions they arouse, we might still appreciate the way in which the message is conveyed and enjoy the process of learning the news.

Another instructive illustration shows more clearly how Santayana's approach leads him astray. He tells us that "a map is not naturally thought of as an aesthetic object; it is too exclusively expressive." He adds that the map can nevertheless be made into a work of art if we concentrate upon the qualities of the first term. If we draw the map with delicate lines, using subtle tints and balancing land and sea masses, we may eventually have a beautiful object: "a thing the charm of which consists almost entirely in its meaning, but which nevertheless pleases us in the same way as a picture or a graphic symbol might please." [29] But surely this is mistaken. One does not make the symbolic function of a map aesthetic by making its colors and lines more attractive. Just as one may delight in a map that has a lovely design without knowing that it is a map and without being able to understand what it represents, so too one may enjoy its symbolic function without having the slightest interest in the materials and decorative pattern that make up the first term. For we may be pleased by the excellent way in which the map does its work, or because it enables us to learn geographical facts, or because it employs interesting techniques to make its particular kind of representation.

Furthermore, Santayana's analysis leads him into an unwholesome distinction between pure and impure expression. In purified expression, he says, the second term is intrinsically aesthetic; in impure expression, it is not. Santayana does not deny that, for the sake of interest, unpleasant truths should be expressed. But he does hold: that unpleasant truths are aesthetically impure; that works of art can be aesthetic only in spite of the representation of evil, never because of it; and that the formal and material components of the first term account for any aesthetic effect the expression of unpleasant truths may actually have — "while we are saddened by the truth we are delighted by the vehicle that conveys it to us."

While I agree that an artistic vehicle can often provide aesthetic effects in itself, I also think that expressiveness can make a unique contribution which Santayana overlooks. To trace the functioning of an expressive relationship is to use our intellect in a certain way, to see that *this* means *that* and not another thing, and to perceive the exact manner in which the artist has effected this connection. We might not delight in either an expressed truth or in the expressive object that serves as its vehicle, but we might enjoy learning the truth simply because we like to live with our eyes open even if what we see is painful. As a result, unpleasant truths cannot be aesthetically impure in the way that Santayana suggests. If they are themselves dissatisfying, they are not aesthetic as second terms. But if they function as materials for a satisfying expressive pattern, if they participate as second terms that we are, under the circumstances, glad to see expressed in the way that they are expressed, then they contribute to the very purity of aesthetic value. Moreover, the representation of evil is often aesthetic; not because all observers are sadists, but because many of them like to learn about life on every moral level and because the representation seems authentic. And this effect, once more, does not depend on formal or material constituents of the first term; it depends on the special function of expressiveness, which is actually a formal component in the larger context to which the two terms themselves belong.

Once we see that expressiveness contributes values of its own, we may go on to show how it assumes aesthetic relevance in terms of the three types of aesthetic effects. For the needs of the present analysis we may limit the expressive function to representation, although expressiveness includes much more and is often nonrepresentational.

As aesthetic effects, representational symbols do not all function alike, usually because they are made to represent in different ways and/or in conjunction with different kinds of second terms. Different types of symbolization, as they occur in aesthetic experience, figure as the three kinds of aesthetic effects with respect to representation. Although many emotional aesthetic effects are related to the form and materials of a work, particularly the form, we often react emotionally towards the mere representation of second terms. The way in which something is represented may arouse suspense, anticipation, and excitement in general. At the same time, the representation may be experienced as a sensible or cognitive aesthetic effect. It is a sensible effect when it is what I shall call "sensible representation," and a cognitive effect when it is what I shall call "cognitive representation." Let us now distinguish between sensible and cognitive representation.

Sensible representation occurs when the second term is represented only with respect to few relations or related contexts; cognitive representation occurs when it is represented in terms of many relations and many related contexts. In sensible representation we get only a rough idea, a simplified or stylized interpretation of the second term; in cognitive representation we get a complex and detailed description in terms of a wide network of relations on various levels of significance. For instance, if we looked at a painting and merely saw the face of someone we might be able to recognize later, someone whose face we could distinguish from other faces but without learning much about him, this actual or imaginary person would have been represented in sensible representation. If, however, the painting supplied us with a great deal of information about this person, told us about his status in life, his character, his occupation, his significance as a historical or symbolic personage, he would have been represented in cognitive representation as well. Sensible and cognitive representation may occur simultaneously, but they are different ways of representing different kinds of second terms. Both may be precise and determinate but they involve different degrees of interpretation.

Whether or not sensible and cognitive aesthetic effects in representation occur together, each of them may be accompanied by relevant emotional aesthetic effects. Thus, with regard to sensible representation, we find that Conrad and Henry James are able to excite in us (partially through the skillful use of formal patterns) a sense of wonder, dread, or mystery at the same time as they present a determinate but scanty description of some horrifying state of affairs. Likewise, much of whatever moving appeal there is in Matisse's paintings results from the use of highly stylized sensible representations, of the human face for instance. For the most part, Matisse was not interested in portraying the detailed contours of actual or imagined faces, and he did not try to depict a mood, emotion, or trait of character. That is why he could limit himself to pink ovals which serve in the sensible representation of some nondescript man or woman. By using stylized figures of this sort, his paintings arouse human interest in a way that nonobjective art might not have at the same time as they focus most of our attention upon their formal and material components.

Cognitive representation may also be accompanied by emotional aesthetic effects. For instance, Racine, Dostoyevsky, and Proust, unlike James and Conrad, excite a variety of feelings in us precisely through their explicit, detailed, and analytical descriptions of human situations. Similarly, the portraits of Rembrandt get much of their emotional impact from the artist's ability to portray, through cognitive representation, the character and personality of complex individuals: in the case of his later self-portraits, of a man whose long and bitter experience has culminated in wisdom, resignation, humor, and a sensitive disillusionment. In relation to expressiveness as a whole, cognitive aesthetic effects are compatible not only with sensible aesthetic effects, but also with emotional ones, and all three may occur simultaneously. These aesthetic effects, like those of materials and form, are based on interpretation. The expressive function is not intuited, and yet its aesthetic effects are undeniable elements in the appreciation of a work of art.

IV

The relationship between Santayana's proposed elements of beauty reconstitutes a unity, but it is by no means the unity that correctly defines the nature of a work of art. This specific relationship is implied in Santayana's treatment of the first and second terms in expression, pure and interesting effects in materials, and indeterminate and discursive types of form. In order for there to be a work of fine art, instead of servile art, he says, the second term must be compounded with, and subordinated to, the first term in expression. A production can be fine art only if it has proper form and materials: a work that has discursive form, or one whose materials are merely interesting, cannot be fine art. What Santayana means by proper materials and form is not entirely clear; but he does say that something could be a work of fine art even if it merely satisfied the principle of purity in materials and had an indeterminate form. The tone of a tuning fork may be aesthetic, and, implicitly, a work of fine art, because it has purity, though hardly any interest. And similarly, an indeterminate form, however inadequate, may organize what Santayana would consider to be a work of fine art, whereas a discursive form cannot.

This kind of preferential relationship among the elements is faulty, I think. It does violence to the function of expression, and it is based on a mistaken conception of what a work of art is. Santayana's distinction between the process of servile art and the process of fine art leads him to the conclusion that a production is specifically aesthetic or "fine" only if it presents essences for intuition. Consequently, materials are not aesthetic insofar as they are merely interesting, form is not aesthetic insofar as it is merely discursive, and the combination of form and materials is not aesthetic insofar as it is merely expressive. In this way Santayana's conception of the process of fine art directs his conception of the work of fine art.

As I have already suggested, the epistemological distinction between fine and servile art cannot be drawn. But even further, I would say that the physical object that results from a creative process need not be a work of (fine) art, or even aesthetic. The physical object produced by a process of art we may refer to as the "art product." Now, for the purposes of aesthetic analysis, let us distinguish between calling something an art product, or physical object, and calling it a work of art.

In ordinary language we have two different ways of talking about paintings, statues, poems, musical compositions, etc.: sometimes we treat them as physical objects; sometimes as works of art. Perhaps I should have spoken of physical "entities," since poems and pieces of music are configurations of marks on a page and patterns of sounds in the air rather than physical "objects"; but we need not boggle at the word. Also, we may ignore the interesting fact that poems and musical compositions are not entities of the same sort as paintings and statues (a poem or a piece of music can occur in different places at the same time whereas a painting or a statue cannot). My point is that we cannot describe a painting, poem, statue, or musical composition as a work of art if we take it as nothing more than a physical object in general and an art product in particular. We call the painting a physical object when we think of it as pigments on a canvas; we call it a work of art when we think of how the pigments would participate in someone's aesthetic experience. In relation to the carpenter that measures the canvas and the historian that describes the pigments' form and representation, the painting is just a physical object; it is a work of art only in its capacity to enter into satisfying experiences of the relevant sort.

Thus, the art product, like any other physical object, may be studied as an historical document, an autobiographical report, a manifestation of cultural and technical developments. It may also be described in terms of its own components — as Santayana does when he analyzes what he calls the work of art into its materials, form, and expression. *As* an art product, the Cézanne hanging on a wall is just a piece of canvas covered with pigments that are designed to represent fruit lying on a table. As a *work of art*, however, the Cézanne has a capacity to give aesthetic experience. Since beautiful objects are not all works of art, this aesthetic capacity is of a particular sort, and it requires further definition.

In attempting to define or characterize the work of art, we must refer once more to the three types of aesthetic effects. It was in terms of them that we analyzed the aesthetic elements with respect to materials, form, and expressiveness. Now we may define the work of art by reference to their unity or totality. To be a work of art an object must tend to provide the three kinds of aesthetic effects and in harmonious combination. By the harmonious combination of aesthetic effects I mean their organization into a satisfying totality. No production is beautiful as a work of art unless it has the capacity to provide a complex of aesthetic effects that are enjoyable as a whole.

If a physical object, even an art product, could not meet these requirements, we would not call it a work of art: we would say that it was either a worthless production or a mere instrumentality. When the phrase "work of art" is not used as a synonym for "art product" (as I have defined that term), it usually designates a certain kind of beautiful object. Unless we were referring to it as an art product, we would not call something an ugly or (aesthetically) bad "work of art." We would ordinarily say "that sonata is bad *music*" or "that portrait is a bad *painting*," implying that neither of them is actually a work of art. If we were sympathetically inclined, we might call the product an "exercise" or a preliminary "study," and we might even admit that it is not without aesthetic merit. But we would not call it a work of art unless it could give the wide range of satisfaction indicated by the three types of aesthetic effects.

In describing the work of art this way, we diverge from

Santayana's formulation in two respects. First, we define the work of art in terms of the aesthetic effects that occur in experience, as opposed to the components of a physical object. Second, in contrast to Santayana's insistence upon the prime importance of materials and form in a work of art, we do not require the subordination of one type of aesthetic effect to another or of one component to another. As a result, the unity of aesthetic elements that we specify is different from the unity that Santayana specifies. Any harmonious coördination of the three kinds of aesthetic effects meets our requirements. In different works of art different kinds of aesthetic effects will predominate and in relation to different components, but this only proves that works of art are not as uniform as Santayana thinks.

Furthermore, although Santayana holds that beautiful materials, form, and expression usually accompany one another, he also maintains that an object need only have beauty of materials or form in order to be a work of art. The sound of a tuning fork he would not consider "interesting," but since it has beautiful materials he would probably treat it as a work of art, although a meager one. This, however, seems unreasonable to me. The sound of a tuning fork may have purity of a sort and it may be aesthetic; but it emphasizes materials to the exclusion of everything else and it is unlikely to provide anything more than sensible aesthetic effects. Such an object lacks the complexity and diversity that we usually require for something to be taken as a work of art: however pleasant a tone may be, it does not amount to music. And the same is true of things that produce emotional and cognitive effects. In general, an object that was highly satisfying, but only in terms of one or another aesthetic effect, would not be a work of art. All three types must participate; more we cannot say until we examine the quantitative and qualitative standards of the greatest or ideal art. (Cf. Chapter 7.)

Although anything that occasions harmonization of the three types of aesthetic effect may be a work of art, one can still distinguish between different kinds of art. A chair is not the same as the painting of a chair, and a scientific treatise is not, usually, a sonnet sequence. All of these productions may be works of art, but if so they are of different kinds. Works of art may be distinguished from one another in at least two ways: First, on the basis of what they present to an aesthetic experience, their component materials and form and whatever expressiveness they may have; second, on the basis of the specific aesthetic effects, in each of the three types, to which they give rise. Let us look a little further at each kind of distinction.

We never have trouble distinguishing between a work of art that is known as a chair and the kind that is known as a painting: their materials, forms, and expressive functions are obviously different. A painting is composed of organized colors or surfaces, but a chair is composed of the legs, the seat, the back, etc. The patterns in a painting are limited to two dimensions; those in a chair are three-dimensional. And finally, the picture of a chair represents a chair, which itself does not usually represent anything. Although some works of art cannot easily be distinguished on the basis of materials, form, and expressiveness, this sort of distinction is one that is commonly employed and with sufficient success for all practical purposes.

But works of art are distinguishable from one another not only in terms of the components that they present to an aesthetic experience, but also in terms of the aesthetic effects that eventuate. Although an actual chair may lack the representational values that the painting of a chair usually has, it provides a great many aesthetic effects which the painting cannot supply. Like the components in the painting, the form and materials of the actual chair may be pleasing to the visual sense; but they may also be pleasing to the tactual and kinaesthetic senses beyond the capacities of a painting. In this fashion, additional aesthetic effects within each of the three types are instituted, and the actual chair is the work of art that it is, and not the kind that the painting is, precisely because it provides the harmonious unity of just such aesthetic effects.

I spell out these ways of distinguishing between works of art because I wish to show that there is no point in Santayana's distinction between fine and servile art. A comfortable chair can be aesthetic and a work of fine art, just as a well-drawn painting can. The chair is a different kind of art; but its aesthetic value is not diminished by the fact that it provides comfort and pleases as an instrumentality. Neither is a scientific nor scholarly treatise inherently servile, however abstract and discursive it may be.*

Even human action, which is a kind of production, may be a work of fine art. If dancers, in the course of their activity, enjoyed their own motions, experiencing thereby the three kinds of aesthetic effects harmoniously combined, their actions would constitute a work of art that only they could appreciate. Their movements would enter into an aesthetic experience that differs from any aesthetic experience undergone by a spectator. The materials would not be dance steps but kinaesthetic and muscular sensations of one's own, organized as something felt rather than something seen. Whether dancers often have this kind of aesthetic experience I do not know. But we might take it as the model of how human actions themselves may constitute a work of fine art. When the organism is functioning properly, what one feels, thinks, perceives, and does takes on aesthetic relevance. In an ideal existence one's entire life would be an artistic process that also satisfied as a work of art. If one's life were sufficiently governed by intelligent creativity, it would be continuously artistic; if it furnished pervasive and harmonious aesthetic effects in each type, it could also be a work of art. This kind of art must not be confused with the kinds known as music, literature, painting, etc. The produc-

---

* At times Santayana *seems* to say something similar. For instance, in *Three Philosophical Poets* he makes the following remarks: "One extension of art, then, would be in the direction of doing artistically, joyfully, sympathetically, whatever we have to do. Literature in particular (which is involved in history, politics, science, affairs) might be throughout a work of art. It would become so not by being ornate, but by being appropriate; and the sense of a great precision and justness would come over us as we read or wrote. It would delight us; it would make us see how beautiful, how satisfying, is the art of being observant, economical, and sincere" (p. 213). Taken at its face value, this passage would contradict almost everything else in Santayana's aesthetics, including statements in other parts of the same book.

tions are different and clearly distinguishable. But as long as they satisfy in their totality, they may all be aesthetic; and as long as they harmonize the various kinds of aesthetic effects, they may all be works of fine art.

Santayana's analysis requires the subordination of interpretation to intuition and of the distinctively expressive to the distinctively aesthetic. In discarding this entire approach, we have identified the elements of beauty with the aesthetic effects that participate in the experience of a work of art. The artist must try to foresee how his production will be received, what aesthetic effects it may be expected to provide, and how these aesthetic effects will be combined. Whomever he takes as the authoritative observer, much of his art will be devoted to the task of making something that can be experienced as satisfying in a variety of ways. He will also keep a standard of artistic excellence in mind, but just what it should be we have yet to decide.

7

THE STANDARD OF ARTISTIC EXCELLENCE

In the role of literary critic, as well as philosopher, Santayana is much concerned about the nature of great art. The standard of excellence that he employs is never explicitly stated, but may easily be reconstructed from his opinions about the aesthetic effects of particular works of art. The four levels of poetry which Santayana describes in *Interpretations of Poetry and Religion* are especially germane. His literary criticism was, to a large degree, written with this classification in mind. He analyzes the subject matter and techniques of the poets with whom he deals, classifies their work in terms of the four levels, and evaluates accordingly. In Santayana's later writing, however, his critical theory seems to have changed — so much so that we shall have to consider whether the doctrine of essences may have led him to a standard of excellence significantly different from his earlier one.

I

The first level of poetry, which Santayana describes in the early essay "The Elements and Function of Poetry," is the level at which sheer sound is most important. The lowest common denominator, the stuff of poetry, is words; and sound is the chief sensuous material of words. On this level the prime poetic value is euphony. Euphony is said to have three forms. Its highest form, since poetry approximates music, is song. Unfortunately, human speech has sacrificed song to the exigencies of communication. All that remains, therefore, is the euphony of vowels and consonants and of the rhythm of speech — euphony that results from the succession of sounds and the effects of rhyme and metre.

Poetic ability on this level has the same relation to great poetry, Santayana declares, as "scales and aimless warblings bear to great singing — they test the essential endowment and fineness of the organ which is to be employed in the art."[1] Still, euphonious effects are essential to great poetry since they provide the sensuous background and basic musical quality.

Illustrating this level of poetry, Santayana cites passages from Shelley's "Revolt of Islam" and Keats' "Endymion" which do not convey any definite meaning but only "a kind of objectless passion which is little more than the sensation of the movement and sensuous richness of the lines."[2] On the following page, however, Santayana admits that in these lines there is already more than mere sound and metre. This brings him to the second level.

The quality of poetry on this level Santayana calls "euphuism," by which he means "the choice of coloured words and rare and elliptical phrases . . . the fanciful, rich, or exquisite juxtaposition of phrases."[3] This quality of precious vocabulary and highly exquisite style explains why the passages from Keats and Shelley were actually poetic, although on a low level. The lack of euphuism in the following couplet by Pope leads Santayana to conclude that mere euphony does not make poetry:

> *In spite of pride, in erring reason's spite,*
> *One truth is clear, Whatever is, is right.*

Here there is no grievous fault of sound or metre, and yet, according to Santayana, "we should hesitate to say that such writing was truly poetical."[4] For although the required element of euphony is present, the couplet is "too intellectual": exact reference interests Pope more than any rich and fanciful suggestion. Pope makes insufficient use of vague words and elusive meanings, and of the emotive quality that poetic discourse should possess. The Symbolists, on the other hand, lean so heavily on the device of euphuism, Santayana claims, that they tend to overlook the other levels on which poetry may exist.

Having reached the third level, we definitely move beyond the rudiments of poetry. Poetry on this level is more complex than merely euphonious or euphuistic verse, but it too concentrates upon a distinctive aspect of poetry in general: the imaginative and intuitive appreciation of essences. The lines depict what is given in immediate experience. Instead of accepting his common-sense beliefs, the poet reduces them to the intuitions from which they originated. It is the impact of sensuous experience that interests him, not the conceptualization of substance. Having surrendered all desire either to understand the world or to act within it, this kind of poet collects and records the sensuous impressions which the intellect can neither portray nor utilize without distortion. He allows himself to return to the pathetic fallacy, restoring to the object before him the emotional quality with which the child or primitive experiences it. Since poetry on this level is a mode of communication, it must include a kind of representation. But what is represented (or "intended," as Santayana would probably say) is not substance or the object of any belief, but rather an essence of some sort. The poet is not interested in conveying "information."

There are two kinds of essences with which Santayana seems to associate the third level of poetry:

First, moods and particular images. The poetry of Walt Whitman, we are told, largely consists in portraying simple qualities as they impinge upon the senses. In Whitman's work we find "the swarms of men and objects rendered as they might strike the retina in a sort of waking dream. It is the most sincere possible confession of the lowest — I mean the most primitive — type of perception." [5] Elsewhere, in the midst of an article on American philosophy, Santayana declares that Whitman "reduced his imagination to a passive sensorium for the registering of impressions." [6] The Symbolists, too, are "fascinated by pure sense," the simple qualities felt in an immediate experience. In accordance with their emphasis upon euphuism, they do not attempt to convey meanings so much as to present a field of qualities associated with some emotion or sensation. "For they play with things luxuriously, making them symbols for their thoughts, instead of mending their thoughts intelligently, to render them symbols for things."[7]

Second, passions and the feelings that arise in the course of action. Robert Browning is taken to exemplify the kind of poet who expresses man's active and irrational nature. More sophisticated than Whitman, Browning is not limited to sensation and the simplest qualities: intricate feelings and the excitement of an active life is what he portrays. By means of these essences, he conveys a "sense of character" and emotional situation. Because he cannot "rationalize emotion" or understand how it can be wedded to a more philosophical outlook, his poetry, like Whitman's, is "barbaric." The barbarian is one who "regards his passions as their own excuse for being; who does not domesticate them either by understanding their cause or by conceiving their ideal goal."[8] Whitman and Browning alike are barbarians, or poets of barbarism, reveling in the irrationality of rudimentary sensation and undisciplined passion. With a slight difference they resemble the modern artists whom Santayana discusses in a paper called "Penitent Art." There he points out that the fear of reason has caused modern painters either to renounce representation entirely or to present "a pregnant hint, some large graphic sign, some profound caricature" instead of a complete and explicit portrait of the object.[9]

Accordingly, Santayana suggests that the third level of poetry is no more adequate in itself than either of the previous ones. Its ultimate failure, as evidenced by poetry such as Browning's, results from difficulties inherent in its treatment of the passions. Human character and emotion are of special importance to a poet; but they must display themselves in terms of an objective environment and by means of dramatic situations. For imagination to have its fullest and most rewarding operation, the outer world must be "bathed in the hues of human feeling, the inner world expressed in the forms of things."[10] But in order for the poet to fulfill the second of these conditions, he must externalize his emotions, he must discover "correlative objects" that will serve to express them. And this inevitably commits him to a wider interpretation of experience than is attempted by poetry on the third level.

Santayana's emphasis upon correlative objects, similar in almost every respect to T. S. Eliot's subsequent theory of the "objective correlative," brings him to the level of rational poetry.

On this level poetry tries to construct a reasoned and reasonable world outlook. Sensitive to the immediate aspect of experience but not limited to it, the poet knows how to integrate sense and passion into a conception of nature. He employs euphonious and euphuistic devices and seeks to penetrate to the essential and intuitive core that underlies convention, but now all this is directed towards the presentation of a philosophical, ontological, or religious point of view. Still, as *poetry* his work does not convey information, and the reader need not use discursive reason in order to appreciate it.

There are three tasks that the rational poet must undertake and accomplish. First, he must subordinate characterization to plot: he must develop and portray character by describing circumstances in which it manifests itself. The rational poet resorts to dramatic situations and intersubjective occurrences, rather than soliloquy or introspection, in order to show the nature and significance of a character. Like Aristotle, Santayana believes that narrative is the most important element in fiction. Second, the rational poet must place the characters within a material and historical setting. The causes and conditions of their emotions can only be explained in terms of their cultural traditions and natural surroundings. The greatness of Virgil and Dante resulted from their awareness of the forces at work within their country and their age. All the classic poets, we are told, have "the topographical sense." Instead of portraying nature as a landscape painter might, they keep the reader constantly aware of the natural forces that move heaven and earth and that direct society. They do not describe the countryside directly, but only through myth and fable. In this way they communicate the cultural and historical import of the place, and this is more significant than listing physical characteristics. At the same time, Santayana warns us, the poet may fall into the dangerous practice of describing the land-scape in moral terms. He might not catalog the physical minutiae of an outdoor scene, but he might limit himself to the inspirational or recuperative effect that the landscape has upon human beings. Here it is that Wordsworth fails. Instead of dealing with "the cosmic process . . . genesis, evolution, and natural force in its myriad manifestations," Wordsworth "dwells on adventitious human matters." [11] A truly philosophical poet makes neither a physical nor a moral snapshot of nature; he locates the scene by means of allusions, generally mythological, that relate it to a definite way of seeing the world. This in turn leads to the third task of Santayana's rational poet: he must present a prophetic, philosophical, or religious interpretation. Rational poetry must be philosophical poetry.

In discussing this requirement of poetry in its "higher function," Santayana seems to hold conflicting views. He says that the rational poet must "build new structures, richer, finer, fitter to the primary tendencies of our nature, truer to the ultimate possibilities of the soul." [12] But several pages later he insists that "the highest ideality is the comprehension of the real" and that "poetry is not at its best when it depicts a further possible experience, but when it initiates us, by feigning something which as an experience is impossible, into the meaning of the experience which we have actually had." [13] The first statement would commit Santayana to the belief that an interpretation of nature that did not accord with human ideals could not be truly rational. At other times, however, he asserts, as above, that the mythical creation of the poet is significant or truthful only as it symbolizes *actual* events. Because poetry is imaginative, its construction will not lend itself to verification. But, Santayana now says, it will be an interpretation of nature, of the world in which we live, and it will not necessarily be idealistic. The rational poet must be religious and metaphysical; but he may also be a pessimist. This conflict between the Platonistic and naturalistic sides of Santayana's philosophy pervades all his literary criticism. How his divergent statements could be reconciled I do not know.*

It is on the basis of this final requirement, that poetry in its highest reaches must be philosophical and religious, that Santayana criticizes Shakespeare. Shakespeare he interprets as a renaissance man who had to choose between Christianity and nothing, and who chose nothing. Santayana denies that either religious sentiments or a philosophical, metaphysical scheme are to be found in Shakespeare's writings. He calls him a positivist, devoid of any specifically religious insight. He does not deny that Shakespeare possessed considerable wisdom, imaginative power, and even metaphysical ability. What he finds lacking is any "cosmic consciousness." In contrast to Homer and Dante, who had a theory of human life and who saw man in his relations to the universe, "Shakespeare's world . . . is only the world of human society." [14] And even with respect to the experience that *Hamlet* expresses, Santayana concludes that "here is no necessary human tragedy, no universal destiny or divine law." [15]

In passing beyond the immediate aspect of experience — if not beyond experience as a whole — the fourth level of poetry is committed to expressiveness in a way that the first three levels are not. Its function is not only to interpret our immediate experience, that is, to use essences as symbols, an operation that occurs in all our ordinary, practical dealings with substance, but also to formulate an ontology or metaphysics that will account for experience itself. This, however, requires the kind of laborious and discursive thinking that was reserved for the intellect, rather than the imagination. How then can philosophical poetry be a work of fine art? How can it even be aesthetic?

In answering these questions, Santayana points out that "if we think of philosophy as an investigation into truth, or as

* But cf. "Santayana As A Literary Critic," my Introduction to *Essays in Literary Criticism of George Santayana* (New York: Charles Scribner's Sons, 1956), pp. ix–xxviii. In that essay I deal more fully with the present issue, and from a somewhat different point of view.

reasoning upon truths supposed to be discovered, there is nothing in philosophy akin to poetry."[16] And yet, philosophical poetry is possible and highly desirable, he maintains. For the *vision* of philosophy may be poetic and imaginative. Philosophical activities of investigation and reasoning are "only preparatory and servile parts, means to an end,"[17] but they may terminate in intuition — "a steady contemplation of all things in their order and worth. Such contemplation is imaginative. . . . A philosopher who attains it is, for the moment, a poet; and a poet who turns his practiced and passionate imagination on the order of all things, or on anything in the light of the whole, is for that moment a philosopher."[18]

With respect to its subject matter, therefore, philosophical poetry would meet the basic requirement for all fine art. It would not convey information so much as express a contemplative insight into the universal order. It would use the discursive parts of philosophy as material perfected by a servile art and subservient to poetry's imaginative flight.

With respect to its technique, philosophical poetry would also meet the basic definition. Like poetry on the other levels, it would lavish attention upon the sound of its words. In its medium it would not be worse poetry. But instead of being meaningless music, it would sing the insights of ultimate truth. It would be more concrete and immediate than ordinary discourse, and more significant and penetrating than unreflective verse. Rational poetry, we are assured, "would present in graphic images the total efficacy of real things."[19]

Before going on to examine Santayana's standard of excellence from a slightly different point of view, we might pause here to notice how Santayana's epistemological approach affects his conception of poetry in general. In *Reason in Art* Santayana distinguishes between two different uses of language — one of them poetry, the other prose. Santayana distinguishes poetry from prose in the way that he distinguished imagination from intelligence and fine art from servile art. From his treatment of rational poetry, however, we can see how intimately Santayana wishes to bind poetry to prose. Far from considering them incompatible, his entire analysis and criticism is concerned to show how they work together, as well as the advantages that accrue from their coöperation. By using the discursive parts of philosophy, poetry may speak with authority about the actual world. By adding interest to the purity of its music, poetry can meet the needs of religious expression. Santayana does not recognize any inherent conflict between poetry and prose. But he does consider them to be different sorts of discourse, one instrumental to the liberal operation of the other, one of them servile art and the other fine art. Even with their final tight integration, they are split by the same kind of cleavage that separates immediate from mediate experience and essence from existence.

II

Santayana's conception of great art, or, more specifically, great poetry, consists of three requirements, which we may derive from preceding discussions:

First, great poetry must utilize a perfectly determinate form. The words must contribute to an explicitly unified pattern of discourse. The sounds must be organized according to definite rhythmic schemes. The images invoked must form a picture, or series of pictures, that is centered in itself as the unity of a manifold.

Second, great poetry must be composed of the most suitable materials. It must employ sounds that are melodious and musical, words that are rich and suggestive, and images that are graphic and stimulating. In each of these respects the needs of a determinate form listed under the first requirement are uppermost in importance, and the effects of euphony, euphuism, and image-making must be subordinated accordingly.

Third, great poetry must express a significant world outlook. It must present a meaningful interpretation of both the human condition and the cosmic scene. But this philosophical vision must not be laborious or discursive, and it must subserve the requirements of formal and material beauty.

These three requirements may suffice for great poetry, but they cannot account for the very greatest poetry. In *Three Philosophical Poets* Santayana analyzes the work of Lucretius, Dante, and Goethe. These three are all philosophical poets and all great poets; but the efforts of each are imperfect and need to be supplemented by the virtues of the others. They are great poets because they express, in beautiful and determinate form, a large and penetrating vision; each of them is subject to criticism, however, for being limited in his outlook and unable to incorporate the intuitions of the other two.

In Santayana's interpretation, "Goethe is the poet of life; Lucretius the poet of nature; Dante the poet of salvation."[20] Goethe portrays experience in its immediacy, its infinite diversity, and its apparent absurdity. He depicts a world that is bounded by the ego, that is constituted by human feelings and ideas, and that tends to be subjectivistic and impressionistic. To his vision must be added that of Lucretius, whose naturalism gives him an insight into the ground or substance of things. Although he tends to subordinate human feeling and experience to the causes and conditions that underlie them, he has a truthful understanding of life. His finger is on the pulse of matter and he knows the secret workings of both Venus and Mars, both genesis and destruction. Still, Lucretius is not especially perceptive of values. To Dante is given the knowledge of good and evil, the ideal and the anti-ideal. More than either of the others, Dante understands the life of contemplation and spiritual harmony. In summary, here are the three great poets whose work Santayana examines: "Goethe, with human life in its immediacy, treated romantically; Lucretius, with a vision of nature and of the limits of human life; Dante, with spiritual mastery of that life, and a perfect knowledge of good and evil."[21]

It does not require much imagination to realize that these three poets, as interpreted, represent three sides of Santayana's own nature and that their visions correspond, more or less, to the three principal categories of his philosophy. Goethe sees the foreground of essences; Lucretius understands substance;

Dante appreciates the moral and religious discipline needed for the purification of spirit. Just as essence, matter, and spirit are coördinated in a specific arrangement and interrelation, so too does Santayana place the three great poets in a hierarchical order. His "sense of what is real and important" shows him a way of integrating the poetic virtues of all three. Santayana thereby makes explicit his conception of the greatest poet.

In this hierarchy, Goethe is at the bottom and Dante at the top. At the same time, it is not only the level on which a poet travels that counts, but also what he brings into that level. Santayana recognizes that Goethe on the lowest rung is in some respects more inspired than either Lucretius or Dante. More than either of them, especially Lucretius, he is able to depict the variegated plenitude of life, the "magical medley . . . of images, passions, memories, and introspective wisdom that Lucretius could not have dreamed of." [22] Lucretius in turn is more sane and rational than Dante with his childish supernatural views. Dante's idea of nature "is not genuine; it is not sincerely put together out of reasoned observation." [23] It is egocentric and anthropomorphic. It places man at the center of the universe and takes the mirror of his purposive and teleological nature to be a window into the world. In this respect, Dante resembles Shelley, another poet whom Santayana considers to be great despite his ignorance of the material structure in things. Like Dante, Shelley expresses the potentialities of man, his moral and spiritual aspiration, his contemplative upper half. But like him, too, Shelley was limited by an "obtuseness to things dynamic — to the material order." [24] Nevertheless, the principles to which Shelley (and Dante) appealed are needed for a true expression of man: "they are good principles for fiction, for poetry, for morals, for religion." [25] Shelley was able to achieve purity of thought and expression; Dante's powers of idealization made him "the type of a supreme poet" and enabled him to touch "the ultimate goal to which a poet can aspire." [26]

Integrating these different visions, the ideal poet would arrange them in the prescribed hierarchy at the same time as he benefits from the values of each level. Thus, just as he usually takes idealization to be the most aesthetic element, and just as his conception of rational poetry emphasizes the presentation of norms or moral goals, rather than a merely realistic portrayal of nature, here too Santayana favors the expression of an ideal. The greatest poet will appreciate the textural wealth of sensation and experience, and he will recognize the nonpurposive character of the physical world; but ultimately, all this will be subordinated to a vision of the good and the contemplation of perfection.

Santayana is aware of the difficulties in uniting these insights, but he insists that it can be done: "This union is not impossible."[27] He outlines two directions that rational art must follow. First, it must integrate itself with activities that buttress life: industry, science, business, morality, politics, history. It must contribute the element of fine art to all our activities so that everything we do becomes a work of art. In this direction "the philosophical or comprehensive poet, like Homer, like Shakespeare, would be a poet of business."[28] But work and business is not enough; the complete poet has a second and higher responsibility. He must express "the ideal towards which we would move under . . . improved conditions."[29] This ideal includes the art of playing well, in addition to working well. It is based on the art of business but far transcends it in the direction of spiritual liberation. This is the ultimate end of the greatest poet, who will, however, move in the other direction as well, harmonizing and refining both insights. Of him one may truly say: "*Onorate l'altissimo poeta*. Honour the most high poet, honour the highest possible poet. But this supreme poet is in limbo still."[30]

This statement cannot, however, be taken as Santayana's final word in the matter. Some eleven years after *Three Philosophical Poets* appeared, he published an article called "On My Friendly Critics."[31] In it Santayana devotes a single paragraph to his current views about the standard of excellence in poetry. How these views, different from those he had formerly held, fit in with the other aspects of his later philosophy, we shall presently see. The pertinent parts of the paragraph run as follows:

> So anxious was I, when younger, to find some rational justification for poetry and religion, and to show that their magic was significant of true facts, that I insisted too much, as I now think, on the need of relevance to fact even in poetry. Not only did I distinguish good religion from bad by its expression of practical wisdom and of the moral discipline that makes for happiness in this world, but I maintained that the noblest poetry also must express the moral burden of life and must be rich in wisdom. Age has made me less exacting, and I can now find quite sufficient perfection in poetry, like that of the Chinese and Arabians, without much philosophic scope, in mere grace and feeling and music and cloud-castles and frolic. . . When living substance is restored beneath the surface of experience, there is no longer any reason for assuming that the first song of a bird may not be infinitely rich and as deep as heaven, if it utters the vital impulses of that moment with enough completeness. The analogies of this utterance with other events, or its outlying suggestions, whilst they may render it more intelligible to a third person, would not add much to its inward force and intrinsic beauty. Its lyric adequacy, though of course not independent of nature, would be independent of wisdom. If besides being an adequate expression of the soul, the song expressed the lessons of a broad experience, which that soul had gathered and digested, this fact certainly would lend a great tragic sublimity to that song; but to be poetical or religious intrinsically, the mystic cry is enough.[32]

This could mean that what is religious or poetical "intrinsically," that is, according to the definition of poetry, need not include expression or representation. But this much Santayana had always maintained. There would be no occasion for him to recant an earlier position. Since he refers to "the noblest poetry," I believe that he wishes to revise his previous conception of poetic excellence. He now wishes to say that although philosophical poetry is more than just a lyric cry, it is not necessarily greater or more perfect than less rational poetry. If this is what Santayana means, the present view contrasts sharply with his characteristic position in *The Life of Reason*: "The noblest art will be the one, whether plastic or literary or dialectical, which creates figments most truly representative of what is momentous in human life." [33] It would seem, then, that Santayana really had two standards of excellence, an earlier and a later one.

III

Santayana's earlier standard of artistic excellence, culminating in his vision of the greatest poet, was conceived during the period when he was most interested in developing the implications of the life of reason. It is marked with the optimistic and ambitious belief in magnificent harmonizations. His standard is very strict and his ideal of *l'altissimo poeta* correspondingly remote. The later standard, which denies that the noblest poetry need "express the moral burden of life" or be rich in wisdom, fits in well with the older Santayana's increased sympathy with a life of sheer contemplation. The first standard employs the conception of harmony as a rationalizing influence; the second standard limits itself to harmony as the criterion of any particular perfection, as inward integration and precision. The first standard includes the requirements of determinate form and suitable materials, but it goes beyond them in demanding an outlook in which a truthful understanding of the world is combined with the search for ideals. The second standard, denying that philosophic scope is necessary, defines the noblest art in terms of "adequacy" and "completeness." Thus, the bird song is infinitely rich if "it utters the vital impulses of that moment with enough completeness," and it must have "lyric adequacy" and be an "adequate expression of the soul."

Just as formerly we had to ask what made an interest harmonious or perfect or precise or inwardly integrated, so too we must now ask what makes a work of art adequate or complete apart from any practical wisdom or philosophical truth that it may happen to express. In our earlier discussion we found that Santayana considered an interest to be harmonious or perfect if it was directed towards a contemplated essence. Here too it is clear that a work which accorded with Santayana's second standard of excellence would be one that combined the simple and complex essences of suitable materials and determinate form. In other words, it could be any work of art that had aesthetic value, regardless of how much or how little expressiveness it might also have. Santayana's later standard limits itself to the first and second requirements of his earlier standard. Let us, then, examine the later standard first and then move on to the additional requirements that are included in the earlier standard.

According to Santayana, there is only one kind of form that is worthy of great art. Santayana considers indeterminate form and discursive form as distinctly inferior to typical form, which alone presents a complex essence freed of all extraneous relations. For only typical form organizes the most suitable materials into a perfectly determinate pattern: a unity that is simple, idealized, well-knit, and direct or precise in a way that neither indeterminate nor overly-determinate forms can be. By means of the following arguments, I shall try to show that what Santayana calls indeterminate or overly-determinate form may be as definite and clear-cut as what he calls determinate or typical form, and that none of these forms is necessarily more aesthetic than any other:

First, Santayana's criticism of indeterminate form is based on the belief that form can be disintegrated into material components and that when this happens, as in the paintings of the impressionists, one encounters indeterminate form. In such paintings, he says, the spectator must unify the materials by means of his own interpretative faculties. What Santayana overlooks is the fact that materials are always seen in *some* organization: otherwise they could not be determinate in consciousness even as materials. Furthermore, since the perception of form is not the intuition of an essence, all painting — and not just the impressionists' — would be alike in requiring interpretation.

As a result of his erroneous approach, Santayana's criticism of the impressionists is, I believe, ill-founded. The impressionists do not present a sense-datum that the observer is supposed to make into a perceptual object; neither do they appeal to the spectator's interpretative faculties any more than other artists. The impressionists did not paint uninterpreted essences, and they did not create materials without determinate form. Instead, they painted a scene as it appeared to them under certain conditions and after certain, often rapid, interpretations. Monet's haystacks are not the materials or simple essences out of which the spectator is supposed to reconstruct anything. They are representative of substantial haystacks that appeared this way at different positions of the sun, and as they were seen and interpreted by the artist. As time went on, the paintings of the impressionists became more and more abstract. But this does not mean that the percipient has to make a special act of interpretation in order for their paintings to become coherent. It only means that they were moving away from the use of iconic or literal representation, so that the spectator who seeks exact likenesses is looking for the wrong thing. Not only do the forms of the impressionists organize their colors in a determinate fashion, but also they organize them in the only way that could enable these painters to convey the meanings that they wished to convey.

Second, Santayana's antipathy towards discursive form seems to be a dislike of detailed or complex structures. He is certainly justified in emphasizing the need for selection: the artist who dazzles us with a succession of highly intricate details causes us to lose sight of the whole in which they are supposed to fit. But a priori there is no reason to think that a complex pattern cannot be properly unified. It is fashionable in our age to prefer uncomplicated structures and streamlined shapes to heavily-laden ornament or figuration. But our age is also a self-conscious age that is embarrassed by magnificent complexity and lavish or splendid detail. When a complicated structure becomes dull, it ought to be sacrificed in favor of simplicity. But the same should be said for simplicity, which often lacks richness and variety. Consequently, unless Santayana means to identify discursive form with any form whose complexity does not satisfy, I think that he is mistaken to deny that discursive form can have its own kind of aesthetic unity. Even though it is structured out of many details, each of which requires considerable attention, the total pattern may be both determinate and aesthetic.

Third, Santayana's belief that the most determinate and desirable form is typical form seems to emphasize idealization to the exclusion of realistic representation. But since Santayana talks out of both sides of his mouth, the naturalistic as well as the Platonistic, I find his conception too unclear to warrant criticism. At times, he seems to mean that typical form presents something that has universal appeal, something that is easily recognized to be "true to" life — typical in the sense of being characteristic or pervasive. But if this is what Santayana means, I cannot imagine why he thinks that the appreciation of typical form excludes interpretation. To see something as being true to life is to see it in terms of a great variety of relations, and by means of a process that evaluates the object's expressive function. Judged to be true to life, an object becomes more determinate for consciousness than it was before. Having passed through enquiry and mediate experience, it is anything but a bare or directly presented essence.

Finally, Santayana seems to think that the best forms are those that are tightly organized and follow rigid conventions. Against "romantic formlessness" Santayana pits "classical unity." In making his judgments, Santayana does not seem to be expressing a mere preference. He does not seem to be choosing the sonnet form, let us say, rather than *vers libre* simply as a matter of personal taste. On the contrary, Santayana *seems* to be distinguishing an inherently better or more beautiful form from an inevitably worse one. In the next chapter we shall see more clearly what Santayana really means. Here I should like to suggest that if he meant to say what he seems to say, he would be committing a most noteworthy error.

For there is no way of deciding beforehand what pattern,

organization, technique, or type of unity will be most suitable for a work of art. Much romantic art succeeds precisely because it is not limited by the restrictions of a conventional pattern. And in general, while the artist should profit from the devices of traditional forms, he will not make a complete and satisfying work of art unless he can manipulate these forms in accordance with his own needs. Of two possible forms the more desirable one is the one that contributes to the greater satisfaction, however unconventional the form may be. Likewise, the most suitable materials are not restricted to visual or auditory effects, but only to those that satisfy most. And the same may be said about techniques of expression or representation. In any particular instance, all three variables must be considered. With some materials a certain form may tend to be dissatisfying, although it is highly aesthetic with others. With some forms a particular way of representing may be unsuitable, although not with others, etc. No standard forms, materials, or types of expression may be ordained a priori. The artist must use his intelligence in order to decide which combination he will employ. The critic, assessing a particular combination on the basis of its total aesthetic appeal, should realize that each of the components can be evaluated only in terms of its ability to satisfy under the circumstances of this particular combination. Unless he sees what the artist is doing or trying to do, his evaluation cannot be just. Whether the artist ought to be doing what he is doing, whether he ought to make just this combination of aesthetic effects and not another, is a critical and moral problem that we shall consider in the following chapter.

Let us now return to Santayana's first standard, which differs from his second in requiring philosophic scope and moral or prophetic insight. Both of these requirements, let us not forget, are subordinated to the ideal of typical form, so that the core of the two standards remains the same. The later Santayana merely sloughs off the two requirements that we are now examining.

Santayana's original insistence upon philosophic scope is, I believe, a desirable one; but I would prefer to interpret "philosophic scope" more broadly than he does. Santayana seems to believe that a poet cannot be philosophical unless he has developed and put into verse a complete metaphysical or religious system. With this interpretation, a poet like Shakespeare does not fare too well. Still, Santayana himself gives Shakespeare credit for expressing a great deal of wisdom, and in the same volume in which he denies that Shakespeare has a religion, he uses him as the shattering contrast to Browning: "The poet (Shakespeare), without being especially a philosopher, stands by virtue of his superlative genius on the plane of universal reason, far above the passionate experience which he overlooks and on which he reflects; and he raises us for the moment to his level, to send us back again, if not better endowed for practical life, at least not unacquainted with speculation." [34] And yet, despite his "superlative genius on the plane of universal reason," Shakespeare is not credited with any philosophic scope.

Using language as Santayana suggests, we may agree that Shakespeare is not a "philosophic poet." For he is not a philosopher in the way that Dante, Goethe, and Lucretius, and perhaps Shelley, were philosophers. Nevertheless, I wonder whether a distinction cannot be made between a philosophical poet, in the above sense, and a poet who has philosophic scope. The latter would have a world outlook as well as an understanding of human nature although he might not be a philosopher, might not have a complete and rigorous system worked out, and might not be especially interested in religion. Shakespeare, like many other great writers, was not disturbed by religious and metaphysical problems; not because he was insensitive to them, but because he was more interested in moral problems. The problems of purpose, of significant behavior and justifiable decision, were, for him, most important. Hamlet holds religious beliefs and expresses them on occasion, Macbeth likewise; but the problems that confront Hamlet and Macbeth are not specifically religious ones. Hamlet's desperation is caused by his inability to act reflectively and his inability to decide whether a life of troubled action is worth living; Macbeth's progressive misery results from an initial miscalculation about the changes in his own personality that would result from actions like the murder of Duncan and Banquo. In this connection, it is interesting to note that, as an illustration of how Shakespeare depicts life "without a meaning," Santayana quotes the lines of Macbeth that begin "To-morrow, and to-morrow, and to-morrow." But these lines are not a statement of Shakespeare's philosophy; they are the words of a wretched, half-crazed Macbeth whose very despair indicates the depths to which his unfortunate action has carried him. The speech itself is a "correlative object" for Macbeth's condition, and Shakespeare's ability to use it as such manifests his superlative power as a dramatist and a thinker.*

Consequently, I would deny that writers like Shakespeare cannot have a significant world outlook or that their avoidance, relatively speaking, of religious problems prevents them from having philosophic scope. Furthermore, I would argue that it is not necessary for a great artist, or even the greatest artist, to be a philosopher or metaphysician. The great artist must understand the world and be able to sympathize profoundly with its human and other occupants; but he may or may not have refined analytical powers, and he may or may not be interested in the problems of technical philosophy.

This sword cuts both ways. On the one hand, Santayana's early standard is rendered unacceptable by his insistence upon philosophical or religious poetry. On the other hand, his later standard is insufficient because it considers philosophic scope

* In a later article "Tragic Philosophy" (1936) Santayana quotes Macbeth's lines again but now denies that Shakespeare was thereby expressing his own "settled doctrine." At the same time, Santayana more or less repeats his earlier belief that Shakespeare had no philosophic scope: "Even in a Hamlet, a Prospero or a Jaques, in a Henry VI or an Isabella, the poet feels no inner loyalty to the convictions he rehearses; they are like the cap and bells of his fools; and possibly if he had been pressed by some tiresome friend to propound a personal philosophy, he might have found in his irritation nothing else to fall back upon than the animal despair of Macbeth." (Triton ed., Vol. II., p. 278.)

to be unnecessary for the noblest poetry. Once we recognize that the appreciation of form cannot be dissociated from interpretation, we see that any perceived "expression of the soul" must be meaningful to some degree. But even further, I would suggest that an *adequate* expression of the soul, which seems to be Santayana's later criterion of excellence, must present a significant world outlook. It must express a mature and reasoned attitude towards life, and it must be able to place man in his social and natural context.

The justification for this emphasis upon philosophic scope derives, as we shall see presently, from the fact that a work with philosophic scope is able to provide a greater network of intense and varied aesthetic effects in the category of expression than a work without it. Still, although philosophic scope is necessary for the greatest art, it is not sufficient by itself. "Mere grace and feeling and music and cloud-castles and frolic," as Santayana suggests, are good things too. Their contribution to the greatest art is also important, and we must not forget them when we come to the final recokning. But first I should like to resolve a final difficulty in Santayana's earlier standard.

As we have seen time and again, Santayana is ambiguous about the function of norms. When he insists that the greatest poetry must be prophetic and visionary, he sometimes seems to mean that it must be revelatory of the truth, and so realistic, and sometimes that it must be aflame with moral and spiritual programs, and so idealistic. By putting Dante at the head of his hierarchy, Santayana would appear to favor the idealistic over the realistic.

Whatever Santayana may actually believe, it seems clear that one cannot expect all of the greatest works to tend in either one or the other directon, and that, in any event, the cleavage between the realistic and the idealistic in art cannot, or should not, be too profound. A realistic work that had philosophic scope would have to recognize ideals that govern human action; conversely, an idealistic work would have to show that its suggested ideals were relevant to actual conditions. When idealistic art ignores significant human problems, it becomes childish or sentimental or fantastic. When realistic art shows an insensitivity to values, it omits an essential part of the story and cannot be adequately philosophic. Aside from these considerations, I fail to see how preferment can be given to works of art that either do or do not advance ideals. Every artist has the right to propagandize and even to recommend political action. If he did not speak his heart and advocate what seems important to him, he could not make an adequate expression. On the other hand, if he merely wishes to paint a realistic picture, he will botch the job if told to raise a banner. The greatest art may be realistic or idealistic, and possibly both at different times or simultaneously in different respects. As long as it has philosophic scope, it need not be exclusively one or the other.

IV

We see, then, that neither of Santayana's standards is wholly acceptable. In seeking a standard of excellence to take their place, I suggest that we first recall our definition of a work of art. We said that nothing could be a work of art unless it provided a unity of the three kinds of aesthetic effects harmoniously combined, that is, integrated so as to provide satisfaction in their totality.

Now, a standard of artistic excellence should be a guide to artists and spectators alike. It should inform the artist about the total effect his production must achieve if it is to succeed aesthetically, and it should prepare the spectator for the kind of aesthetic experience that a superlative production makes possible. For either of these purposes, the standard must be related to an analysis of aesthetic experience. By-passing the technical problems that are involved in the making of art products, it must define excellence in a work of art by reference to its asethetic elements alone. Thus, if a work of art provides a harmonization of aesthetic effects, a great work of art must provide an outstanding harmonization of aesthetic effects.

This outstanding harmonization, being itself the total aesthetic effect, must be highly satisfying. The more it satisfies, the more intense and powerful its impact, the greater will the work of art be. Shall we say, then, that the greatest art is the most satisfying? If we were limiting ourselves to quantitative considerations, we would have to conclude that the most beautiful work of art is the one that tends to give most satisfaction, the one that is most eagerly and continually accepted. But this criterion, I suggest, must be supplemented and modified by another. Qualitative considerations are also important. No matter how much satisfaction an object may provide, it is not a work of art unless our experience tends to include each of the three kinds of aesthetic effects. Similarly, the standard of excellence requires not only the joint participation of emotional, sensible, and cognitive aesthetic effects, but also their mutual coöperation. If any one of them tends to limit the others, the balance and variety of effects is lacking. A work of art in which there were few sensible or cognitive effects would tend towards an unarticulated vagueness. If there were few cognitive or emotional effects the work would tend to be trivial and unexciting. If there were few emotional or sensible effects, the work would be cold and forbidding. The great work of art will be the one that harmonizes considerable enjoyment in each of the three modes. The greatest work of art tends to provide the greatest amount of satisfaction with respect to *each* kind of aesthetic effect, compatible with the need for harmonizing all three kinds.*
This standard is, of course, only an ideal, but it is worth considering because it is an ideal that most people ordinarily assume, or logically presuppose, when they talk about excellence in art. In terms of this ideal we can specify the *sine qua non* of the greatest art. It also gives us a basis for com-

---

* It might well be argued that, as a matter of fact, an object could be most satisfying as a totality only if it did provide the greatest amount of

paring different works of art. Works that have voluminous aesthetic effect with respect to the sensible, emotional, and cognitive, and that combine these aesthetic elements harmoniously, are greater, more beautiful, than works that have less aesthetic effect with respect to the sensible, emotional, and cognitive or fail to combine them with as enjoyable a total effect.*

This second requirement, that all three types of aesthetic effects must participate in similar degree, adds the needed qualitative restriction to our standard. All the same, it would be a mistake to overlook the fact that in every totality one or another type of aesthetic effect is going to predominate. Some works of art have more of the emotional, others more of the sensible, and still others more of the cognitive type of effect. This is both inevitable and desirable, since it adds to the variety of great productions. By recognizing such variety, we incorporate a relativistic principle into our standard. Though all three types must participate in force, any one of them

---

satisfaction with respect to all three kinds of aesthetic effects compatible with their harmonious combination. I am *inclined* to favor this view myself, but I think it desirable to frame a standard of excellence that will not depend upon it.

* Nevertheless, there are at least two sorts of questions that we cannot answer simply by reference to the standard of artistic excellence:

First, of two objects, one of which tends to provide satisfaction in all three modes and is a work of art and the other of which tends to provide satisfaction in only one or two modes but is more satisfying than the work of art, which is more beautiful?

Second, of two works of art, one of which tends to provide roughly the same amount of satisfaction in all three modes but as a totality is not highly satisfying and the other of which tends to provide little satisfaction in one or two modes but a great deal in the remaining one(s) and as a totality is highly satisfying, which is more beautiful?

In order to answer questions such as these, we must appeal to criteria other than the standard of artistic excellence. Just what they are, or ought to be, I am not quite sure. Ordinary usage is of little help in such matters — it is far too porous; and I am not clear about the grounds on which one might make a recommendation. With respect to both questions, however, we may be comforted by the fact that, usually and for the most part, objects that provide roughly equal amounts of satisfaction in all three modes are more satisfying than objects that provide satisfaction in only one or two modes or a great deal of satisfaction in one or two modes and only little satisfaction in the other one(s).

might predominate. On this level, it will be impossible to compare works of art or arrange them hierarchically. A work that predominated in one respect would not necessarily be greater than one that predominated in another respect, although at different times and under different circumstances we might prefer one work or the other.

A work of art that met these requirements would be excellent in all components. Its form, materials, and expressive function would work together, constituting a totality that was not only a coalition, but also a consummate unity. No work of art need necessarily employ representation. But it is unlikely that there could be a great work of art, one that serves to harmonize voluminous satisfaction in the three types, without expressiveness of one sort or another. And for the greatest art, expressiveness would seem to be indispensable. Without it, a great wealth of emotional, sensible, and cognitive effects would be lost to aesthetic experience. Above all, the greatest art depends upon aesthetic effects contributed by the level of expressiveness that I have called "philosophic scope." By means of philosophic scope, expressiveness institutes aesthetic effects, especially but not exclusively cognitive ones, which increase in number as the mind is forced to reach out in all directions. The proper expression of a world outlook provides the sensitive percipient with greater and greater delight as he finds in his own experience, and that of others, the implications of seeing things in the prescribed manner. There is no limit to the aesthetic effects of philosophic scope.

In the case of arts like music, it may seem strange to require philosophic scope. But although the greatest music does not convey the same kind of meanings as the greatest literature, it gives us a sense of life in all its complexity. When we hear great music, we hear more than organized sounds: we also hear the expression of a sense of reality. It is in terms of this that music may be said to have philosophic scope. Music is not meaningful in the terms of linguistic communication, but only in its own terms. And the same may be said about the greatest abstract painting and sculpture.

Philosophic scope must not be confused with literal truth-values. A great work of art may be full of lies, and it may concoct the most fanciful fiction. But if it has philosophic scope, it will use this fiction as the device for communicating a significant interpretation of life. This interpretation itself may be erroneous, as the world outlooks of great poets like Dante, Goethe, Lucretius, and Shelley all were, I believe, in many important respects. The greatest poet need not hold the most acceptable theory of physics or astronomy, and he may believe in all kinds of strange or conventional nonexistent gods. He need only express an interpretation that evinces an understanding of the common-sense world. If he chooses to go beyond our ordinary world, he is at liberty to roam as far as he can without making his construction irrelevant to the basic and pervasive conditions that we see about us. However distorted a work may be from the point of view of science or metaphysics, it can have philosophic scope and be true to life as long as it remains an imaginative interpretation of the everyday world.

As an imaginative interpretation, the great work of art would not fit Santayana's description. The doctrine of essences leads Santayana to the belief that great poetry, and indeed all poetry, is distinctively imagistic. There is much to be said for this conception of poetry, but more that could be said against it. For although much poetry does use imagery, much of it does not. It has been suggested that even the finest poetry is more often nonimagistic than otherwise. Whether or not this is so, there is no reason to believe that all great poetry owes its aesthetic impact to the effects of imagery.

Consequently, I would not agree with Santayana when he says that the discursive, nonimagistic parts of philosophical poetry are preparatory and servile, merely instrumental to a picture-like intuition that poetry must provide in order to be distinctively poetic and imaginative. For even if it does not communicate by means of imagery, discursive reasoning may be poetic, imaginative, and aesthetic in its own right. Nor is there any poetic element which expresses a "steady contemplation of all things in their order and worth," presumably the intuition of a highly complex essence. In philosophical poetry imagistic and nonimagistic effects are combined for the sake of expressing a significant world outlook. But just as the imagistic is not instrumental to the nonimagistic, neither is the nonimagistic instrumental to the imagistic, nor discursive reasoning subordinate to any ideal end of pictorialization. Subordination of this sort would lead to a distortion of facts and a pseudo-intellectual or superficially philosophical production. The two modes of discourse must be combined harmoniously, preference being given to one or the other only in view of what the poet is trying to do. When both modes are properly employed, they contribute to a philosophical poem that is successful *because* of the nonimagistic (as well as the imagistic) aspect and not in spite of it.

But, having said all this, let us remember that the enjoyment of philosophic scope must not be emphasized to the exclusion of other aesthetic effects in the great work of art. Expressiveness must be integrated with form and materials: the greatest art has emotional appeal and "surface" attraction as well as philosophic scope. Not only does it convey a sense of reality, but also it gives us an emotional uplift and delights our senses.

Through its emotional appeal, a great work of art need not cause a complete upheaval, reducing us to tears or provoking an extended catharsis. Instead, the work need only retain our excited interest throughout its progression. Great art — especially in music and literature — often builds up suspense by first shocking or surprising us. It sometimes begins by plunging us into an arresting, problematic situation, usually the statement of an intriguing but incomplete theme. We are then led through a series of adventures, variations, or experimental probings that complicate our initial interest. A whole network of emotional effects is established as we are filled with vague forebodings and indeterminate expectation. When sufficient stridency and excitement have been stirred up, the work begins its downward movement, resolving the initial problems and releasing our tense emotions. Having purged our feelings, we now relax and cast an indefinite glance at the development that we have pursued. When people speak of their aesthetic experience of "form," it is often this dialectic of predominantly, but not exclusively, emotional aesthetic effects that they are referring to. In one way or another and in varying degrees, the greatest works of art provide a satisfying emotional outlet. At the same time as we retain the status of observer, we become engaged participants in the work's own development. When it has reached a successful culmination, we undergo a kind of sympathetic consummation ourselves.

The delight in materials also contributes to our enjoyment of the greatest works of art. The brightness of Klee's colors, the delicate sheen of Vermeer's, the marble texture of the Venus de Milo, the woodwind sounds in Mozart serenades — especially, though not exclusively, by means of sensible aesthetic effects, these materials can produce the most exquisite enjoyment. Nineteenth-century aestheticism, insecure about emotions and contemptuous of reasoning, laid the greatest emphasis upon the "beauties of sense," by which it generally meant sensible aesthetic effects with respect to materials. Having spent itself by the end of the 1920's, aestheticism is on the defensive today. A revival might be beneficial. The greatest art is often predominantly sensible, and even when sensible effects are not foremost, they make their own indispensable contribution.

Philosophic scope, emotional appeal, and sensuous attraction coöperate in the greatest art. Although they might seem to correspond to the expressive, the formal, and the material, and to the cognitive, the emotional, and the sensible, it would be fruitless to devise too neat a system of classification. Emotional and sensible aesthetic effects play a considerable role in relation to expressiveness and with regard to philosophic scope; cognitive and sensible aesthetic effects are important in relation to the formal element and with regard to emotional appeal; and cognitive and emotional aesthetic effects have their place in relation to the material component and with regard to sensuous attraction. In the experience of the greatest art, all three types of aesthetic effects form an harmonious totality that has its own integrity and its own progression. But the exact nature of the harmonious integration, the predominance given to one or another aesthetic effect, is something that need not be alike for any two of the greatest works. To make a choice between alternatives we would have to consider factors of morality and criticism over and above the standard of excellence itself.

8

THE NATURE OF CRITICISM

Santayana's aesthetics culminates in a theory of criticism. Taking issue with Croce's view that aesthetics is an individual and unique science, Santayana denies that it is a science at all. In the place of an aesthetic science one finds "the art and function of criticism." By criticism Santayana means "a reasoned appreciation of human works by a mind not wholly ignorant of their subject or occasion, their school, and their process of manufacture."[1] Because a work of art is an object that enters into a variety of relations, the critic cannot limit his judgment merely to an assessment of beauty. He must be a moral critic, even a moral philosopher, whose function it is to determine the role that the object ought to play in human experience.

I

With respect to judgments of beauty, Santayana denies that the critic can appeal to any quality of beauty or aesthetic excellence that would necessarily appear to all other observers. He denies that aesthetic judgments can have a universal application and he denies that there is widespread agreement in particular evaluations. He claims that any resemblance between critical opinions depends upon the similar "origin, nature, and circumstance" of the critics themselves. "It is unmeaning to say that what is beautiful to one man *ought* to be beautiful to another. If their senses are the same, their associations and dispositions similar, then the same thing will certainly be beautiful to both . . . But no two men have exactly the same faculties, nor can things have for any two exactly the same values."[2]

The desire to attain agreement about aesthetic values Santayana considers to be dogmatism, or insecurity, or just a lack of sensibility. The man who *knows* what is fine does not wish to impress others with the rightness of his judgment: he realizes that their appreciations may be different from his, but feeling no necessity to change the enjoyments of either himself or those who disagree with him, he is secure within his own taste.

Still, Santayana does not want to eliminate the possibility of a desirable kind of critical dispute. While he denies that mass appreciation is indicative of excellence in a work of art, he suggests that "the true test is the degree and kind of satisfaction it can give to him who appreciates it most."[3] And it is obvious that by "appreciates" he here means "is sensitive to" or "understands." What matters, then, is the *degree* and *kind* of satisfaction undergone by a discriminating critic.

When, in another place, Santayana discusses the "criterion of taste," he lays great emphasis upon the degree and kind of satisfaction. A criterion of taste Santayana takes to be the awareness of what it is that delights us, how our appreciation is conditioned by our nature and our interests, the kind of enjoyment others have and which an affinity between their nature and ours makes possible for us, and finally, the way in which an object that delights us may or may not be harmonized with the rest of our interests. In describing the criterion of taste, Santayana mentions three principles of choice. By means of them he outlines a natural history of "good taste."

Good taste is originally formed in moments when "aesthetic emotion is massive and distinct."[4] Our ability to decide, to know what is worthy of choice, is initially dependent upon some stirring experience that we have had in the presence of an object. The first principle emphasizes the degree of satisfaction and the "authority of vital over verbal judgments." But although it is the "volume and intensity" of our own appreciations that determines what we shall henceforth choose, the ability to discriminate may be acquired under tutelage. Having been introduced to the beauties of art and nature by one who intensified our appreciation through the example of his own superior enjoyment, we tend to treat his judgments as the norm, since they were "the source and exemplar of all our own." [5] On this first level we take degree of satisfaction to be the standard, and we do not (it would appear) restrict our criterion to the "vital judgments" that we have made ourselves. What our tutor has felt, even if we have not, helps us decide what is really good. How Santayana would distinguish a judgment based merely on the tutor's experience from a "verbal judgment" I cannot tell.

Though dependent on the volume and intensity of appreciation, good taste includes much more. A vivid feeling may be "inwardly confused or outwardly confusing": the second principle regards its possible inward confusion; the third, its outward confusion. Inward confusion Santayana seems to identify with internal discords that occur when "elaborate things are attempted without enough art and refinement." [6] Such objects are in bad taste because they lack purity and simplicity, whether or not they stimulate a massive enjoyment. These second level virtues of purity, simplicity, inner perfection, clarity, articulateness, etc. are possessed by "wildflowers, plain chant, or a scarlet uniform." [7] Such objects may be too simple to find a considerable place in the life of reason — on the third level they may have to be subordinated to other things — but in themselves, as "natural joys" and "elementary beauties," they have an inherent dignity and worth.

In seeking the purity of that which escapes inward confusion, good taste looks for objects that are properly formed. Purity is apparently identified with a determinate form that makes a thing into an harmonious unity and not merely a manifold.

We may now begin to see how this aspect of Santayana's philosophy ties in with his theory of value, discussed in Part II of this study. His appeal to the perfection, precision, inner integrity, and harmonious nature of an interest, as constituting the standard of value, is similar to the second requirement for a criterion of taste. The present analysis also resembles his treatment of elements in the work of art. The first level of the criterion of taste dealt with the degree of satisfaction, a quantitative factor parallel to the materials of beauty. The second level deals with the type or kind of satisfaction, the highest of which is based on form and determinate unity. The third level, as we shall find, deals with the object's moral significance, its external relations to other things, similar to the expressive element in a work of art.

On this third level, good taste guides us towards objects that are "outwardly fit" as well as inwardly pure. Our aesthetic appreciations cannot stand by themselves. They must be compared with other enjoyments that are possible in these or similar circumstances. However perfect an interest may be in itself, it can always be harmful to other interests; just as two contiguous paintings may ruin the effect that each would have if they were put in different places. Good taste requires the harmonization of interests. Consequently, the final level in the criterion of taste involves a social and moral standard. The critic must evaluate an aesthetic effort in terms of its pertinence, the width of its appeal, its capacity to serve mankind, and its general suitability under the circumstances. The life of reason demands an interest in the consequences of an experience as well as its inner integrity, and good taste "cannot abstract from tradition, utility, and the temper of the world." [8]

Correspondingly, Santayana insists that the critic must be a moralist and not merely a person who is sensitive to beauty. Any occurrence of beauty may itself be criticized, and art is always subject to moral censure. Attempting to justify the existence of art, Santayana begins by pointing out that, on the whole, artistic endeavor is innocent. "Now art, more than any other considerable pursuit, more even than speculation, is abstract and inconsequential." [9] Art may give expression to social changes long after their occurrence, but is unlikely to cause them. In the individual, art "registers passions without stimulating them." [10] The artist who deals with erotic or religious subjects will not produce a lascivious or pious work, but rather a work of beauty. "In so far as he is an artist in truth," he will make something that gives expression to sexual and devotional interests without occasioning the kind of action that would satisfy them. Art is "liberal": the enjoyment it furthers is aesthetic, intrinsically valuable. And finally, art is a typical and symbolic example of "perfect activity." Art is "a rehearsal of rational living, and recasts in idea a world which we have no present means of recasting in reality." [11] In this way art shows the practical world what it could make of itself. Since it lives in fancy only, art cannot create this better world; but aside from the fact that practice may always use aesthetic figments as a blueprint, art finds its rationale elsewhere. "What nature does with existence, art does with appearance." [12]

In this fashion, Santayana justifies the existence of art. He suggests that Plato overemphasized the influence of arts like poetry, taking the Homeric stories too seriously and failing to realize that "left to themselves they float in an ineffectual stratum of the brain." [13] Nevertheless, Santayana agrees with the bases of Plato's moral objections. For Plato was specifically concerned with the third level of the criterion of taste. He saw the necessity for judging appreciations morally, and to this extent Santayana agrees with him.

Furthermore, Santayana claims that an interest in art, like an interest in the aesthetic quality of experience, ought to be harmonized with other interests. All too often, art becomes an indulgence and an impediment. The interest in art that either an observer or a creator may have often tends to separate him from the workaday world of honest, though practical, activity. Santayana points out that such a person may become a dilettante or virtuoso, but that he is unlikely to become a complete, intelligent, or happy man. The artist is basically a craftsman, and his home should be in the midst of society, not on its bohemian fringes or in some remote empyrean. An interest in art should crown an interest in useful practice. But although art must be harmonized with industry and science, its own function is supreme: "In industry man is still servile, preparing the materials he is to use in action . . . In science he is an observer, preparing himself for action in another way, by studying its results and conditions. But in art he is at once competent and free; he is creative." [14]

Santayana holds similar views about the work of art itself. A mere work of art, one that has no usefulness in practical, everyday living, is a "baseless artifice." Instead of being socially significant, it becomes artificial and esoteric. It is usage that makes works of art most attractive and that gives them their "highest expression." Art objects that are incapable of having practical uses tend to be ephemeral and slight: "there has never been any art worthy of notice without a practical basis and occasion, or without some intellectual or religious function." [15] For instance: "architecture may be useful, sculpture commemorative, poetry reflective, even music, by its expression, religious or martial." [16] In a more rational society it would be recognized that works of art can be useful, and useful objects would be works of art. Useful arts would not be isolated from fine arts, nor practical goods from aesthetic ones. But although the useful and the fine arts would be harmonized and coördinated so that particular objects could be both useful and fine, the distinction between useful art and fine art is one that Santayana retains. Only fine arts are specifically "ideal," for only they are dedicated to that which is distinctively aesthetic.

Thus, Santayana's theory of criticism merges with his conception of morality. He says that criticism and the criterion of taste must organize our multiple interests " with a view to attaining the greatest satisfaction of which our nature is capable." [17] No moral, or other, judgment can require a species or an individual to change its being: morality is only concerned with the perfection of one's nature, that is, the fulfillment of one's innate capacities. "All that morality can require is the inward harmony of each life." [18] In its ultimate function, good taste endows one's total experience with the same kind of purity and integrity that exists in every harmonious appreciation. One's life then possesses determinate form and unity.

II

In order to clarify Santayana's theory of criticism we shall have to examine his moral theory at some length. For it is there that we get the best idea of what he means by "harmony." We have already discovered that Santayana uses the word in two different ways. Sometimes he uses it to mean the condition of interests which have been made mutually compatible through the mediating operation of reason or intelligence. It is in this sense that he considers an interest in harmony to be the prerequisite to the life of reason. At other times, however, Santayana uses the word to mean inward integration, the "condition of any specific perfection." In this second sense, harmony is the prerequisite not to the life of reason but to "precision in interest or passion itself." *

Although in his various statements about intrinsic value Santayana sometimes used "harmony" in one sense and sometimes in the other, we concluded that the second sense was probably more suitable on that level. On the level of morals, however, we are confronted by a further difficulty. It was the "relativity of morals" that Santayana claimed to be defending when he made explicit his second meaning for "harmony." And yet, he had devoted *The Life of Reason* to the elaborate exposition of what harmony, in its first meaning, would require. To many readers it had seemed obvious that harmony, as the ideal of a life of reason, was a standard in accordance with which Santayana recommended that all men act. How else could one interpret his condemnation of barbarism and the life of unreason? Still, as a relativist, Santayana says that "we may prefer discord, if none of our passions consents to surrender anything." How can Santayana, as a moralist, reconcile his two different conceptions of harmony?

* Cf. pages 65–69 above.

It is this kind of difficulty that underlies the polemics of Santayana's critics, Vivas, Edman, and Munitz. The problem, as they present it in the Schilpp volume, turns on the supposed conflict between Santayana's earlier and later philosophy. In his earlier work, Santayana is understood to have used a standard of intelligence for the sake of determining what would be an "objectively moral act" under specified circumstances — that is, an act that might justifiably be recommended for all persons similarly situated. In his later philosophy, however, Santayana is thought to have renounced the ideal of intelligence for one that advocates an interest in contemplated essences, an interest that is accepted and recommended not because it harmonizes best with other interests but because it is one in which purity, precision, and perfection are uniquely revealed. In his book on Santayana's moral philosophy, Munitz states the critical position as follows:

Santayana has described the spiritual life in two opposite and incompatible ways: on the one hand, as a life of understanding, in which cognitive intent . . . is directed upon the ideals of truth and clarity of meaning; and on the other, as an escape from existence, as a disintoxication from all ideals, as a reversion to the immediately given that in itself possesses no meaning or significance.[19]

Like the other critics, Munitz holds that Santayana's later philosophy, with its recurrent reference to spirituality, offers a second moral standard that is both contradictory and inferior to his former standard of harmony through reason.

Santayana's reply, in "Apologia Pro Mente Sua," resolves the difficulties that disturbed his critics, although, as I shall try to show, his explanation poses further problems. In his reply Santayana appeals to the relativity of morals in a new context. Not only does moral relativity consider all interests intrinsically valuable if only they are inwardly integrated, but also it asserts that the choice between a perfect passion that does not harmonize with our other interests and one, perhaps less attractive, that does harmonize must be left to the man who has to choose. A man should do what it is in his nature to do; the life of reason may be good for some, but for others it may be detrimental to their ultimate destiny — and the same is true of spirituality.

Actually, this kind of moral relativity received expression in many of Santayana's works. It was, however, usually accompanied by statements that *seemed* to advocate, as objective and dogmatic standards, first the life of reason and later the life of pure spirit. The following quotations give some of Santayana's clearest utterances about moral relativity:

It is prudent to be rational up to a certain point, because if we neglect too many or too deeply rooted impulses in ourselves or in the world, our master-passion itself will come to grief; but too much rationality might be fatal to that passion at once . . . . the impulse to be rational and to establish harmony in oneself and in the world may be itself a "higher" impulse than others, in that it presupposes them; yet the romantic impulse to be rash, or the sudden call to be converted, might be thought "higher" than rationality by many people. Reason alone can be rational, but it does not follow that reason alone is good. The criterion of worth remains always the voice of nature, truly consulted, in the person that speaks.[20]

Spirituality is the supreme good for those who are called to it. . . . Just as the value of an artist must be judged by the world, in view of all the interests which his art affects or subserves, while the artist himself lives only in his own labour, irresponsible, technical, and visionary; so the value of spiritual life in general . . . . must be judged morally by the world, in view of its own ambitions, while the spirit judges the world and its ambitions spiritually.[21]

[With reference to the contemplation of essences:] Is it *better* to do this than not to do it? It is certainly better if you are committed to that task, or love that employment; but if you ask me whether it is better to be so committed, or so to love, I am speechless. Is it better to live than not to live? . . . My own feeling rather prompts me to think life and to think contemplation and to think riches a good when they come spontaneously, and an evil when they are constrained or distracted; but this is only a way of avoiding the question, and leaving it to each spirit at each moment to judge for itself. I am not a dogmatist in ethics.[22]

If Santayana is not a dogmatist in ethics, he cannot maintain *any* objective moral standard. His moral relativism would prevent him from making recommendations about what other people ought to do. How, then, are we to interpret his earlier defense of the life of reason and his later concern for the contemplation of essences? I think that they should be taken more as expressions of Santayana's own momentary interests than as theoretical or doctrinal positions in ethics. However confusing his language may have been, Santayana never really considered rationality or spirituality to be *the* objective moral standard. As a young man, Santayana sided with the rational world and judged spirituality, like everything else, in terms of its consequences. His judgment was severe, as may be seen from his treatment of mysticism. Also, he was confident that rebellious interests could be harmonized without too much trouble, and a stable political order imposed upon them. As an older man, Santayana shed that illusion: he came to realize that a life of reason was a precarious achievement and its victories often slight and dubious. His renewed interest in the ontological underpinning for his general philosophy deepened his sympathy with the contemplative life and even mysticism. He could now imagine the arguments of one who stood against the world and chose renunciation rather than harmonization. He came to appreciate the message of the Indians as well as that of the Greeks, although he himself still preferred the latter: "I frankly cleave to the Greeks and not to the Indians, and I aspire to be a rational animal rather than a pure spirit." [23]

We may say, then, that Santayana more or less retained his preference for the life of reason. But, in any event, he never suggested that his preferences were to serve as the bases of an objective moral code. When he defends the life of reason, as a young man, or takes the part of someone who aspires to be a pure spirit, in his later years, he is mainly presenting the implications of a possible way of life. He does not tell the

reader which one *he* ought to follow, and at times he specifically denies that "ought" can be used in this way at all.

Still, this does not prevent Santayana from being a moral
dogmatist on another and more revealing level. For he says
that we ought to do that which it is really in our nature to do,
that we ought to take our stand, whether it be with the world
or against it, in the light of what we *are*, as distinct from what
we *think* we are. The criterion of worth, as we have seen,
comes from the voice of nature "truly consulted." Concerning the antagonism between a master-passion and an interest
in achieving harmony, he says: "the ethics of this conflict
are the same as in other conflicts: to know oneself, and to
impose on oneself or on others only the sacrifices requisite to
bring one's chosen life to perfection." [24] It is, presumably, with
this in mind that he elsewhere asserts that the wise moralist
speaks with authority because he knows us better than we
know ourselves.

In the final analysis, therefore, it would appear that Santayana does believe in an objective standard of moral value
and that he is not, to this extent, a moral relativist. He ordains
that our preferences are morally justifiable only if they result
from knowledge of what we really are and what we really
want. And this, on its own level, virtually reinstates the ideal
of a life of reason. The barbarian, controlled by his master-
passion, does not wonder about the consequences of sub-
mitting to it. Unhampered by any knowledge of himself, he
succumbs to the romantic impulse to be rash, and perhaps,
succeeds in a way that he could not have otherwise. To require
him to decide whether he has truly consulted the voice of his
own nature is to require him not to be a barbarian. For this
demands more than the modicum of reason needed to assure
the continued existence of his master-passion. It demands the
ability to assess and criticize the master-passion; and that can
only be done by the honest and careful use of intelligence.

Consequently, I would not agree with Santayana's pragmatist critics who complain that his later philosophy relinquished the objective standard of intelligence. In the only

sense in which Santayana consistently maintained that standard as a young man, he also did as an old man. Like the pragmatists themselves, he was, both early and late, a relativist insofar as he denied that one could determine, a priori, which way of life is best for some individual. But also like them, he was a dogmatist in maintaining that a valid decision could not be made without a veridical insight into the individual's nature.*

This combination of moral relativity with moral dogmatism I find adequate, except that I would ask both Santayana and his critics how the veridical insight is to be attained. What is the criterion or decision-procedure that enables us to determine the truth or falsity of statements about a person's "real nature"? We are back to the problem raised during our discussion of harmony in its first meaning. According to Santayana, and Dewey as well, I believe, the good life for an individual is one that truly harmonizes his various interests and passions. Unfortunately, what they mean by "harmony" is not clear. As the word is ordinarily used, one might well say that, somehow or other, *every* interest can be harmonized with an indefinite number of other interests. But neither Santayana nor Dewey would consider all interests equally desirable: they would insist that most of them are not *truly* harmonious, most of them do not accord with one's *real* nature. And yet, how are we to decide that *true* harmony has actually occurred? How are we to determine what makes one harmonious way of life better than another?

In *Dominations and Powers* Santayana makes his most thorough attempt to grapple with this problem. There he says: "Primal Will and Circumstances, not the man's wishes or the reformer's prescription, determine the true interests of each person. And this is also the criterion by which the genius or folly of the directive imagination would be determined."[25] By primal Will in man Santayana means the agency of primitive

---

* In my essay "The World of George Santayana" (*The Hudson Review*, Autumn 1954), I give a longer, and more elaborate, analysis of what Santayana means by the "true nature" of a person.

needs and impulses that motivate the psyche to exploration and activity, even though the organism does not know what it wants or what would satisfy its need. We cannot stop to compare Santayana's position with a satisfaction theory, but we should notice how he defines Will: "the universal movement of nature, even if quite unconscious, in so far as running through a cycle or trope it precipitates a result that seems to us a consummation."[26] But Will, he continues, is blind and irrational by itself. It must be ruled by intelligence; the rational justification of any action derives from the likelihood of its attaining practical success. "That which makes an action rational is the material possibility of carrying it out successfully. In a word, *Circumstances* render oné action rational and another irrational."[27] No impulse is intrinsically right, Santayana now maintains, and none is intrinsically wrong, except in relation to its suitability to the actual world. "You have a right to be what you are and to become what you can become."[28]

The combination of primal Will and suitability under the circumstances Santayana offers as the objective standard of moral value. He explicitly rejects, as I think he always had, any relativity of morals which denies that true and authoritative judgments about one's nature can be made. Authoritative judgments disclose the rational justifiability of one act or impulse rather than another, and this depends upon feasibility in the relevant circumstances. Santayana goes on to admit that in a sense his position supports the maxim that Might is Right. For any successful act is right. At the same time, Santayana insists that actually his doctrine is more complex. The man who believes that Might is Right will land himself in moral contradictions if he thinks that sheer license pays off. Such a person "may always do as he likes, but he will seldom get what he wants. He will prove himself a fool, in little things and in great, if he persistently pursues what Circumstances deny him."[29]

This seems to be Santayana's clearest statement of his ethical views. It closely resembles the pragmatist emphasis upon the rightness of opportune acts and the necessity for considering the consequences of one's behavior. But towards Santayana and the pragmatists alike we must still direct one final question: What is the criterion for choosing between interests or impulses all of which are feasible under the circumstances, all of which *could* be carried out successfully? Of two or more interests, any of which might succeed, which one ought to be chosen?

It is this kind of question that neither Santayana nor Dewey answers. I have elsewhere * tried to show that Dewey's theory of value (as well as his ethical and political philosophy, which also claims that objective goods can be discovered solely by means of a critical method that judges the consequences of an act and its feasibility under the circumstances), actually presupposes standards that determine the way in which a decision is to be made. Assuming that there are an indefinite number of different interests that could be suitable under most circumstances, and that could therefore fit into some harmonious system or other, I tried to show that Dewey's a priori standards made it impossible for all but a few interests to be morally or objectively acceptable under *any* circumstances. I did not, and do not, claim that presuppositions are undesirable, or that Dewey's were repugnant, but only that his method of determining what is or is not objectively valuable was based on standards of which he did not seem to be aware and that the very existence of these standards made it impossible for objective values to be discovered simply by means of the process of evaluating circumstances. Something similar could be done with Santayana's ethical and political philosophy, I believe. Although this is not the place for developing this suggestion, I would refer the reader to Russell's essay on Santayana in the Schilpp volume. Russell there points out that Santayana's *The Life of Reason* pretends to define rational conduct in terms of the harmonization of interests but actually presupposes that rational conduct serves to institute a cultivated and aristocratic society. Russell concludes that, taken as ethics, Santayana's

* *John Dewey's Theory of Value*, Widener Archives, Harvard University.

statements "imply that culture is to be sought even at the cost of a vast accumulation of human suffering."[30]

Regardless of what Santayana's a priori standards may turn out to be on closer inspection, I should like to suggest that his *official* theory, like Dewey's, cannot, or does not, provide an answer to my question. Apart from his a priori standards, Santayana does not offer any criterion for choosing between the various interests that could be carried out successfully on some occasion. And this, I think, is a most serious shortcoming. For Santayana's ethical theory cannot really meet the arguments of one who believes that Might does make Right. The person with sufficient might will alter the circumstances according to his own designs. Then, *anything* he desires will be attainable, and hence, on Santayana's theory, morally justified. Santayana might continue to deny that such a person, doing what he likes, gets "what he wants." But circumstances are arranged so that he *does* get what he wants. Santayana might reply that the individual does not get what he *really* wants. But Santayana has also told us that primal Will and Circumstances determine the "true interest of each person." If Santayana were consistent, he would have to applaud every domination and become a universal camp follower.

The dilemma in which Santayana and the pragmatists find themselves, required to treat every successful act as morally justifiable or else to presuppose some moral standard that manages to put them on the side of the angels after all, is eliminated once we realize that neither primal Will *nor* Circumstances is suitable for determining where one's true interests lie. Both needs and the situations in which they arise are subject to change. At times an individual will sacrifice his interests rather than try to change circumstances that are inimical to their successful completion. At other times, however, he may put primal Will first and do everything in his power to arrange the circumstances accordingly. The moral situation is always fluid. The individual must not only know what he currently is, but also what he wants to make of himself. He can change himself, as he is presently constituted, or he can change the environment. He can succumb to an impulse that would succeed under the circumstances, or he can choose an impulse that would succeed under more favorable circumstances. Which should he prefer? To this kind of question there is no single valid answer. With the pragmatists we must insist that antecedent to, and apart from, each moral situation no one can, or *ought*, to recommend that the individual change either himself or the circumstances. The dynamics of the situation must decide. But once we have said this, we must go on to recognize that the individual who is not completely stymied by the alternatives, like the ass of Buridanus starving to death between two bundles of hay, will rely on some prior standard in order to be able to choose at all, and that we ourselves have done so in recommending that one *ought* to rely on the dynamics of the situation. What, then, is this standard?

The moral, and therefore critical, standard that I would suggest is related to my earlier definition of intrinsic value as satisfaction. In a moral situation we are forced to choose between different values: between the satisfaction that would result from changing ourselves and the satisfaction that would result from changing the environment. What we ought to choose, I would *initially* say, is that action which provides the greater amount to satisfaction. To this extent, the standard is quantitative, the ideal lying in the direction of most satisfaction. We frequently forego intense satisfactions, but only because of their distasteful consequences; and when we choose a lesser satisfaction, it is generally because it conduces to future experience, ultimately an entire life, that harmonizes the greatest satisfactions possible. Harmonization itself I have already defined as any satisfying coördination.

Still, a merely quantitative standard is not enough. Although we may agree that a life of greater satisfaction is better than a life of lesser satisfaction, we may not believe that a life of constant excitement is more desirable than a calmer, less neurotic, one. Here, as with the standard of artistic excellence, we are faced by a problem about the qualitative aspect of our choice.

Until we resolve this difficulty, we cannot claim to have given an acceptable standard of morality.

Before suggesting a way out, I should like to return to Santayana's theories about the nature of criticism and the criterion of taste. The reader may already feel that our digression has carried us too far afield; yet, by means of it we are now in a position to understand Santayana's philosophy of art better than we could have otherwise.

III

Santayana's views about criticism seem to take two different paths. On the one hand, he claims that it is unmeaning or absurd "to say that what is beautiful to one man *ought* to be beautiful to another." On the other hand, he also maintains, just two pages later, that the "true test" of what is beautiful depends on the degree and kind of satisfaction undergone by the most appreciative critic. These two assertions are not contradictory in any formal sense, but they seem to pull in different directions. Pepper, for instance, thinks that Santayana's first statement might be construed to deny any "objective basis" for criticism; the second he accepts and amplifies: "a work of art of great aesthetic value is one that affords a great deal of immediate pleasure to a highly discriminatory taste." [31]

These two different approaches to aesthetic criticism can be reconciled, I think, in the same way that we reconciled Santayana's different approaches to morality. On one level, Santayana is what may be called "a critical relativist"; on another level, he is a "critical dogmatist." He is relativistic inasmuch as he recognizes that differences of origin, interest, and circumstance among men cause them to find beauty in different places. This accounts for the fact that many of the greatest works of one age are boring to the next, and that even within an age critics of the greatest sensitivity, intelligence, and integrity frequently differ in their appraisals. At the same time, Santayana realizes that not everyone's opinion has "rational justification."

One cannot criticize Bach properly without having a knowledge of counterpoint. Just as Santayana would not specify a way of life that is best for all men, neither would he recommend a work of art that all men would or should find beautiful; but just as a reasonable moral decision is based on an intelligent evaluation of the circumstances, so too does an adequate critical judgment depend on refined appreciation and discriminating taste. One's "true interests" are determined by primal Will and Circumstances; the "true test" of a work of art is the degree and kind of satisfaction that it provides the one who understands it best. The aesthetic judgments of different critics may differ, but if they are all equally discriminating about the work at hand, their disagreement merely signifies that they have different likes and dislikes and are satisfied by different kinds of things. An objective aesthetic judgment — that is, a valid or rationally justifiable one — would be any judgment made by a highly discriminating critic on the basis of his own interests. And it is only in this sense, I think, that Santayana would try to justify his own literary criticism.

Although this interpretation of Santayana's critical theory has been pieced together out of occasional statements, it represents the position that he generally seemed to hold. The theory invites discussion in relation to the following questions: First, who is the authoritative or ideal critic? Second, what things ought we to enjoy, which aesthetic experiences ought we to cultivate? At the same time as I find Santayana's desire to combine critical relativism with critical dogmatism entirely commendable, I cannot help feeling that his philosophy of art suffers from the same methodological difficulties as his moral philosophy. An examination of each of the questions may serve to point them out.

In trying to determine the qualifications of an authoritative critic, we turn to a problem previously deferred. Our definitions of beauty, the work of art, and the great work of art have all been incomplete thus far because we have not specified in whose experience the physical object is to be aesthetic. We have said what aesthetic experience would be like in each case, but whose aesthetic experience was authoritative or the "true test" we have not yet indicated. Although Santayana barely deals with this issue, his conception of rational justification gives us a starting point. Let us see how his position needs to be modified.

In discussing evaluations of art, Santayana says that critical debates are never ended since a critic may always appear with a "fresh temperament or a new criterion."[32] But though Santayana recognizes these two factors which contribute to the critical experience, he does not subject them to sufficient analysis. As a result, he ignores the fluid and unterminated character of the aesthetic situation. The critic's temperament, preferences, prejudices, likes and dislikes must themselves be criticized; and the same holds for his "criterion," his type or degree of perception and discrimination. Not every judgment that satisfied Santayana's conception of rational justification would necessarily be authoritative: some of them could have been made by critics who were unduly subject to personal limitations. On the one hand, many discriminating critics are scornful of religious verse simply because they dislike the sentiments expressed; and the recent revulsion from proletarian literature is due to a change in the world situation more than a change in the reading public's aesthetic awareness. On the other hand, critics that are favorably disposed towards a work, or are not prejudiced against it, may be guilty of *too much* discrimination, too much technical knowledge, too great a concern for minutiae, and in short an attitude that is far too professional or intellectual. A critic who suffers from technical inbreeding and is so highly cultivated in his own specialty that he cannot appreciate the more pervasive, and possibly less precise, values of a work, is often as unreliable as an insensitive boor. Both offend against the standard of intelligence that is inherent in good criticism.

The ideal critic, the one whose aesthetic experience we may take to be authoritative, would be the critic who overcame both these difficulties with respect to the object in question. On the one hand, his temperament, prejudices, likes and dislikes, etc. would not be such as to prevent him from taking an interest in this kind of thing or from enjoying it to the full. On the other hand, he would be equipped with powers of discrimination and perception that opened his eyes to many important values in the object without fixating them on every minor blemish. Each object requires its own kind of ideal critic: a good judge of the baroque may be worthless for jazz, just as a good judge of music may be worthless for painting. To discover which real, live critics actually resemble the ideal, we would resort to the empirical techniques ordinarily used to decide whether a man is discriminating and impartial.

We may now say that something is beautiful (aesthetically good, aesthetically commendable) only if it would participate in the aesthetic experience of an ideal critic. An object cannot be beautiful in some respect or as a work of art or as a great work of art unless it has the capacity to provide the requisite satisfying experience to a critic whose preferences and powers of discrimination do not bar him from the fullest enjoyment of this particular object. As the word "beautiful" is commonly employed, people do not *always* have this meaning in mind: in one of its characteristic uses, the term makes no reference to the qualifications of an observer. But this is not the use that applies when we *give reasons* for a judgment in the way that people generally do. When aesthetic evaluations have an objective and authoritative thrust — which is to say, most of the time — words like "beautiful" refer to the experience of critics who are appropriately qualified. On no other basis could we explain our refusal to credit the aesthetic judgment of the man whose political views blind him to the merits of a novel or of the ignoramus who boasts that he doesn't know anything about music but he knows what he likes.

By defining "beautiful" in terms of the aesthetic experience of an ideal critic, we specify the conditions that are relevant to giving (good) reasons. But these are only necessary, not sufficient, conditions. To say that something is beautiful is to say that *some* ideal critic would find it satisfying; it is not to say that whatever satisfies an ideal critic is beautiful. For that would mean that the judgments of ideal critics could never be doubted, which is an assumption that our evaluative use of language certainly does *not* make.

That no such assumption is made is evident from the fact that we ordinarily expect disagreement among ideal critics themselves. We recognize that different ideal critics could make different judgments on the basis of different aesthetic experiences. Although their antecedent attitudes and powers of discrimination must not prevent them from being able to like a work and to perceive its values intelligently, it does not follow that their evaluations will be at all similar. An effect that one critic enjoys another may find distasteful, a point of view that seems significant to one may seem childish to another. A critic who allowed a preference for literal truth to affect his judgment would not be ideal or authoritative. But different ideal critics might hold different world outlooks, with the result that a work could have philosophic scope for one critic but much less significance for another. In general, an ideal critic who accepts the world outlook presented in a work of art will tend to appreciate the work much more than an ideal critic who holds a different philosophy. Not only would the critics have different interests, but also their different conceptions of what is universally relevant or true to life would lead them to divergent evaluations.* Even within the same outlook, critics may have different beliefs about the nature of an orthodox or faithful representation. Because no two individuals, however ideal as critics, are perfectly alike, their interests, preferences, and interpretations are sure to be somewhat different. They will not look for the same things, they will not see the same things, they will not care about the same things. If their judgments are similar, it will be due to resemblances between them other than the fact that both are ideal critics.

Consequently, we cannot hope to define evaluative words

---

* Santayana expresses a similar view in "Tragic Philosophy," *op. cit.*, p. 275, *et seq.* Cf. also Henry David Aiken, "The Aesthetic Relevance of Belief," *The Journal of Aesthetics and Art Criticism*, Vol. IX, No. 4, June, 1951, especially pp. 308–310.

in terms of necessary and sufficient conditions. In our ordinary use of words like "beautiful," we imply that an ideal critic would enjoy the object; but we rarely indicate *which* ideal critic and we generally leave open the possibility of disagreement among ideal critics. For the sake of arbitrating between them, we might *introduce* a further standard of aesthetic judgment. This, however, would take us beyond ordinary usage, and far beyond the limits of this study. For the present we need only realize that although aesthetic evaluations are justified by reference to the hypothetical experience of ideal critics, one is always free, on strictly aesthetic grounds, to reject any particular evaluation by a particular ideal critic.

Our definition is, then, inherently limited. Still, it may help to explain the use of aesthetic language. If someone said: "The paintings on the ceiling of the Sistine Chapel are very great works of art," we could use our analysis to make the following explication: "If a person were highly perceptive of paintings, sufficiently sensitive and discriminating to appreciate their philosophic scope, emotional impact, and sensuous attraction, and in general, their values with respect to expression, form, and materials, but also judicious enough not to be misled by overly precise technical considerations, and if this person were not temperamentally or otherwise averse to religious paintings, or the anthropomorphic representation of divinity, or the renaissance creed of Christianity, etc., then this person would tend to undergo an extremely satisfying experience that could be characterized as the harmonious integration of voluminous enjoyment with respect to emotional, sensible, and cognitive aesthetic effects, when he observed the paintings on the ceiling of the Sistine Chapel."

IV

Let us now return to the second question: What things ought we to enjoy and find beautiful? Although it may be true that only the judgments of ideal critics are authoritative aesthetic judgments, it might also be true that in particular cases we ought not to experience what they would. Their judgments might have rational justification in questions of beauty without being justifiable as recommendations to choose or study one work of art rather than another. That is to say, the judgments of ideal critics inform us about objective aesthetic value, but not, necessarily, about objective moral value. It is this cleavage between aesthetic and moral values that Santayana recognizes when he adds a third principle to his criterion of taste. The first principle required voluminous satisfaction, and the second, inward perfection. These two principles we have superseded, or elaborated, by giving an analysis that was not based on Santayana's epistemological distinctions. A person has good taste to the extent that his judgments approximate those that an ideal critic could be expected to make on the basis of his own aesthetic experiences. In asking how the recommendations of ideal critics can be justified, we move on to the third principle of good taste and return to the moral issues we previously considered.

We have already seen that different ideal critics will make different recommendations. Which one should we take? As judgments about beauty or aesthetic excellence, they may all be authoritative. Physical objects or art products are neither good, bad, nor indifferent, except in relation to someone's aesthetic experience; and in specifying an authoritative kind of aesthetic experience, we never expected all its instances to be alike in every detail. Because they are not alike, as evidenced by the variety of different, but equally justifiable, evaluations, we must choose among ideal critics.

This kind of choice is an ethical, and not a strictly aesthetic, one. Once again, we find ourselves in the moral situation, forced to question both our impulses and our circumstances. Our impulses tell us to retain our own preferences and our own world outlook and, therefore, to emulate ideal critics who resemble us as we are presently constituted; the circumstances consist of works that other ideal critics find highly aesthetic and which we are unable to appreciate. Shall we try to change ourselves in order to become sensitive to a greatness that we cannot now perceive, or shall we cultivate our garden, expending our energy on the search for more of the greatness that we can and do appreciate? Shall we stand by our present interests and beliefs, or shall we sacrifice them whenever they keep us from looking for something better?

Up to a point, this kind of question is merely theoretical. As a matter of fact, we cannot jump out of our skins. Our likes and dislikes, as well as our world outlook, are largely determined by the conditions that have made us what we are. Our capacities are not unlimited, and our human nature is not entirely malleable. Nevertheless, both our preferences and our world outlook are subject to criticism. The tenets of a world outlook are largely empirical beliefs whose cognitive warrant varies with new developments in our conceptual system and in our experience of the common-sense world. And although a world outlook is ultimately based upon sheer commitments of some sort, these commitments can be justified or criticized in the way that likes and dislikes are. Like all other interests, they are subject to the criterion of satisfaction throughout a lifetime.

This brings us back to the moral standard already proposed: individuals should follow that course of action which contributes to a network of experiences, ultimately an entire lifetime, that will be as satisfying as possible. At an earlier stage of the argument, we refused to content ourselves with a merely quantitative standard, as this one seems to be, but we failed to supply the qualitative restrictions. Now, however, we may say that a life of greatest excitement or most intense enjoyment is not necessarily best. Even if a life of emotional orgy were most satisfying, it would not be most desirable. For it would tend to throttle sensible and cognitive elements and make it impossible for one's life to be a great work of art. Thus, the standard of artistic excellence also serves as a standard of moral excellence. For some individual the life most worth living would be that life which harmonized, so that it could be aesthetic in its totality, the most satisfying cognitive, emotional, and sensible aesthetic effects which this individual could possibly experience.

Adhering to this standard, a person who had to choose among critics, or decide which interests and discriminatory powers to develop, would consider the implications in terms of future satisfactions. It will not do merely to advise him to broaden his interests and increase his perceptive abilities. Since most people make so little use of their capacities, this advice is, of course, sound. But it is equally important to recognize that new interests often drive out the old ones and that a person who becomes more critical also becomes more intolerant of imperfections. Great art often spoils our enjoyment of lesser works. The man who appreciates Bach may not sneer at the productions of jazz or Boccherini, but his listening hours are limited, and the more he devotes himself to Bach, the less time he will have for composers he considers inferior. Boccherini will have to suffer, which is a shame. The man's choice can be justified if, in the long run, he can count on Bach for a richer satisfaction than Boccherini; but this fact does not diminish the inevitable loss.

I offer this standard only as a tentative approximation, since this study is not devoted to ethics and cannot enter into all the difficulties that beset a formulation of this sort. In particular, I have said nothing about duty, justice, and the demands of society. Nevertheless, the standard may serve to indicate the way in which a whole lifetime can be made into a great and significant work of art. In these terms, one need not, and cannot, justify art as a whole, any more than life as a whole. A good life, a life worth living, is a type of great art. Arts, such as music, painting, poetry, etc. are morally justifiable to the extent that they contribute to what would be, for some individual, the most satisfying life of which he is capable. A priori, they are not to be ranked higher than any other arts. But, as a matter of fact, the special arts that have traditionally gone by the name of "fine arts" tend to make a significant and outstanding contribution towards a life that, for most persons, would be eminently worth living. In general, they are better suited for the production of great works of art than most other human occupations — though even here, we may find that the arts of industry, scholarship, human relations, and social action resemble the so-called fine arts more than we suspect.

In the attempt to justify arts such as music, painting, literature, etc., I would not agree with Santayana that they are innocent, detached from practical concerns, or uniquely liberal. They are not innocent: for they focus experience, making it intense at the same time as it has direction, exciting as well as meaningful. They teach us how to *perceive*. They also teach us lies, as Homer and Dante do, but they strengthen our grip on the world by allowing us to enjoy even the wildest misconceptions. They are not detached from practical concerns: for they change our way of seeing things and thereby alter our goals and aspirations. They not only register emotions but also stimulate them. All of the greatest art arouses passions in order to carry them through a complete and satisfying development. What otherwise might have been dissipated and lost is now used to the fullest and its very existence redeemed by intelligent employment. Nor is this kind of art unable to reform the world. Whether or not it incites to immediate action, which it occasionally does, its very ability to excite and to educate gives it a kind of practical efficacy. Finally, no art is uniquely liberal: for there is no servile process to be contrasted with what Santayana means by fine art. Nor does art play with shadows, doing with appearance what nature does with existence. A work of art is not an ideal fiction. It is an imaginative reconstruction of the common-sense world. It does not prefigure reality but directly contributes to it.

With Santayana's belief that an interest in what he calls fine art ought to be harmonized with other interests and that works of (fine) art ought to be useful as well as aesthetic, I am entirely in agreement. But once we recognize that fine art cannot be distinguished from servile art in the way that Santayana desires, we have no reason to insist on their being united. It does make sense, however, to point out that there are more arts than those that interest aesthetes, and that practical productions can be beautiful as well as instrumental. We cannot contrast an interest in art with an interest in science or philosophy, since these may also be artistic; but we can say that the man who restricts himself to arts like music, painting, poetry, etc. without venturing beyond them is unlikely to attain the heights of either significant creation or intelligent appreciation. The artist and the spectator must both possess the powers of the critic. If their experience is to take on the greatest value, it must include cognitive, emotional, and sensible aesthetic effects. The harmonization of these elements would result in a life of reason that was also a life of beauty. But which effect must, or should, predominate, no one can say until he examines the individual situation.

We see, then, that there are respects in which our criterion of taste is dogmatic and respects in which it is not. The criterion is dogmatic insofar as it specifies a standard of artistic excellence, insofar as it limits authoritative aesthetic experience to that of an ideal critic, and insofar as it suggests a standard of morality. But in other ways the criterion is relativistic. On principle it refuses to lay down a detailed program for either the artist or the spectator. It does not maintain that the life of the poet, painter, musician, etc. is necessarily more exalted than the life of the physicist, mathematician, historian, etc. It does not recommend that everyone become an artist in any of these or other fields. Nor does it pretend to know exactly what kind of work an artist ought to prepare himself for, or what particular objects he ought to make. Likewise, it denies that an interest in any one art or type of art is necessarily preferable to interests in others. And it does not claim that different observers ought to adhere to the recommendations of the same ideal critic.

In all these issues there is no standard for determining whether an emotional, sensible, or cognitive type of experience ought to predominate, and there is no standard for prescribing a class of uniquely desirable interests. In every case there will be certain preferences and, perhaps, certain world outlooks that are given to enquiry. Decisions should be made in the light of these givens, and with regard to their intimate appeal for the person who has them. At the same time, the givens must be criticized in terms of the moral standard. Under particular circumstances, any one of them may have to be sacrificed. But our judgment in this matter, as in every other, is never final, always fallible, and at best relevant only to the particular situation in question.

In conclusion let me remind the reader that Santayana's philosophy has been misconstrued by most of his critics, particularly those that favor pragmatism. On the one hand, Santayana's pragmatist critics fail to recognize the extent to which he accepts many of the basic tenets of pragmatism; on the other hand, they fail to admit, or make explicit, the extent to which they are themselves committed to a kind of intuitionism not wholly different from Santayana's. Although Santayana's critics realize that he combines a modified Platonism with a modified naturalism, their mistaken conceptions about the way in which he effects this combination have often prevented them from appreciating the genuine merits of his philosophy.

Having said this, however, I must also remind the reader that my attempt to work out an approach somewhat different from Santayana's was based on criticism of several of his most fundamental views. Santayana's approach leads to a whole series of indefensible distinctions in epistemology, aesthetics, and the philosophy of art. These distinctions, in my estimation, are not only unsuitable for the resolution of the specific problems to which they are addressed, but also false to experience as a whole. Aesthetic theory, and aesthetic practice, cannot reach fruition unless they are loyal to the variegated pattern of ordinary experience. Epistemological distinctions, such as Santayana's, force experience into an artificial, unrewarding mold. Here, as elsewhere, let us learn how to dispense with them.

NOTES

NOTES

Preface

1. George Santayana, "A Brief History of My Opinions," reprinted in the Preface to Volume VII of the Triton Edition of his works (15 vols., New York: Charles Scribner's Sons, 1936–1940) and also in *The Philosophy of George Santayana*, ed. P. A. Schilpp (Evanston and Chicago: Northwestern University, 1940), pp. 20–21.

Chapter 1. Mediate and Immediate Experience

1. George Santayana, "Apologia Pro Mente Sua," Schilpp volume, p. 497.
2. *Ibid.*, p. 523.
3. George Santayana, Preface to Volume VII of the Triton Edition, reprinted in the Schilpp volume, p. 29.
4. C. A. Strong, *The Origin of Consciousness, an attempt to conceive of the mind as a product of evolution* (London: Macmillan and Co., 1918), p. 38, his italics.
5. George Santayana, *Scepticism and Animal Faith: Introduction to a system of philosophy* (New York: Charles Scribner's Sons, 1923), p. 47.
6. George Santayana, *The Realm of Essence*, reprinted in *Realms of Being* (New York: Charles Scribner's Sons, 1942), p. 1.
7. *Ibid.*, p. 3.
8. *Ibid.*, pp. 10–11.
9. *Ibid.*, p. 6.
10. *Ibid.*, p. 23.
11. Cf. Charles W. Morris, *Six Theories of Mind* (Chicago: The University of Chicago Press, 1932), pp. 233–236; for Santayana's counter-attack, directed against Dewey, cf. George Santayana, "Dewey's Naturalistic Metaphysics," *The Philosophy of John Dewey*, ed. by P. A. Schilpp (Evanston and Chicago: Northwestern University, 1939), pp. 245–261, esp. pp. 255–258.
12. *Scepticism and Animal Faith*, p. 3.
13. *Ibid.*, p. 16, his italics.
14. John Dewey, *Logic: The Theory of Inquiry* (New York: Henry Holt and Co., 1938), p. 517.
15. *Scepticism and Animal Faith*, pp. 150–151, 121, and 117, respectively.

16. Clarence Irving Lewis, *An Analysis of Knowledge and Valuation* (La Salle, Illinois: Open Court Publishing Co., 1946), pp. 188–189, his italics.
17. *The Realm of Essence*, p. 18.
18. *Scepticism and Animal Faith*, p. 95, his italics.
19. *The Realm of Essence*, p. 18.
20. Gardner Murphy, *Personality: A Biosocial Approach to Origins and Structure* (New York and London: Harper & Brothers, 1947), pp. 333–334.
21. "Apologia Pro Mente Sua," p. 502, his italics.

CHAPTER 2. BEAUTY AND THE SENSE OF BEAUTY

1. Eliseo Vivas, "From *The Life of Reason* to *The Last Puritan*," Schilpp volume, pp. 313–350; Irwin Edman, "Humanism and Post-Humanism in the Philosophy of Santayana," Schilpp volume, pp. 293–312; Milton K. Munitz, "Ideals and Essences in Santayana's Philosophy," Schilpp volume, pp. 183–215; Paul Arthur Schilpp, "Santayana on *The Realm of Spirit*," Schilpp volume, pp. 377–398. For a brief reference to critics who have doubted the unity of Santayana's philosophy as well as those who have criticized his early formulation in aesthetics, cf. Raimundo Lida, *Belleza, Arte y Poesía en la Estética de Santayana* (Universidad Nacional de Tucumán, 1943), pp. 46–47, note. Lida himself relates Santayana's early formulation to the aesthetics of Lipps and Lotze.
2. "Apologia Pro Mente Sua," p. 538.
3. George Santayana, Preface to Volume VII of the Triton Edition, "On the Unity of my Earlier and Later Philosophy."
4. "Apologia Pro Mente Sua," p. 555, his italics.
5. Bertrand Russell, "The Elements of Ethics," in *Philosophical Essays* (London: Longmans, Green & Co., 1910), p. 11.
6. George Santayana, *Winds of Doctrine: Studies in Contemporary Opinion* (New York: Charles Scribner's Sons, 1912), p. 140.
7. *Ibid.*, p. 141.
8. *The Realm of Essence*, p. 8.
9. *Ibid.*
10. George Santayana, *The Sense of Beauty: Being the Outlines of Aesthetic Theory* (New York: Charles Scribner's Sons, 1896), p. 12.
11. *Ibid.*
12. *The Sense of Beauty*, pp. 14–15.
13. *Ibid.*, p. 16.
14. *Ibid.*

15. *Ibid.*, p. 17.
16. *Ibid.*, p. 18.
17. *Ibid.*, p. 19.
18. *Ibid.*, p. 20.
19. *Ibid.*, pp. 28–29.
20. *Ibid.*, p. 36.
21. *Ibid.*, p. 48.
22. *Ibid.*, p. 49.
23. Reprinted in a later article entitled "An Aesthetic Soviet." Cf. George Santayana, *Obiter Scripta: Lectures, Essays and Reviews*, edited by Justus Buchler and Benjamin Schwartz (New York: Charles Scribner's Sons, 1936), pp. 253–255.
24. George Santayana, "The Mutability of Esthetic Categories," *The Philosophical Review*, vol. XXXIV (May 1925), p. 284n, my italics.
25. *Obiter Scripta*, p. 225.
26. John Dewey, "Philosophy as a Fine Art," *New Republic*, vol. LIII, no. 689 (February 15, 1928), pp. 352–354.
27. John Dewey, "Values, Liking and Thought," *Journal of Philosophy*, vol. XX (November 8, 1923), p. 622.
28. John Dewey, *Experience and Nature* (La Salle, Illinois: Open Court Publishing Co., 1926), pp. 396–397.
29. *An Analysis of Knowledge and Valuation*, pp. 401–402.
30. G. E. Moore, *Principia Ethica* (Cambridge University Press, Second Impression, 1922), p. 92.
31. Cf. John Wisdom, *Interpretation and Analysis in Relation to Bentham's Theory of Definition* (London: K. Paul, Trench, Trubner & Co., 1931).

CHAPTER 3. AESTHETIC VALUE

1. Cf. Schilpp volume, p. 233, and Milton Karl Munitz, *The Moral Philosophy of Santayana* (New York: Columbia University Press, 1939), p. 53.
2. Munitz, *The Moral Philosophy of Santayana*, p. 53.
3. "Apologia Pro Mente Sua," p. 577.
4. *The Sense of Beauty*, p. 18.
5. *Winds of Doctrine*, p. 146.
6. *Ibid.*
7. George Santayana, *Dominations and Powers: Reflections on Liberty, Society and Government* (New York: Charles Scribner's Sons, 1951), p. 40.
8. George Santayana, *The Life of Reason: Or the phases of human progress;* Volume I: "Introduction and Reason in Common Sense"; Volume II: "Reason in Society"; Volume III: "Reason in Religion";

Volume IV: "Reason in Art"; Volume V: "Reason in Science" (New York: Charles Scribner's Sons, 1905); Vol. I, p. 223.

9. *The Life of Reason*, Vol. I, p. 56.

10. George Santayana, "Fifty Years of British Idealism," *Some Turns of Thought in Modern Philosophy: Five Essays* (New York: Charles Scribner's Sons, 1933), pp. 59–60.

11. George Santayana, *Platonism and the Spiritual Life* (New York: Charles Scribner's Sons, 1927), p. 3.

12. *Ibid.*, p. 14.

13. *Dominations and Powers*, p. 95.

14. *Winds of Doctrine*, p. 146.

15. *The Life of Reason*, Vol. I, p. 267.

16. George Santayana, *The Genteel Tradition at Bay* (New York: Charles Scribner's Sons, 1931), pp. 61–62.

17. *Ibid.*, pp. 62–63.

18. "Apologia Pro Mente Sua," p. 577.

19. *The Life of Reason*, Vol. V, p. 234.

20. Schilpp volume, p. 334.

21. "Apologia Pro Mente Sua," p. 578.

22. *The Realm of Spirit*, p. 549.

23. *Ibid.*, p. 664.

24. *Dominations and Powers*, p. 169.

25. *The Realm of Essence*, p. 6.

26. *Platonism and the Spiritual Life*, p. 53, his italics.

27. *The Realm of Spirit*, p. 664.

28. "Apologia Pro Mente Sua," p. 578.

29. *Ibid.*, p. 579.

30. "Apologia Pro Mente Sua," p. 501, his italics.

31. *The Realm of Essence*, p. 7.

32. George Santayana, "What is Aesthetics?", *Philosophical Review* (May 1904); reprinted in *Obiter Scripta*, pp. 32–33.

33. *Obiter Scripta*, p. 256.

34. *The Realm of Essence*, p. 10.

35. *Obiter Scripta*, p. 33.

36. *Ibid.*, p. 38.

37. *Scepticism and Animal Faith*, p. 140.

38. *Ibid.*, p. 17.

Chapter 4. Aesthetic Effects

1. *The Sense of Beauty*, p. 21.

2. *Ibid.*, p. 50.

3. John Dewey, *Art as Experience* (New York: Minton, Balch and Co., 1934), p. 55.

4. *Ibid.*, his italics.

5. *An Analysis of Knowledge and Valuation*, p. 438.
6. *Ibid.*, p. 439.
7. "A Pluralistic Analysis of Aesthetic Value," *The Philosophical Review*, vol. LIX (October 1950), p. 498. Cf. also Stuart M. Brown, Jr., "C. I. Lewis's Aesthetics," *Journal of Philosophy*, vol. XLVII (March 16, 1950), p. 145.

Chapter 5. The Creative Process

1. *The Life of Reason*, Vol. IV, p. 4.
2. *Ibid.*
3. *Ibid.*, p. 35.
4. *Ibid.*, p. 13.
5. *Ibid.*, p. 24.
6. *Ibid.*, p. 22.
7. *Ibid.*, p. 32.
8. *Ibid.*, p. 30.
9. *Ibid.*, p. 32.
10. *Ibid.*, p. 15.
11. *Realms of Being*, p. x.
12. Preface to Volume VII of Triton Edition, Schilpp volume, p. 8.
13. *Scepticism and Animal Faith*, p. 258.
14. *Experience and Nature*, pp. 86 and 81, transposed, his italics.
15. *An Analysis of Knowledge and Valuation*, p. 203.
16. *Ibid.*, p. 473n.
17. George Boas, "Santayana and the Arts," Schilpp volume, p. 259.

Chapter 6. Aesthetic Elements in the Work of Art

1. *The Sense of Beauty*, p. 66.
2. *Ibid.*, p. 71.
3. *Ibid.*
4. *Ibid.*, p. 72.
5. *Ibid.*, p. 74.
6. *Ibid.*
7. *Ibid.*, p. 81.
8. *The Life of Reason*, Vol. IV, p. 15.
9. *The Realm of Essence*, p. 70.
10. *Ibid.*
11. *Ibid.*, p. 71.
12. *The Sense of Beauty*, p. 131.
13. *Ibid.*

14. *Ibid.*, p. 135.
15. *Ibid.*
16. *Ibid.*, p. 96.
17. *Ibid.*, p. 114.
18. *Ibid.*, p. 197.
19. *Ibid.*, p. 195.
20. *Ibid.*, p. 197.
21. *Ibid.*, p. 222.
22. George Boas, "Santayana and the Arts," Schilpp volume, p. 249.
23. Katherine Gilbert, "Santayana's Doctrine of Aesthetic Expression," *Philosophical Review*, XXXV (1926); reprinted in Katherine Gilbert, *Studies in Recent Aesthetics* (Chapel Hill: The University of North Carolina Press, 1927), p. 118.
24. "Santayana and the Arts," p. 254.
25. *The Sense of Beauty*, p. 267.
26. "Santayana's Doctrine of Aesthetic Expression," p. 123.
27. Charles Hartshorne, "Santayana's Doctrine of Essence," Schilpp volume, p. 158.
28. *Scepticism and Animal Faith*, p. 148.
29. *The Sense of Beauty*, p. 21.

CHAPTER 7. THE STANDARD OF ARTISTIC EXCELLENCE

1. George Santayana, *Interpretations of Poetry and Religion* (New York: Charles Scribner's Sons, 1900), p. 256.
2. *Ibid.*
3. *Ibid.*, p. 257.
4. *Ibid.*, p. 258.
5. *Ibid.*, p. 178.
6. *Winds of Doctrine*, p. 203.
7. George Santayana, *Three Philosophical Poets: Lucretius, Dante, Goethe* (Cambridge: Harvard University Press, 1910), p. 58.
8. *Interpretations of Poetry and Religion*, p. 176.
9. *Obiter Scripta*, p. 157.
10. *Interpretations of Poetry and Religion*, p. 265.
11. *Three Philosophical Poets*, p. 59.
12. *Interpretations of Poetry and Religion*, pp. 270–271.
13. *Ibid.*, p. 284.
14. *Ibid.*, p. 154.
15. *Obiter Scripta*, p. 67.
16. *Three Philosophical Poets*, p. 8.
17. *Ibid.*, pp. 10–11.
18. *Ibid.*, p. 11.

19. *The Life of Reason*, Vol. IV, p. 112.
20. *Three Philosophical Poets*, p. 204.
21. *Ibid.*, p. 206.
22. *Ibid.*, p. 207.
23. *Ibid.*
24. *Winds of Doctrine*, p. 176.
25. *Ibid.*, p. 171.
26. *Three Philosophical Poets*, p. 133.
27. *Ibid.*, p. 211.
28. *Ibid.*, p. 213.
29. *Ibid.*
30. *Ibid.*, p. 215.
31. First printed in *Journal of Philosophy*, vol. XVIII (December 22, 1921), pp. 701–713; reprinted in *Soliloquies in England and Later Soliloquies* (New York: Charles Scribner's Sons, 1922), pp. 245–259.
32. *Soliloquies*, pp. 254–255.
33. *The Life of Reason*, Vol. IV, p. 122.
34. *Interpretations of Poetry and Religion*, p. 193.

Chapter 8. The Nature of Criticism

1. *Obiter Scripta*, p. 37.
2. *The Sense of Beauty*, pp. 41–42.
3. *Ibid.*, p. 43.
4. *The Life of Reason*, Vol. IV, p. 194.
5. *Ibid.*, p. 195.
6. *Ibid.*, p. 197.
7. *Ibid.*
8. *Ibid.*, p. 202.
9. *Ibid.*, p. 169.
10. *Ibid.*, p. 170.
11. *Ibid.*, p. 172.
12. *Ibid.*, p. 173.
13. *Ibid.*, p. 175.
14. *Ibid.*, p. 229.
15. *Obiter Scripta*, p. 38.
16. *The Life of Reason*, Vol. IV, p. 210.
17. *The Sense of Beauty*, p. 218.
18. *Ibid.*
19. *The Moral Philosophy of Santayana*, p. 88.
20. "Apologia Pro Mente Sua," p. 563, his italics.
21. *Platonism and the Spiritual Life*, p. 40.
22. "Apologia Pro Mente Sua," p. 585, his italics.

23. *The Realm of Essence*, p. 65.
24. Preface to the Triton Edition, Schilpp volume, p. 27.
25. *Dominations and Powers*, p. 128.
26. *Ibid.*, p. 40n.
27. *Ibid.*, p. 313, his italics.
28. *Ibid.*
29. *Ibid.*
30. Bertrand Russell, "The Philosophy of Santayana," Schilpp volume, p. 465.
31. Stephen C. Pepper, *The Basis of Criticism in the Arts* (Cambridge: Harvard University Press, 1946), p. 52.
32. *Three Philosophical Poets*, p. 133.

INDEX